Praise for Dr. Sue Morter and

The Energy Codes

"*The Energy Codes* offers deep insights and po[...] brilliantly merge the ever-blending worlds o[...] reveal the truth of our being and the depths of [...] book, which I strongly encourage you to read, Dr. Sue Morter will help guide you to living more fully and expressing your true potential."

—Jack Canfield, coauthor of the Chicken Soup for the Soul® series and
The Success Principles™: How to Get from Where You Are to Where You Want to Be

"I have just found a book that *practicalizes* and *functionalizes* the metaphysical insights and mystical wisdom of all the best spiritual literature of the past half century. *The Energy Codes* by Dr. Sue Morter offers shockingly simple, yet wonderfully masterful, explanations that turn all the What's True info into a single How To revelation that can change lives virtually overnight. Spiritual knowledge is one thing, spiritual tools are another. For those ready and willing to build a new life, *here are the tools*. Powerful, incisive, extraordinary writing."

—Neale Donald Walsch, *New York Times* bestselling author
of *Conversations with God*

"In this wonderfully powerful book, Dr. Sue Morter bridges the realms of science, spirituality, and true personal transformation. Her years of research, investigation, and practice will change you and your life for good. When you apply these practical and effectively proven tools, you will heal your mind, your body, and your reality. I loved reading it!"

—Dr. Joe Dispenza, *New York Times* bestselling author
of *You Are the Placebo: Making Your Mind Matter*

"Simply, Sue Morter is the real deal. Her authentic insights, integration and embodiment of sacred truth is evident as you hear her teach and have the privilege of being one of her clients. In this book she masterfully integrates spirituality and science in a way that is life-changing. Sue pours her years of research and experience into this powerful literary contribution that will assist in your transformation like no other. You are holding in your hands right now a powerful key to real transformation. Use it."

—Michael Bernard Beckwith, founder, Agape International Spiritual Center
and author of *Spiritual Liberation* and *Life Visioning*

"Every once in a great while, a book comes along with such truth, clarity, and genius that it can powerfully transform your life. *The Energy Codes* is such a book. It's an owner's manual for understanding who you truly are and for creating lasting happiness, optimal health, and a most miraculous life."

—Marci Shimoff, #1 *New York Times* bestselling author
of *Happy for No Reason* and *Chicken Soup for the Woman's Soul*

"Brilliant and relatable, *The Energy Codes* is filled with powerful, profound and transformational principles and practices that are both accessible and relevant. Dr. Sue Morter is an extraordinary enlightened visionary, bridging the gap between heaven and earth, and inviting us fully into our creatorship. I highly recommend this book!"

—Anita Moorjani, *New York Times* bestselling author of *Dying to Be Me*

"Dr. Sue Morter, one of the most exciting and original health practitioners out there, takes a truly holistic view of health by focusing on the body's dynamical and interconnected energy systems, including the role of the soul's purpose and the power of certain key movements to radically shift energy. Take a daily dose of the seven principles in *The Energy Codes* and enjoy a powerful prescription for living in radiant wellness and harmony."

—Lynne McTaggart, internationally bestselling author of
The Field, The Intention Experiment, and *The Power of Eight*

"In the midst of a growing transition in human health and consciousness, Dr. Sue Morter's *The Energy Codes* establishes new ground with a multidisciplinary approach to healing. Blending the movement arts of yoga with energizing breathwork, deep belief, and heart expanding meditations, she takes her readers into the greatest healing experience of all—the lifting of the mind into a heightened discovery of the true self and mission."

—James Redfield, #1 *New York Times* bestselling author of *The Celestine Prophecy*

"This book shows you why passionately embracing your energetic nature—your Soulful Self—is the most important thing you could ever do. A must read!"

—Janet Bray Attwood, *New York Times* bestselling author of *The Passion Test*

"[A] valuable 7 'codes' exercise program that enables you to fully express your creative magic in manifesting your life. Dr. Morter's book is a virtual scientific treasure map for finding health, happiness, and love at the end of the rainbow."

—Bruce H. Lipton, PhD, cell biologist and bestselling author of
The Biology of Belief, Spontaneous Evolution, and *The Honeymoon Effect*

THE ENERGY CODES

The 7-Step System to Awaken Your Spirit,
Heal Your Body, and Live Your Best Life

DR. SUE MORTER

Foreword by Jill Bolte Taylor, PhD

ATRIA PAPERBACK

NEW YORK   LONDON   TORONTO   SYDNEY   NEW DELHI

ATRIA
PAPERBACK

An Imprint of Simon & Schuster, Inc.
1230 Avenue of the Americas
New York, NY 10020

Copyright © 2019 by Dr. Sue Morter
The Energy Codes, Energy Man, JourneyAwake, and The Quantum Flip
are registered trademarks of Dr. Sue Morter LLC.

All rights reserved, including the right to reproduce this book or portions thereof in any form whatsoever. For information, address Atria Books Subsidiary Rights Department, 1230 Avenue of the Americas, New York, NY 10020.

First Atria Paperback edition March 2020

ATRIA PAPERBACK and colophon are trademarks of Simon & Schuster, Inc.

For information about special discounts for bulk purchases, please contact Simon & Schuster Special Sales at 1-866-506-1949 or business@simonandschuster.com.

The Simon & Schuster Speakers Bureau can bring authors to your live event. For more information or to book an event, contact the Simon & Schuster Speakers Bureau at 1-866-248-3049 or visit our website at www.simonspeakers.com.

Interior design by Kyoko Watanabe

Manufactured in the United States of America

9 10

Library of Congress Cataloging-in-Publication Data

Names: Morter, Sue (Patricia Sue), author. | Taylor, Jill Bolte, 1959-
Title: The energy codes : the 7-step system to awaken your spirit, heal your body, and live your best life / Dr. Sue Morter ; foreword by Dr. Jill Bolte Taylor.
Description: First Atria Books hardcover edition. | New York : Atria Books, 2019] | Includes bibliographical references.
Identifiers: LCCN 2018042567 (print) | LCCN 2018051898 (ebook) | ISBN9781501169328 (eBook) | ISBN 9781501169304 (hardcover)
Subjects: LCSH: Energy medicine. | Alternative medicine.
Classification: LCC RZ421 (ebook) | LCC RZ421 .M67 2019 (print) | DDC 615.8/52—dc23
LC record available at https://lccn.loc.gov/2018042567

ISBN 978-1-5011-6930-4
ISBN 978-1-5011-6931-1 (pbk)
ISBN 978-1-5011-6932-8 (ebook)

Medical Disclaimer

For my mother and father,
Marjorie Ruth Kibler Morter and Dr. M. T. Morter Jr.
I thank you from the depths of my Soul.
And may we keep the dream alive. . . .

CONTENTS

Foreword by Jill Bolte Taylor, PhD   xi

Introduction   1

Part I

A NEW WAY OF SEEING—THE QUANTUM FLIP

CHAPTER 1
Project Awakening: Shifting from Pain to Bliss   13

CHAPTER 2
Your Role in Creating Your Life   39

CHAPTER 3
The Invisible You: Bioenergy Basics   64

Part II

A NEW WAY OF BEING— THE ENERGY CODES PROGRAM

CHAPTER 4
The Anchoring Code: Getting Back in Your Body   97

CHAPTER 5
The Feeling Code: The Language of the Soul   125

CHAPTER 6
The Clearing Code: The Healing Power of the Subconscious   153

CHAPTER 7
The Heart Code: The Universal Solvent   180

CHAPTER 8
The Breath Code: The Power of Life Itself   203

CHAPTER 9
The Chemistry Code: The Alchemy of Embodiment   233

CHAPTER 10
The Spirit Code: Where the Many Become One   263

Part III

A NEW WAY OF LIVING—THE EMBODIED LIFE

CHAPTER 11
Making the Quantum Flip, One Day at a Time   293

CHAPTER 12
Life on the Front Side: Living as the Soulful Self   313

References   321

Resources   325

Acknowledgments   331

FOREWORD

Every once in a great while, I happen upon another life traveler whose experiences and beliefs resonate so boldly with my own that I literally jump up and down and burst into song. My first meeting with Dr. Sue left me not only singing, but vigorously dancing my happy dance. It's truly a pleasure to gaze into the eyes of another who perceives life, and our relationship with our brain, in a similar way.

In 2008, my TED talk "My Stroke of Insight" became the first TED talk ever to go viral on the Internet. That presentation struck a chord with millions of people all around the world, not simply because I was a brain scientist at Harvard who experienced and recovered completely from a severe brain hemorrhage, but because of the lessons we gleaned about the relationship between science and spirituality at a neurological level.

As stated by Louis Pasteur, *fortune favors the prepared mind*, and just as I was the right person with the right background and education to gain maximum insight into the brain from my experience with stroke, Dr. Sue is exactly the right person to garner wisdom from her extraordinary experiences with energy medicine, meditation, illumination, and embodiment.

Dr. Sue's father, Dr. M. T. Morter Jr., was a highly respected chiropractic physician who explored and defined many of the cutting-edge principles underlying the scientific field of bioenergetics. He developed the BioEnergetic Synchronization Technique (B.E.S.T.), which functions by stimulating the body's natural healing capacities. For him, this pursuit of bioenergetic training was cognitive, clinical, and intuitive.

Dr. Sue grew up immersed in the developing conversation, and for her, bioenergetics became a way of living, an awakening, and a *deep knowing*. Armed with a traditional chiropractic education, supported by tens of thousands of hours of clinical practice, Dr. Sue has emerged as a true leader in the unfolding field of quantum medicine. I know this firsthand, because she helped me rebalance my own wounded brain so I could complete my recovery. After receiving sessions with Dr. Sue, I felt like I'd come home for the first time in the seventeen years since the stroke.

Thank goodness our society requires that any evolving science must be both challenged and appropriately tested by the status quo. However, while traditional science demands the application of the scientific method—which by its own definition requires that results be both linearly tested as well as replicated—unexplained miracles of healing are happening on a regular basis because *the world around us does not obey the laws of linearity.*

It is truly exciting to exist in a time when established neuroscientists are utilizing innovative methods to help us better understand the biology underlying the success of the nonlinear healing modalities.

Near the end of my TED talk, I shared that I was motivated to recover from that devastating stroke because I pictured a world that was filled with beautiful, peaceful, compassionate, and loving people—people who knew that they had the power to choose, moment by moment, whom and how they wanted to be in the world. Dr. Sue is one of those people, and her life's mission has become helping others embody the same.

In my language, peace is just a thought away. By consciously choosing to run the circuitry of our whole brain, we have the power to experience deep inner peace. Within the following text, Dr. Sue presents techniques that will train you to do exactly that—and for this gift to humanity, I am forever grateful.

Enjoy the ride of your life!

Jill Bolte Taylor, PhD

THE ENERGY CODES

INTRODUCTION

I was sitting with my eyes closed in a darkened ballroom with hundreds of fellow meditators surrounding me, when suddenly I found myself weight-less, suspended high above Earth, engulfed in a radiance so intense that it was as if I were on fire with light. I could feel my absolute vastness. I could see 360 degrees—in every direction—in a light so bright it was ten times brighter than the brightest day in the desert that I had ever seen. Gone was my sense of having a body; instead I was a crystalline ray of light. And, seeing the vastness with my mind's eye, I knew that I *was* that. I was the universe itself and all that it entailed. The brilliant, all-encompassing radiance permeating my being *was* me. I could see the Earth beneath me, about the size of a marble, and every breath I took allowed light to become a loving presence that flowed through my system and into the Earth. I was immense and at one with all of creation.

Yes, this experience totally rocked my world!

From the time I was a little girl, I'd heard my parents talk at the dinner table about energy: everything is energy, and energy is what we humans are really made of. My father was a pioneer in "energy medicine," a bril-liant chiropractic doctor with an internationally renowned body of work, a legend in his field. As a child growing up in his shadow, I always wanted to be around him and continually looked for his approval. As a young adult, I worked alongside him in his health-care practice and attended his popular seminars. I went from being an observer of my father's work to being an active partner, and after I became a licensed chiropractor, I spent many hours of meaningful time with him. We shared a deep devotion to humanity and a continual excitement about the new energy practices we were discovering to help the people we served.

But even with all my exposure to the concept of energy, I'd never known this infinite vastness of energy. After this personal experience of it, my reality changed. The concept of energy suddenly took on a much deeper meaning. Instantly, I knew that this was *who I really was*: this pure, intelligent energy—blazing and alive. Peaceful. Eternal. Outside of time and space. I was wise and absolute. My existence was effortless. There was nothing I lacked or wanted for; I was totally, utterly whole and complete. It was a state of exquisite perfection, which I knew was my home. More real than any reality I'd ever known, it was the only place I ever wanted to be.

And what a stark contrast it was to my life experiences to date, which had felt downright torturous at times, and at best like a steep uphill climb. Everything took so much effort. Every day, at some deep level, I felt like I was being sent to the battlefield in a fight for my life. As a child, dealing with these feelings, I developed a debilitating shyness, which at every turn caused me to feel terrified and insecure. I watched softball from the sidelines for two summers because I was afraid of "doing it wrong" on the field. When I finally did step up to bat, I hit home runs. I took this to mean that I should always watch and learn as much as I could before stepping in, because otherwise I might fail. In junior high and high school, I played it safe by becoming an overachiever, always doing things "right" as a way to feel safe and to get approval from others for being a "good person." I was a cheerleader, played sports, got great grades, won "best actress" in state drama competitions, and was voted "most popular" and "most likely to succeed." But despite all my efforts, and even the considerable validation I received, my fear of not being good enough never decreased. In fact, most of the time I was downright terrified.

By my midthirties, having become my best version of a good doctor, citizen, and friend driven by perfectionism and overgiving, I felt exhausted. Though I had attained professional and financial success, I lacked joy, love, fulfillment, and a true sense of self. I was suffering physically, too, especially from almost daily migraine headaches that left me unable to lift my head off the pillow, let alone go to work. More and more often, I found myself wondering, *Is this really all there is?*

Then one day, something inside me snapped. While God had never been a part of my worldview, I was now desperate enough to be willing to let go of doing things my way and to reach out for help. That evening, I walked out onto my balcony, looked up to the heavens, and almost demanded: "You show me, as I am clearly not getting this life thing very well!"

In that very moment of surrender, something shifted. I felt lighter, and right away my life began to improve. A series of serendipitous events took place—people started inviting me to meditation retreats and to have conversations about consciousness and the study of enlightenment and offering books and instructions on how to engage in life in an entirely different way. As I went to the meditation classes, awakenings began immediately shifting my perspective of what was real. Not long after, I was in that ballroom having the profound experience that would forever bring me out of the suffering and struggle that my life had too often been up to that point.

I suspect that you have also had your fair share of struggle and troubles that brought you to the brink of exhaustion and that you can relate to that part of my experience. Perhaps you've had a broken heart or have not found lasting love. Maybe you've suffered from physical illness or pain, financial struggle or stress, disappointment or disillusionment. There are so many ways we can suffer: from low self-esteem, anger, sadness, resentment, or regret; from the inability to let go of the past and live in the present; from guilt, shame, or the inability to create what we would most truly love to have in our lives; from anxiety, depression, loss, or abuse; from the loss of our true sense of self.

The reason I know with certainty that you've experienced some of these feelings and conditions is that we all have. They *are* the human condition . . . that is, *until they're not!* The wonderful truth is that, as a species, we're evolving beyond this. Collectively, we're sitting at the edge of a pivotal breakthrough in human consciousness. Living from the perspective of the painful, small, insecure self we've always known is not our only choice. Another option is built into us—we're actually wired for another perspective for living in which we are equipped with full awareness of our true greatness.

How you can systematically switch over to that far more rewarding perspective is what I'll be sharing with you in *The Energy Codes*. I'll show you that there's a happier, more successful version of yourself that's available to you right here and now—the same as the version of myself that I experienced that day in the ballroom. That version I know with every ounce of my being is the true reality of who I am . . . and who you are too. Because it's not just my truth; it's also yours. It's who we *all* truly are.

The best part is that, not only can we perceive this reality from time to time through a spontaneous breakthrough while meditating, we can actually *live as that reality*, reliably and consistently, throughout our daily, waking, walking lives. That's the promise of what I call the Energy Codes. What you're going to learn as you begin to use the Energy Codes isn't how to reach the occasional exalted state. As exciting as that may sound, the power of the Energy Codes is far more compelling and much farther-reaching than that. No, as you do this work, you'll be making the one change that transforms everything in your world for the better. You'll be implementing the one solution that makes every problem you ever had go away.

Hard to believe? Sound too good to be true? I assure you it's real. When you live from the perspective achieved through the Energy Codes, your life becomes meaningful, and, even more than that, it becomes fulfilling. Every day is fueled by a powerful sense of purpose and passion. Your health improves dramatically: symptoms resolve; you feel energized, vital, and alive. You have simple and effective tools for dealing with any pain or illness that arises. You feel clear, positive, empowered, and deeply connected to yourself and to the rest of life. Feeling self-love and self-worth is your constant inner state. Living as your whole self, rather than just as your rational, conditioned mind, you make choices according to your deep inner wisdom, which is readily accessible to you. Every endeavor is an exciting adventure in which you are the predominant creative force. You are your life's creator, consciously manifesting what you would truly love. Life is magical, filled with wonder, awe, and trust.

I know this to be the case because I live it every day, and I've helped thousands of others learn to live it too. I began experiencing profound results like these immediately after my exalted experience in the ballroom, an awakening of consciousness, in 2001. I was suddenly able to solve long-standing problems in my life. In fact, I didn't even see problems *as* problems anymore. I could easily understand how any challenge was serving my evolution and awakening—my highest good. My life became happier and healthier, far surpassing anything I'd previously known. I had spontaneous healings: my migraine headaches simply disappeared, and within a few months, the painful scoliosis I'd had since birth began to correct—today it's totally gone. During the next few years, injuries such as two compression fractures, one in each of my arms, and a horrible ankle sprain mended quickly and without traditional treatment methods of immobilization. Instead of being held back by perfectionism, I began to flow in collaboration with life, feeling a profound sense of ease. I was no longer in a hurry. I trusted the timing of circumstances unfolding. I no longer felt the need to prove myself by improving upon all I came in contact with; instead, I noticed the perfect beauty that existed inherently within everything. Fulfillment, rather than success, was my objective; yet success seemed to happen naturally as a by-product.

My patient base grew without efforts to generate new business, and the challenges of difficult cases resolved. People healed and referred their families and friends. Amazing new staff members came to the clinic without my having to search for them. An invitation from the governor's office to fill a position on the licensing board (Indiana Board of Chiropractic Examiners) came, as well as invitations to speak at professional conferences. Life was expanding on every level with grace and ease.

I was so excited by the positive changes that I wanted to be able to return to my exalted experience again and again. More, I wanted to learn how to *reside* there. It became my mission to figure out how to do that—not only for myself, but so that others could also experience the truth of who they are and reap the astounding benefits. For the next several years, I turned my life into a living laboratory, made many discoveries, and began sharing those discoveries with others. Before long, everyone involved started seeing amazing results. I knew I was onto something significant. Something huge. Revolutionary even. In fact, for me, it was the fulfillment of the whole purpose of human life!

Since the beginning of our days on earth, we humans have looked for ways to engage with our true, limitless nature as spiritual beings (our soul, or Soulful Self) and transcend the small, limited, fearful, and pain-riddled identity (our ego, or Protective Personality) where we spend so much of our lives. As I started to work with others (using early versions of the methods you will learn in this book), and they began to find their own renditions of the breakthrough I'd achieved, I knew I was on the path to finding the keys that would unlock that potential in all of us. People began to share that their meditations were progressing beyond simply a relaxing of the mind and a centering within a peaceful state; they were now beginning to experience expanded realities, "seeing" with their inner eye and having access to deeper wisdom than they had previously known. They were reporting that they were not as inclined to engage in arguments, but rather would see from a higher perspective new solutions that benefited everyone involved. They found it easier to love, have compassion, and forgive. And, emotionally and physically, they, too, began to heal.

And while I'd stumbled upon a profound version of who we are that I was aware is usually reached only by devout yogic meditators, I knew that we were *all* meant to live from this place—that it's there for *all* of us to discover, if only we know how.

Developing the Energy Codes

Fortunately, my exalted experience left an indelible impression on my mind and my body. When I came back into my body in the ballroom that day, I could still recall in intricate detail what it had felt like inside of me, and I knew that the way to return to it was to re-create its characteristics there— in my body and in my consciousness. The particular way of focusing my mind; a slowed and intentional breath; an immense feeling of being centered in my core; a devotional disposition; and an intimate, tender, loving presence were all integral pieces of the puzzle. I replayed and scrutinized every nuance of my experience, then would practice re-creating those nuances and observe what might reveal itself in my awareness as I did so.

I spent my evenings in lengthy, sometimes all-night meditations, and my days in consultations with my patients and clients, implementing what I had learned on the previous night's journey within. With each experiment I did, I made careful notes about what seemed to bring my body and mind into, or close to, that expanded state, until I could re-create it at will.

Little by little, workshop by workshop and patient by patient, I decoded what worked for me and for others to tap into our true nature. And, in the process, a series of life-changing principles and practices emerged. Keeping only the most effective and efficient of what worked, I codified the steps that allow us to live as our Soulful Self. Because these all had to do with sensing, anchoring, and increasing the presence of our essential energy within the body, I named these steps the Energy Codes. Since then, I've found through my research that both ancient texts and modern science verify what I've discovered. The Codes are comprehensive and holistic, and best of all, anyone can easily use them.

We are all capable of awakening to this higher dimension of ourselves— and of living to our true potential, enjoying optimal wellness as the constant condition of our lives. In fact, it's part of our life's purpose to do exactly this. *Knowing, experiencing,* and most importantly, *living* as our divinity—not secluded in meditative silence, but in our everyday life—is Heaven on Earth, now ours for the taking.

The knowledge you need is in your hands. Those steps, the Energy Codes, are spelled out for you in simple terms in the pages of this book. Just as they've changed my life and the lives of thousands of others, I know with certainty that they will change yours too.

Discovering Your Magnificence

As you will see, what I wish to share with you is more about what is *right* with you—what is good and true—than it is about anything I learned in school about diagnosing problems and fixing them. Whether focusing on pathology or prevention, our culture has been preoccupied with what's wrong and how to fix it. Mine is a different message. It has to do with the truth of who you really are, and what you're made of. Yes, it will show you how you can heal—physically, mentally, and emotionally—but, better yet, it will also show you how to embrace your own magnificence and the profound truth that there was actually nothing wrong with you in the first place. I want you to experience this on a very deep level and learn how to express it and live it every day.

This is far more important than any accomplishment in your outer life, including winning any trophy or award, breaking any record, acquiring more things, losing weight, or asking for the promotion—or even getting it! The one simple inner achievement that matters more than anything else is this: *to awaken to your true nature.* Seems amazing, perhaps, but this undertaking is at the forefront of our consciousness as a species. It is truly on the cutting edge!

It's also not new. It's foundational to the Bible, the Quran, the Torah, the Upanishads, and many more ancient texts. People from cultures all across the globe have turned to this line of questioning for thousands of years. Many of us become interested, at some point, in who we are and why we are here.

The use of energy as medicine also goes back to the earliest recorded history. Ancient Egyptian hieroglyphs depicted the use of energy for toning and healing the physical body. Ancient Christians used the "laying on of hands" to create miraculous healings. More than five thousand years ago, in ancient India, the Vedas, the oldest recorded commentary on human potential and development, described moving energy in the body and raising our vibrational frequency to facilitate healing and to awaken the consciousness to higher realms. These practices were not imaginary "magic"; rather, they were (and are) based on the truth that *we are beings of energy*!

Today, scientific research is revealing what ancient practitioners knew long ago. Science is proving the existence of the human energy field; this field is as real and as sensitive as our physical skin—and it affects our physical reality in dramatic ways. We are discovering, for example, that it is through our energy field that our very DNA gets its instructions about how to act. We see this in the findings of Dr. Bruce Lipton, for instance, who, working at Stanford University's School of Medicine, revealed evidence that changes in organisms are caused by gene activation from a stimulus coming from the *surface of the cell wall* rather than in the genetic code within the cell nucleus, as was widely believed. This shows us that messages from our cells' environment, including our thoughts and emotional states, generate energy flow of a particular nature at the surface of the cell that determines what the cell will "do." This discovery made a significant contribution to a new branch of science called epigenetics, which basically states that our environment is more important than our genetic inheritance when it comes to our experience and expression of health and well-being. That environment is generated by the energy of our individual thoughts and actions, which lead to the production and movement of molecules of chemistry, which in turn lead to the activation of our DNA and overall cellular function. In other words, by what we think and do that affects our energy, we create our own possibilities for healing!

With these new breakthroughs, the importance of restoring and maintaining our energy flow has become ever clearer. If we want to claim our true potential, we need to build the circuitry in our brains and bodies so that we can live as conscious energy beings. When we do this, we can heal every part of ourselves and begin to masterfully create a life experience of magnificence.

I don't *need* science to tell me that this is so; yet, having grown up in a household where it mattered if an understanding had scientific backing, the conditioned scientist in me delights with each piece of scientific evidence that pours in to validate my experience. It helps my mind catch up with what my heart, gut, and deeper wisdom innately already know. Fortunately, science is now advancing so wonderfully in bridging the gap between the visible, material world and the invisible world of intuition, intention, and spirituality that each of us has the opportunity to experience this "knowing" before we know, and trust it!

The question before us now is: How long will it take us to make this inquiry into our true nature a priority and begin to answer it for ourselves? When will it actually become apparent that knowing and living from that true nature is what matters most? The answer is that it usually takes until the day our pain becomes so unbearable that we begin to look around and ask if life doesn't have more to offer. But I say, why not get interested in living from your truest self now rather than later, so that you can spend the rest of your life in celebration of the greatest accomplishment ever known? This book will walk you step-by-step along the path to achieving that goal.

What's in This Book

In part 1, "A New Way of Seeing—The Quantum Flip," you'll build the foundation you need to successfully shift from living confined by your fear-based self to living as the boundless, whole, creative being you actually are. This section lays the groundwork for how to engage with yourself and your external world so you can tap into your limitless potential and create the life you truly want. With the understanding you'll gain in part 1, you'll be ready to begin doing the work that will move you into your Soulful Self in part 2.

In part 2, "A New Way of Being—The Energy Codes Program," you'll learn the seven Energy Codes that turn on the needed wiring or circuitry inside you that will enable you to live as your Soulful Self. The Codes offer a complete system for healing your imbalances, awakening to your own true magnificence, and—most importantly—living a magical life. In a simple and straightforward way, they'll show you how to embody the truth of who you are and create a life you'll truly love.

Whether this is your first exploration with using energy as medicine or you're well versed in the subject, the Energy Codes' revolutionary methods offer unique insights and protocols that will be life-changing for you and for those whose lives you touch.

In part 3, "A New Way of Living—The Embodied Life," we'll look at how you can integrate the Energy Codes into your daily life, as well as how this new way of living will ultimately amplify your presence in, and contribution to, the world.

Though this book is a powerful transformational tool that draws from the sciences of quantum physics, neurobiology, and energy healing, I've worked hard to make it accessible so that you will *use it*. From the results I've seen, you could be a whole new version of yourself—healthier, happier, more empowered—just a few months, or even weeks, from now. But only if you apply what you learn! The time will pass regardless. Therefore I invite you to truly embrace this work—and I promise that you'll be grateful you did.

Ready to get started? Great, let's go!

Part I

A New Way of Seeing— The Quantum Flip

Chapter 1

PROJECT AWAKENING:
SHIFTING FROM PAIN TO BLISS

"Everything is energy . . . including this lectern," I often say in my talks, and then tap my pen on the wooden surface beside me. With the clicking sound that resounds when the two solid objects connect, I see something click in my audience members' minds.

The most important (and, to many of the attendees, startling) insight offered in these sessions is the fact that, underneath the tangible, physical form of our body, we humans are pure, intelligent, conscious energy—as is everything else in the universe.

We don't tend to think of the floors we walk on, the equipment we use, or the people we meet and interact with as made of energy. But they are. And, more importantly, *we* are. The physical world we perceive with our five senses is actually just energy that is compressed and made dense enough to touch. We label this compressed energy *matter*, but in reality it's no different from other types of energy—light waves, sound waves, or thoughts.

I grew up as the daughter of a pioneer in energy medicine, and I heard and saw many things that validated the energetic reality of our nature. In his long career, my father, Dr. M. T. Morter Jr., served as president of two chiropractic colleges and, as a researcher and educator, worked with hundreds of thousands of patients and practitioners worldwide, always at the cutting edge of advancements. But as mind-blowing as the discoveries I was privy to often were, nothing I saw or heard in my years of working with my father prepared me to know and experience the full reality and implication of what being an *energy being* means. It wasn't until my own profound experience of feeling I was a being of energy that I learned, in the deepest way, what and who I truly am—who we *all* are.

We are *energy*. Our matter, mind, and thoughts are energy. Our flesh and bones are energy. We are integrated, multidimensional beings made of pure energy. And the degree to which we know this truth about ourselves is the degree to which we live either in pain or in bliss.

After my awakening, I realized that there were aspects of my new understanding of who and what we actually are that were not addressed within my father's work. Learning to master myself at the level of pure consciousness and explore life from the inside out at this invisible "spirit" energy level was new to me. So I sought answers from ancient Eastern traditions and the masters of consciousness who practiced there. Eventually I left the family business and went off on my own to teach the profound truths I was living and experiencing. I thought my father understood. He said he did; after all, he'd done the same thing when he'd started his career in health care and branched off from his own family's work. He was disappointed that I'd moved away from the family, and he disagreed with some of my choices, but on the whole, we were two sides of the same coin, both working to heal and empower people around the world.

When Dad passed, I was fifty-one. I was by his side, holding his hand, at the moment of his transition. I didn't want him to go: he was my idol, my hero, my mentor. He developed some of the foundational techniques I use in my practice today. We shared so much, even if we were no longer working side by side. I just couldn't imagine life without him.

Dad's last words to me were, "I love you from the bottom of my heart."

"I love you, too, Dad," I whispered.

Two weeks after he passed, I was in Colorado, leading a three-day women's retreat. Twenty minutes before I had to walk onstage to begin the retreat's first session, I got an e-mail from my brother Ted that read simply, "Here's Dad's will." Since my mother had passed several years before, his will would dictate the distribution of all of their belongings.

As I read through it, I gasped. Aside from my portion of the proceeds from the sale of my parents' home, my two brothers would be the sole recipients of the entire estate.

Did he stop loving me? I wondered. *What did I do to deserve this kind of rejection?* Tears flooded my eyes as I groped for the nearest chair. For several minutes, I just sat there, shaking my head. *How can this be?* I felt shattered. How was I going to go onstage and lead this program in just a few short moments?

It wasn't that I wanted or even needed the money or material things, although to be barred from receiving my mother's teacups and her paintings was a blow. No, it was that being cut out of my father's will felt like the biggest withdrawal of love I could imagine. We'd worked together, discovered together, accomplished so much together. I'd spent my whole young life desiring his approval and attention, and had later devoted many years and thousands of miles of travel to teach his work for him, even though it always meant leaving my own practice. Now, in this moment, it felt as if he had rescinded his support from everything I was and everything I was doing. The pain was deep. It was unbearable.

"Ready, Dr. Sue?" A voice pulled me back into the room, reminding me that I had to go onstage in a moment. *How can I possibly be a facilitator and teacher for others right now?* I questioned again. Then I remembered the very work that I do, and the truths that I teach. I had to pull myself together—mentally, emotionally, and, most importantly, energetically. I had to realign and reintegrate my "shattered" energy so I could feel whole and continue to do the work that is my mission in the world. So I immediately did what I'd spent the last fifteen years discovering and teaching to others.

I applied the Energy Codes.

My body calmed down first, as feelings of safety and peace washed through me. My mind followed, landing gently on the solid sense of self that was like a warm ball of light growing bigger and brighter inside me. Suddenly I knew that I was unharmed by this turn of events. Everything was going to be okay. I knew from experience that what had seemed so devastating a moment ago would ultimately be beneficial to me in a larger, more complete context.

Most of all, I could once again feel the truth of my father's love. I could see that, ultimately, leaving me out of his will wasn't a betrayal. I could experience it as a gift of love, one that would be revealed to me at exactly the perfect time.

As this new perspective took over, a smile broke across my face. From within my core, I felt empowered, energized. I couldn't wait to go onstage and do what I do some 250-plus days a year: share the awe-inspiring discovery of *who we really are* and how we can miraculously transform every aspect of our lives by more consciously living as *that* version of ourselves.

As the weekend progressed, I continued to apply the Energy Codes and remained calm, loving, and fully present. In the weeks and months that followed, if negative thoughts or emotions about my dad's will came up, I again used the Energy Codes to not only work through them, but also benefit from them. I deepened my compassion and understanding for everyone involved in the situation, and ultimately even got a glimpse of the higher purpose behind why it had happened in the first place. (I'll share that with you a little later in the book.)

Now, I have to say, if the news about Dad's will had come to me earlier in my life—before my spiritual breakthrough, and before I developed the Energy Codes—it all would have gone very, very differently. I'd have translated my dad's choice into "What's wrong with me?" or "What did I do to deserve this?" and spiraled into self-doubt. Feeling angry and hurt, I might have withdrawn from my family, possibly ruining our relationships. And because my career was so closely tied to my dad's, I might even have abandoned my life's work. I know for sure it would have been a path of suffering and pain for me.

How do I know this? Because until any of us have had the experience of a greater reality about ourselves, we can only come at life's challenging situations from the perception that we are inadequate, that there is something missing, wrong, or broken about us. Without knowing a version of ourselves that is indeed perfect, whole, and complete—the version I call the Soulful Self—we have no reference point outside of that old story of inadequacy.

Our problem as humans isn't that we are inadequate, wrong, or broken; our problem is that we *believe* we are. This fundamental misconception underlies every other problem, dysfunction, and pain we have. It can turn gifts into burdens, love into unrequited need, and a few challenging moments into lifelong dis-ease.

The good news is, we don't have to live with this untruth anymore. We don't have to keep telling ourselves the same old stories about who we are and what is "real" in our lives. We can realize and reclaim our magnificence and embrace ourselves as the powerful energy beings we are—and create from that place.

We can do this by remembering that we are *energy beings*, and that energy is the key to everything.

Living in Pain or in Bliss

My transformative "ray of light" experience, my spontaneous breakthrough while in meditation, showed me the truth of my essence as an energy being in a way that I couldn't ignore or deny. Suspended above Earth as a radiant being of light, I was in another reality altogether. I had awakened to a different version of perceiving life—and myself in it. It was as if I were scuba diving, looking out from behind a face mask, aware that the underwater world I was now experiencing was more real, and truer, than life on shore. It felt like I'd been in this place forever and was never going to leave it. I was more at home here than in any concept of "home" I ever could have conceived with my mind. Instead of being completely afraid, as I'd been for much of my life, I suddenly experienced myself as completely *complete*. There was nowhere to go, nothing to do; I could simply *be* in my absoluteness, my oneness with everything.

This all-encompassing sense of completeness was a total contrast to how I'd experienced myself to date. As an adult working with my father in his seminars, I found meaning and purpose, but I also suffered from debilitating migraines and a persistent fatigue; for years I napped during my lunch breaks. I was always ready to please, fix, and prevent conflict in any form. Relationships were often arduous, yet I set out to "make them work," even if that meant I wasn't true to myself. After graduating from chiropractic college, I set up a clinical practice and had great success in the outer world, but lacked deep internal joy and real fulfillment. In short, I was suffering. Not because I was doing anything "wrong," but because I was operating according to a set of rules that were not based upon my true nature.

When we struggle, it is not because we are flawed or unworthy, but because we are trying to solve problems, pain, and challenges using the very forces that generated them: the mind and the Protective Personality.

THE PAINFUL PERSPECTIVE OF THE PROTECTIVE PERSONALITY

Until we know ourselves to be energy, or spirit, we believe that we are the body and/or the mind. This single misperception about our identity causes us untold suffering and is at the heart of every problem we have in life. Why? Because so much of our true nature is excluded with this view. Something feels missing, so we perceive that something *is* missing, or wrong, or broken about us. We then spend all our time and effort trying to compensate for feeling inadequate, as I did growing up and for years into my career. Stress, dysfunction, and disease are all by-products of this misperception. We feel like something is missing; we try to prove ourselves right or worthy; we try to fix what's broken. When we don't identify with the energy that we actually are, we can't feel our inherent wholeness and well-being. To gain some sense of orientation for navigating life, the mind then starts to write stories about how something *is* missing, or wrong, or broken about us.

These stories and thoughts, in turn, affect us at an energetic level (because we *are* energy). The power of thought affects our reality; these internal stories are no different. When the mind, instead of seeing how we are integrated with the fabric of the universe and inherently connected to All That Is, writes stories about how we are separate and alone, we perceive ourselves as separate and alone. Thus isolated, we don't feel safe. We think we need protection to exist in the world. We're constantly on guard against threats and scan the external world for all of the places where we aren't getting the approval, acceptance, and love we believe we need to be safe. Rather than creating from our own heart's desire and actively pursuing a life we love, we continually jockey for survival.

This fear-based, survival-centric identity is sometimes referred to as the ego or the false self, but I call it the Protective Personality. Whatever you call it, though, this protective approach to life tends to limit what we are willing to try, because "safety" is its first priority. This makes our relationships with others very conditional, keeps us off-balance, and creates continual stress that eventually takes a major toll, mentally, emotionally, and physically.

On top of this, the battle we fight as the Protective Personality is hopeless, because it's based in that single, destructive belief that *we* are the problem. Although we each have our own tools for coping with this belief, and even circumnavigating it to some extent, none of us is exempt from living from this painful perspective (at least in part). It's simply an aspect of the human condition . . . again, until it's not!

Fortunately, the Energy Codes' most profound purpose is the integration of the Protective Personality with our true nature—the Soulful Self; this integration offers nearly limitless potential for healing at every level of our lives. We are changing the game. We are disregarding the notion that living from the Protective Personality is the only option. We are evolving as a species into a new and more complete way of living, loving, and being.

HEAVENEARTH: OUR EVOLUTION TO
LIVING AS THE SOULFUL SELF

When we start to see ourselves as the pure, magnificent energy beings we are, we automatically begin our journey to experiencing wholeness. It truly is that simple.

When we know we are energy beings, we begin to live away from the fear-based stories our minds create and start living from the *other* option that is available to us—the perspective of our true, eternal nature as the Soulful Self. Rather than focusing externally, always scanning the horizon for what may do us harm, we focus inward on the energy within and around our body and rely on it to show us what is true for us. When we do this, life flows effortlessly. Opportunities for love and expansion are revealed naturally; we only have to lean in, say yes, and let them unfold. We are powerfully loving, and lovingly powerful. We know and feel our oneness with everything and feel separate from nothing. Stress and worry don't exist, because we know, unequivocally, that everything in our life ultimately serves our expansion and well-being.

I speak about this peaceful, magical state from direct experience. My journey into awakening as the Soulful Self followed a pivotal moment of surrender that left me irreversibly changed. My body felt as if it was glowing. My mind wanted only to revel in what it had been exposed to, rather than process it in any way. I'd gained a completely new perspective on who and what we truly are. Although I had not yet begun to integrate my experience (in fact, I initially felt rather disoriented and was taken to a nearby house to lie down), I knew that my reality would never be the same. That proved to be true, and the period that immediately followed the experience was interesting, to say the least!

When I got home that night, I fell into a state of bliss that I never wanted to leave. For many days, whenever I raised my head off the pillow I would be pulled from ecstasy and into a sense of standing under the thunderously whirring blades of a helicopter about to take off. It was as if I'd absorbed a super-high-frequency energy that neither my body nor my mind had a context for. Then, as I laid my head back down or when I would slip into a meditation, I was instantly immersed in the most exquisite state imaginable. Visions of electric and iridescent colors, shapes, and other realms would open up in my mind—the most beautiful sights I'd ever witnessed. These were followed by vignettes of images simultaneously bringing messages and perceptions of all kinds of truths. It was all so grand, brilliant, and pristine! I was in bliss, in a state of *ananda* or *samadhi*, as they call it in the yogic traditions, and I never wanted to move!

For days I remained in bed and simply experienced myself as a being of pure, divine energy. My Protective Personality began to merge with my Soulful Self. I had freedom in my mind and heart, a deep and beautiful relaxation in my body, and I spent many moments in the wonder and awe of pure awareness that we are truly cosmic beings. Still, this process wasn't instantaneous. My subtle-energy opening was only the beginning of my understanding of what it means to *be* the energy being that is the Soulful Self.

After about a week, I'd integrated the high-frequency energy enough that I could sit and stand and walk around. But even then, the world outside my bedroom seemed harsh and loud. I was extraordinarily sensitive to everyday sounds, such as the radio or television, and to fast-moving activities—people hurrying past me, cars zipping by, even waiters bustling around a restaurant. At first my body felt so lightweight, I could barely sense it. Then, as time passed, I began to consciously anchor into my body more consistently, which generated a feeling of incredible strength.

Even so, returning to my everyday life was a challenge. I felt somehow "between worlds" and had no idea how to operate from this place. I was no longer able to just look at people's faces, read their body language, and simply trust their words. I could now see the energy *beneath* the surface veneer they presented. Something else was revealing itself to me that felt more real and true. My attention was drawn to another level of reality that had been imperceptible to me before, except for during a short period of my early childhood.

When I was about six years old, I was playing in a creek bed while the sun shone on the rippling surface of the stream. Tadpoles were sprouting legs in the shallows, and the summer air was perfect and still. I looked at my hands above the water and saw golden light around them, radiating in every direction. At that age, I also frequently saw spheres of colored energy around people—around my dad, for example, when he was working with patients or teaching, or around my mom as she was painting, or around the other kids on the school playground. I thought it was normal and that everyone saw these things.

But after several painful experiences of talking about what I saw and hearing that others hadn't seen the same things, I became afraid that people might think I was strange and reject me. So at around age eight, I simply shut down my connection with these sights. During my twenties and thirties, however, I remembered these beautiful experiences and longed to re-create them, but could not. I wondered if perhaps I'd simply "made it all up," as children supposedly do.

After my opening to the energetic realm, though, not only could I *see* energy again as I had in my childhood, but I could also *sense* and *feel* it. It had been real all along. Only the stories I had told myself about the lights had made me stop seeing them!

Once again, I found myself able to perceive things that others didn't—and once again, I felt uncomfortable about this ability, especially because often I had a hard time making sense of what I saw and felt. I'd ask patients about something I was seeing or sensing, and they wouldn't recognize what I was picking up on. Their energy patterns, which represented an upset emotion such as sadness, fear, or anger, were obvious to me, yet they would say they "were fine" and "everything was great."

Rather than once again hiding my new perceptions, though, I persisted. And I noticed that my patients who "didn't know what I was talking about" during one visit would report back on their next visit that what I had discerned had been the case all along; they just hadn't realized it at the time. For example, during an appointment with my patient Cecile, I'd inquired about the weak energy flow in her system. At the time, she reported that all was well with her relationship, but she returned to say that she'd been in denial about a very real problem with her husband. Similarly, Brian, who, when I asked about the energy drain that I could see surrounding him, claimed he was doing just fine with all the travel for his work, reported back that he'd realized it was time to pursue another career. Countless times people would return to say that they'd been unaware of an issue, but then a "light turned on" following our session.

I was seeing and sensing interference in a person's energy field before even they could perceive its presence. A fragmented energy field would guide me to inquire with a client, which would often lead to an enlightening reveal of their underlying problem, such as a history of childhood sexual abuse or patterns of unhealthy behavior. We could resolve these issues once the light of the patient's own consciousness could shine upon the larger picture. This validation of my insights got my attention. It was as if there was a subtle layer of truth beneath what someone's conscious mind was perceiving, a layer that needed time and attention to become obvious.

Other changes were a bit harder to handle, such as my increased awareness of my own energy field. Sometimes when I was talking with someone, I could sense and see my own energy field around my body; suddenly it would feel like my energy was overlapping the other person's and I was on top of them when actually I was a normal distance away. I would self-consciously back away so as not to be invasive, only to have them step toward me to maintain the normal distance. This was confusing! It felt to me like we were "inside" each other, because our energies were so completely overlapping. I would step away repeatedly and they would follow, until we had "danced" our way across a room or down the sidewalk. (Later, I learned that our energy fields do overlap; until our nervous systems develop the sensory sensitivity—or "circuitry," as I call it—to perceive it, we just don't notice, so we feel as if "nothing is there" in the space between us. But this energy field is actually the most profound way that we are all connected to one another, as one united humanity.)

As awkward as this new way of being felt at times, every interaction I had with the world told me *I was back*. The *real me* was back. I felt more at peace and at home in myself than I had since experiencing those special, mystical moments as a young child. I felt joyful for no reason, warm and relaxed, comfortable day and night. I breathed differently and more deeply than ever before. I knew all was well and that the previously painful circumstances of my work and personal life were going to be different—as if some "answer" had opened up.

I also knew that this newly expanded, *real* me would have to learn how to navigate the contradictions I continually faced—of how to make "rational" decisions while following my inner knowing at the same time, not only for myself as a person but also as a doctor, a friend, and a confidante for many significant leaders in my community. Many times, for instance, I could see that leaders in the larger metropolitan community were not acting with integrity, and this insight allowed me to make decisions that were true for me without feeling any conflict, or any need to try to belong or rebel. Often, as I talked to someone, I could see clearly how they were creating their life circumstances in order to defend and protect a "smaller" version of who they were, as if they were subconsciously insisting on living as a false self, feeding on drama and pain.

Simply put, the reality I could now see—the reality of us as whole, complete, and powerful energy beings—often didn't align with others' perceptions of themselves or how they were living their lives. I realized that I was at a crossroads. I had to decide: Go with what was true, or not? Live in bliss, or return to a life of denial, self-deception, and pain? So much of what I had established in life—my friendships, business, and relationships—seemed to be at stake; yet it was clear to me that my new reality was more important than anything else. It was my truth, and I *had* to go with it.

Moment by moment, by following the energetic messages that were arising from within me, I chose bliss—oftentimes beyond logic or what others called reality. I'd be strongly encouraged by advisors to incorporate particular modalities or equipment into my clinical practice, treatments that claimed to be the "latest advancements" in technology, but if the advice didn't feel right to me, my choice became an easy "No, thank you." Then, months or years later, reports would show that the equipment didn't perform as originally promoted. Or I would be invited to participate in investments, business practices, or conferences that all seemed at surface level to be very good opportunities, but this flow of energy would simply make my decisions for me, leading me to decline many such invitations. Then it would be revealed, sometimes even years later, that the business practice or opportunity was not operating with integrity for those who had participated.

There became a grace—what I call the *wave* of grace—guiding my life. There were many times when I would simply sense to place my attention in a particular direction, and the next thing I knew, often within hours or days, a fabulous invitation in that exact area would come my way—to participate in a documentary film or to speak at a very important conference, for example—with literally zero effort on my part. Additionally, countless times I would sense to connect with someone I hadn't spoken to in months or years, and I would call or send a message only to receive a reply that they had just "that very day" been wishing they could ask me a question or share a concern with me, and "there I was!"

My life became magical, unfolding in an effortless and joy-filled way without any of my previously paralyzing feelings of insecurity, inner conflict, and self-doubt. Finally I'd landed on higher ground, able to dial in to a version of decision-making that required no thinking. I simply went with the palpable energetic impulses that told me in an instant what my true choice was, and, miraculously, these impulses were always right. My gut reaction inevitably proved to be a far better choice than my logical, educated mind alone could have come up with. Starting a new business, moving my office, and releasing work relationships that no longer served the highest purpose of my true vision were all now easy decisions that came from my core. The energy flowing through me became my compass; over time, I no longer needed input from external sources to validate my decisions.

Going through life with this kind of absolute inner knowing and guidance is beyond freeing. Instead of trying so hard to figure things out and bend life to my will, I let my life lead—and it became a revealing, an unfolding, of my right path. A higher wisdom came into play that exceeded the limited vision of my conditioned, educated mind.

As I followed the truth that was coming up inside of me, a new direction for my life began to unfold. I felt led to teach more energy healing classes. Held in the reception room of my clinic, they immediately filled up and became standing-room-only more often than not. I also taught regular meditation classes where I shared with my patients and students the experiences I'd had in my own meditations.

For instance, in the midst of a meditative state one evening I'd noticed a rush of energy that dropped down through the core of my spine and circulated low in my pelvic area, and as it did the center of my brain "lit up" with an experience of full presence while a sense of knowing came over my entire being. So in the next class I guided the group through a similar process. As we practiced what I had done, I watched to see what their energy fields responded to. I could see that my sharing helped people awaken their own ability to shift and manage their energy fields, which in turn brought about changes in their lives. At the next class, they would share stories about the new things that had been happening with them since I'd last seen them.

Week by week, month by month, they were undergoing true transformation. Bonnie, for instance, finally saw that she could leave her job after long-standing indecision. Nicole had breakthroughs that allowed her to drop into a deeply relaxing meditative state that she had never reached in years of trying. And Courtney finally let go in meditation and allowed the energy to flow through her body, which led to the release of a migraine headache pattern that she'd had for twenty years. These results, and many others, unfolded through a regular practice of specific breathing patterns, relaxing the mind, and guided meditation. I observed, noted, and began to codify it all. Clear principles and practices emerged that would eventually become the Energy Codes you'll learn in this book.

In my new life, I also got invited to speak at nearby hospitals about the energy medicine tools I was teaching and sharing in my clinic, long before word of any such topics was breathed in the mainstream of health care. People responded, and more and bigger invitations came. It all happened fast and effortlessly, all because I had surrendered and said yes to the tangible energy and its innate wisdom coming up inside me. I could literally *see* that the energy flowed from one situation into another.

Today, I see all situations that occur as impulses from the universe nudging me toward my greatness. I melt old, unhelpful relationship dynamics and find love where pain and even estrangement previously existed. In addition to having completely healed my migraines and scoliosis, I feel younger than I did twenty years ago. I now not only believe in miracles, I see them happen all the time. And now that I know where those miracles come from and how we can tap that place, I can constantly support the miraculous and the magical in others' lives.

––––––––

Living this kind of grace-filled existence is not only possible, it's our birthright. It's what we and our lives were actually *designed* to be. Therefore, just as it happened for me, it can happen for you too.

In fact, awakening to this personal identity shift—from living as the Protective Personality to the Soulful Self—is *the very purpose of human life*. When the soul meets consciousness, humanity awakens to its truth, and we know peace. This is what we're here for—to discover our soulful, energetic nature and *live as that true nature* here in physical form. We are here to awaken our divinity inside of our humanity. To experience Heaven while on Earth, and to live what I call HeavenEarth—one unified space.

All of this is available to us right this very minute. How? Because, in reality, we *already are* the Soulful Self. We can experience that reality spontaneously, in a nanosecond, just as I did in meditation that day. It is right here, waiting for us to acknowledge it. There is nowhere for us to go and nothing for us to do in order to become the Soulful Self. There are no qualifications, no hoops to jump through, but . . . we simply don't know that. And this not knowing our true nature is the state of being in the Protective Personality.

With the Energy Codes, I'm going to teach you how to awaken to your wholeness and perfection, your true self, your magnificence—and to increase the presence of that true self in your everyday life. When you do, your life will be magically transformed, just as mine was.

Though this shift from Protective Personality to Soulful Self can happen spontaneously (the way it did, in part, for me, and for others who have had similarly profound and transformative experiences), for most of us, actualizing the Soulful Self happens in stages. And while you may or may not have been *intentionally* working toward this goal of awakening before now, the truth is that you have been working toward it all of your life, because it's what you came here to do. Yes, everything that has happened in your life until now has been moving you toward awakening to your true nature. For this reason, I call life Project Awakening.

By understanding how that awakening progresses, you can help yourself to consciously and intentionally facilitate it happening with greater ease, speed, and grace. I have laid it out for you here, in what I have named the Model of Awakening. Being able to "see" where we are evolving from and where we are evolving to can help the mind make the needed shift to more readily perceive, and thus live as, the Soulful Self.

The Model of Awakening

The Model of Awakening reflects the three distinct levels of consciousness we embody as we evolve toward discovering and living our truth. The model also has two sides, like a coin. The Back Side of the Model ("tails" on the coin in the image on page 28), which has two stages, represents the Protective Personality. Here, we're in constant survival mode, employing the reactive defaults in our system, spending all of our energy on strategizing for safety and protecting ourselves. We only reach the Front Side of the Model ("heads") when we surrender our attachment to our nervous system's reactive patterns or circuitry, and build new, higher-capacity circuitry that allows us to fully activate our creative genius, our Creatorship. It's on the Front Side of the Model that we claim and live from the place of our true power—consciously and actively creating our life as the Soulful Self.

TAILS   HEADS

FRONT SIDE	**Creative Genius / Creatorship**
BACK SIDE	Survival / Victimhood → Survival / Self-Help

STAGE 1: VICTIMHOOD

Stage 1 of the Back Side of the Model, found on the bottom left of our diagram, is the perspective of Survival/Victimhood. Simply put, this is where we see life as happening *to* us and believe we can't have any impact. We are completely unaware of ourselves as influencers or creators and therefore feel a strong sense of fatalism and resignation. We believe we are unable to do what we want because of opposing outside forces that seem to be beyond our control. In fact, we may be so far on the Back Side of the Model that we don't even know we're unhappy, or that there is any other way to be. We may simply be going through the motions, believing that this is just what we have to do, because this is the way life is.

For example, in Stage 1 you might blame your unhappiness and feelings of unfulfillment on being born in unfortunate circumstances, not having the college education you wanted, marrying too young and not getting to pursue a particular passion or a career, or simply not having enough money to do the things you really want to do. (Or you may not even think about it or name it at all.) This paradigm is characterized by anger, fear, hopelessness, helplessness, resignation, fatalism, struggle to survive, and the like. Its tagline is "Life is happening to me, and I have no control over it. This is just the way life is." You may not even put this into words; the perception just unfolds as though it is the truth.

STAGE 2: SELF-HELP

This is where most people today find themselves. It's a big step up in consciousness from Stage 1—but it's still on the Back Side of the Model because it's still based in operating reactively out of a *subconscious* perception of inadequacy as the Protective Personality rather than in operating creatively from a place of knowing our true power and magnificence as the Soulful Self.

In this stage, we no longer accept our miserable state as the way life is. Instead, we awaken to the sense that we're in pain and to the possibility that perhaps we don't have to be. Instead of being resigned victims, we get the idea that something could change; we *could* be happier or healthier or more respected and honored. And so we start to look at what we can do to make those changes occur.

In this paradigm, we still see life (both "good" and "bad") as largely happening *to* us, but at least we believe there is *something* we can do about it (at least some of the time). We realize that often we can improve or even fix our situation—and possibly, by choosing some of our thoughts and actions, exert some control over what we experience. With the right mindset, we can make the best of a bad situation, and in doing so, we might find some benefit or gift in our pain. The tagline for this stage is "Though life is happening to me, I choose to make the best of it." It's the view: "Something is wrong, but I will fix it. It won't get the best of me."

I call this Self-Help because in this stage we work hard to heal what we believe is wrong, missing, or even broken within us or in others, and strive to be happier. Many of our coping skills, therapy sessions, and self-help books and programs are operating at this level of consciousness. We diagnose a problem, and then get busy treating it. This paradigm certainly helped me to decrease my own level of pain and attain more of what I wanted at an earlier time in life, and I'm very grateful for that and for the help it has offered many of my patients. But, while this is far better than being completely stymied and has served many of us well for many decades, it's not the advanced state of consciousness that we want to be in, and it does not honor our true capability.

Continuing to look for and find "problems," and spending our resources fixing them, only makes us better at problem-solving. Unfortunately, this leaves us needing problems to fix in order to "know who we are." We don't build our capacity to perceive joy and wholeness without depending on the contrast of pain. We never get ahead of the game. On a deep level, in Stage 2 we're actually still viewing ourselves as coming up short in life; it's only that we now have some tools to compensate for it. We're still not thinking like powerful creators; therefore this paradigm cannot fully serve us moving forward.

Fortunately, we can attain a level of consciousness that takes us far beyond "making the best of whatever life hands us." It's the Front Side of the Model, where we experience who we truly are in all our power and glory. That moment when I was suspended above Earth, bathed in my own radiance, I *knew* this truth about myself—and about all of us. Yes, even you!

STAGE 3: CREATORSHIP

The Front Side of the Model is a very different interpretation of life than the Back Side. This is the place of living in the Soulful Self's mode of Creative Genius or Creatorship. Here you begin to see that there actually is no such thing as a bad circumstance to make the best out of or find a "silver lining" in, since there never was anything wrong, missing, or broken in the first place. Even though the "silver lining" is a beautiful concept and helped us when we were trapped on the Back Side of the Model, it's a very incomplete use of our creative abilities. Instead, on the Front Side, we know that every challenge that happens serves us, and we sense, feel, and know that we have played, at the highest level of the soul, a role in its very creation. There is a purpose for everything and that purpose is to awaken *ourselves* to our true greatness. Yes, we are playing a role in our own awakening process. The greater part of us is inviting the smaller part to meld with it, generating the experience of wholeness that we seek.

From this perspective, life is always unfolding in our favor, to serve our expansion, despite how it might seem or feel in the moment. There are no exceptions. Our Protective Personality begins to melt into this truth as it recognizes that if things were supposed to go differently in our life, they would have. As I often ask the students in my live courses, "How do we know it was supposed to happen?" The answer is: "Because it did!"

Rather than "making the best of" a situation, which implies that something "bad" has happened and we should work at turning it into something "good," what if the truth is that the situation, no matter what it is, truly was never bad in the first place? The more painful a situation is, of course, the more this notion can be a challenge to embrace. That's okay. We'll continue to work with this idea as we progress through the book. For now, I'd just like you to ponder: What if you *were* empowered to see that every event in your life truly occurs *for no other reason than your eventual benefit*? And what if you knew that you were playing a role in this very process so that *you* might awaken *yourself* to a greater reality, one with more freedom and empowerment? What if your greatest pain point was actually hiding the greatest gift you would ever receive? This understanding would indeed change the quality of your life on Earth—which, of course, is why you came here.

If you were empowered to see your life this way—as happening entirely and only for your eventual benefit—you'd be living in flow and collaboration with life. You'd see the bigger plan at work behind the scenes. You'd much more quickly see the gains in any loss. You'd see how losing that job, for example, resulted in finding your true, fulfilling vocation. You'd find that the injury that left you unable to perform taught you compassion and a deeper sense of self. You'd start to embrace the loss of a beloved as a way to deepen your heart to levels you might never have known otherwise. You'd find yourself in profound gratitude for life and all of its mysteries. Ultimately, you'd stop seeing losses as losses at all. You'd know and see that, with every happening, no matter how difficult, there comes a benefit equal to or greater than the suffering it entails. Knowing this, your suffering would dramatically decrease, and maybe even cease to exist at all.

Now imagine that you could know ahead of time how to work with your body, mind, and energy field so that the big experiences never generated pain and suffering in the first place. That is what you will be learning in this book: how to work with *all that you are*, consciously, below the level of the stories told by the Protective Personality, so that each and every life experience becomes a meaningful step that takes you deeper into your wholeness, your truth, and a trusted relationship with the universe.

Interpreting the happenings of our lives through the lens of trust—knowing that "it's all good" and everything is in our favor—*in the moment they occur*, saves us from having to go through the process, over time, of forgiving ourselves or others for the situations we find ourselves in. This is the viewpoint of the Soulful Self, whose tagline is "Everything that happens in my life is always in my favor, and I created it on some higher level of my own consciousness for the purpose of discovering my own magnificence."

———

When we look at life from this perspective of "it's all good," we're on the threshold of the Front Side of the Model. Yet this awakening doesn't happen simply by reframing our beliefs about who we are or changing our thinking about the nature of life alone. There is no "spiritual bypass" of just telling ourselves some rosier story here. Far from it.

For millennia, spiritual traditions have espoused the notion that we are spiritual beings having an earthly, or physical, experience. I'd like to offer another understanding of that point: that, actually, we are spiritual beings having a *spiritual* experience in a physical, energetic world. And that, to experience and live the fullness of our true nature, we must begin consciously living as beings of spirit—as *energy beings*—in this physical aspect of life.

This means we must go beyond knowing intellectually that we are energy or spirit, and actually *embody* our energetic or spiritual nature. We must literally bring our energy to life within the physical body and identify as that energy. When we do this, our transformation to the perspective of the Soulful Self and the Front Side of the Model occurs automatically, in a sudden, radical, and comprehensive shift I call the Quantum Flip.

Embodiment, Not Only Enlightenment, Makes the Quantum Flip

In quantum physics, there is a phenomenon known as a "quantum flip." This describes the ability of an atom, a foundational element in the quantum world, to change directions instantly, without ever slowing down to a zero-momentum state as other matter appears to. You might think of this like rolling a marble up a hill. In linear physics, the marble would roll up the hill a little way and then slow down before reaching zero momentum; then it would slowly start to roll back down, gaining speed as it went. In the quantum physics scenario, however, the marble rolls uphill and then instantly rolls back down without ever slowing to that near-still point. For an instant, the marble would essentially be moving in two directions at once—never going through a process of slowing down and reversing its direction, but rather just flipping into a new direction instantaneously! Yes, atoms can jump back and forth between two stable states of motion that have equal and opposite momentum, without passing through the zero-momentum state that separates them—thus making a "quantum flip."

Getting to the Front Side of the Model and becoming the Soulful Self happens in much the same way. In an instant, we can begin seeing an entirely different world and make our choices accordingly.

Essentially, there are always two directions in which we can look, and either will be true if we follow its particular potential for creating. One will lead us to the Front Side of the Model, and the other to the Back Side. We get to choose, and the quantum universe will support us fully in that choice. It doesn't matter if we've been rolling up the same hill for our entire life; our reality can shift in an instant if we so choose. And, as the quantum flip proves, we don't even have to come to that still point to perform the turnaround!

The mind is very involved in the Quantum Flip. The difference between this method and others you may have studied is that we use the mind in an entirely different way—in close collaboration with the *body* and the spirit. You'll notice my emphasis on *body* here. After all, while we are spiritual beings, we came to this three-dimensional world and took a body. Therefore, the body is going to play a huge role in our liberation from the overactive, fearful mind, and we can and should use it to its full advantage in our awakening. As you will see, embodiment of the Soulful Self involves building new circuitry—circuitry within the body along which the energy of the Soulful Self can flow, and circuitry within the body and the brain that enables the mind to perceive that energy. Living as

THE QUANTUM FLIP
(Two Directions at the Same Time)

the Soulful Self comes down to circuitry—having the communication and sensory circuitry in place to sense, anchor, and activate within the body the energy that is who we truly are.

It's as if each one of us is a city, and our nervous system is the electrical grid. We can't "see" into the places where there is no wiring. The streetlights in those areas will remain off until we consciously bring energy to them and illuminate them. Then conscious energy will flow there, and we will be able to perceive what is happening in those places in a new way.

Achieving this turned-on or light-filled state is a return to our true nature. Spirit *is* light. As spirit beings, we are literally *made of* the high-frequency energy called light. Science today is telling us that even our cells emit light when they perform their functions. Neurons in the brain and spinal nerves have been found to produce photons (tiny particles of light that influence our very atomic structure) when they send impulses to each other, communicating through light. Light channeled by micro-tubules in the tissues helps activate different parts of the brain faster than nerve synapses can do the work. We are truly astonishing and miraculous creatures . . . of light energy!

The reason we don't know our own divinity is not that we aren't divine. It's that we don't have the circuits in place to *perceive* that divinity. Our lack of circuitry limits our ability to experience aspects of our true nature. To embody our wholeness—to know, feel, and live it—we have to build and activate the circuitry in the nervous system to "turn the lights on." We'll do so by working with the energy system directly.

When we really get that everything is energy, including ourselves, we begin to see and exchange with life beneath the physical, material level, on life's subtler levels. Here, where there is fluidity and things shift and flow, change is most readily accessible to us. Here, we have the greatest power to create a life we truly love.

The key to a fully empowered experience of life is embodying the energy that you are. We must not only enlighten ourselves to the truth of who we are as energy beings, we must also embody that truth fully. In the next chapters, you'll learn how being embodied gives you direct access to your intuition, and how living from the intuitive mind rather than the rational mind manifests a life guided by your most creative self. You'll see that this is not only an effective and reliable path to lasting, positive change but also the fastest route available for experiencing your wholeness here in physical form.

With this one key, you unlock your innate creative ability to transform every aspect of your life experience—from your health to your relationships to your sense of self and purpose to the contribution you make to the planet. Without this knowing, however, we remain trapped in a limited view and version of ourselves, one that is locked in struggle, suffering, and pain.

How do we activate the circuitry to sense, anchor, and activate our true nature, the Soulful Self? That's what the Energy Codes are for.

What Are the Energy Codes?

The Energy Codes are a set of practices you can do on your own to generate your own Quantum Flip—to take yourself from confusion, dis-ease, exhaustion, and frustration to empowerment, joy, clarity, wellness, and creative expression. These practices teach you to build new internal circuitry that supports your true nature as an energy being. By reestablishing a natural flow of energy in the body, you create a shift in your identity from Protective Personality to Soulful Self.

The Energy Codes give you the tools to feel and know in your body, mind, and spirit that everything in your life is energy. You will live underneath the level of the mind and its stories, in your core and away from drama and pain. Seeing life from this deep and rich perspective changes the meaning of nearly everything you engage with. As you bring your conscious awareness into your body, you'll find that the Energy Codes are incredibly grounding, which enables you to perceive a higher level of consciousness overall, like the tree deepening its roots in order to grow taller.

By living as the energy being you are, you are able to embody your true gift to the world without hesitation or doubt. For instance, Jamie, a student of the Energy Codes, is now able to make decisions gracefully for her aging mother, which she used to struggle with painfully. Many teens have used the Energy Codes to find their place in the world and have stopped destructive behaviors like drug addiction, eating disorders, and cutting themselves in the attempt to "feel." The need to fit in or belong diminishes when we see and experience ourselves as made of creative energy and as natural leaders, rather than following the crowd or comparing ourselves to others. With your new knowledge of yourself as a creator, you'll experience patience and presence that you've never known before and step into life as the leader you never knew yourself to be.

Practicing the Energy Codes also just feels good! I'll be instructing you in breathing exercises and simple but effective movements and meditations, including some specialized yoga, that will get your energy moving in areas of your body—and your life—where it's been stuck, causing pain, and keeping you from experiencing your truest version of yourself. As the energy flow is restored, you will start to see multiple positive changes right away. These can include: improvements and healing in mental, emotional, and physical dysfunctions and dis-ease; greater energy, motivation, and clarity; balance and well-being in every area of your life; and perceiving your true nature and living your divine purpose. Rather than "thinking" your way through life, you'll find yourself feeling very clear from deep within your core, stepping into life as if it is "meant to be" and is happening in your favor.

Mary, for example, didn't feel she was in the right job to experience true fulfillment in her life. She was surrounded by people who seemed uninspired and spoke all day of things that felt petty and negative. She wanted to quit her job and pursue another career that supported her desire to grow and evolve. Now that she practices the Energy Codes, she realizes that her spiritual practice can be found *within* her current vocation and experiences deep fulfillment each time she does one of the practices in the middle of her day. She now knows that everything in her life is working toward her own awakening. This change in perspective changes her interpretation of what she sees, and therefore what she spends her time thinking about and doing.

Spirit is power—the greatest force of nature—and you are that spirit. The Energy Codes won't change you into something you're not; they'll simply help you express the untapped greatness that you already have within you!

The Energy Codes work with energy, and I have seen them enhance the tremendous benefits of other energy-based methodologies, such as acupuncture, chiropractic, craniosacral, osteopathy, Reiki, acupressure, Rolfing, reflexology, myofascial release, and massage, in my own patient base and in the clinics of doctors, nurses, energy-based psychologists, and practitioners of these modalities who are in my student base. However, my aim is not *just* to enhance your health and well-being, and certainly not limited to "fixing" something that is seemingly lacking or broken in your life. The Energy Codes go further by triggering the Quantum Flip and catapulting you to the Front Side of the Model to live as a conscious, awakened being of energy, and help sustain you in this new way of living.

In other words, this book isn't about using the mind to understand at a story level the truth of who we are. And it is not just about enlightenment. Nor is it simply about healing. It is about *embodiment* and living *as* the creative-genius energy being that you are. It will radically change how you experience and create in every area of your life.

———

The state of your energy has a direct effect on your perspective and the state of your life. I know this because I live it, and I can also clearly see it at work in other people's lives. The same is true about you. Though our Quantum Flip to the Front Side of the Model perspective and living as the Soulful Self doesn't happen intellectually, with the mind alone, opening the mind to a different reality and new worldview is part of the process. We've made a good start with that here in chapter 1 and will continue in chapter 2.

Chapter 2

YOUR ROLE IN CREATING
YOUR LIFE

In chapter 1, you learned that you are energy. That energy is your true nature. That an energy being is who you really are. And you learned that the degree to which you know that you are energy, and *live from that knowing*, determines the amount of pain—or bliss—in which you will spend your life. In this chapter, I'll show you why that's true. We'll look at how, as an energy being, you are the sole creator of your life experience and how, by addressing life at the level of energy rather than at the psychological/ mental level of "story," you can create a life you truly love.

Part of making the Quantum Flip from the Protective Personality to the Soulful Self is *identifying as* the Soulful Self. To do that, you must first become aware that there is an energetic reality going on beneath the story level of your life. To help open your mind to this deeper reality and ready you for the work involved in actually making the Quantum Flip, which you'll do in part 2, I'm going to share the insights and foundational truths that I found along the way.

We are part of a greater truth, a greater state of being, than we are usually aware of. This has been taught since the beginning of time, but while many indigenous cultures live this truth, our modern religious, cultural, and social structures have drawn us away from that spiritual/energetic/ connected reality. Quantum science has supported that knowing by proving that we are all connected to each other, to the earth, and to our physical world. Now it is our cultural and spiritual job to catch up to that science, and to *live as* true energy beings, with the deep knowing that energy is all that exists. In so many ways, this realization is the missing link so many of us have been searching for all along! Fortunately, our time for knowing and living this truth has come.

While the science behind all of this can be complicated, I'm going to keep it very simple. I've distilled the most important principles into what I call the Five Energy Codes Truths. These were helpful to me in the years when I was seeking and finding my true nature as an energy being; I hope that they will help you acquaint yourself with the real you as well.

The Five Truths are:

1. Everything is energy.
2. Your life is a reflection of your energy.
3. You are the creator of your life.
4. Your creation—your life—is always expanding.
5. The purpose of your life is to discover your creatorship.

Let's look at these a bit more closely here.

Truth #1: Everything Is Energy

Everything that makes up the entire universe is merely energy in varying wavelengths, vibrating at different frequencies. The highest frequencies are pure light, ranging from nonvisible to visible to the human eye. Sound frequencies are just more condensed versions of the same energy. Our thoughts and emotions are merely different vibrational frequencies, and even physical form is nothing more than compressed energy. What we experience as "positive" thoughts are energy patterns that are more open and spacious, while "negative" thought energy patterns are denser. Later we will learn how to use each of these patterns to our advantage in managing the outcomes in our life.

Our physical body is composed of an infinite number of different frequencies. The five main circulatory systems of the body—respiratory, hormonal, immune, cardiovascular, and digestive—exist as unique frequencies in the energy spectrum, different still from the frequencies of individual organs that compose them.

Specific energy fields exist at all levels of life, from the level of a whole organism to the various systems of the body to the organs and glands that compose those systems to the cells, molecules, atoms, and subatomic particles within each organ. So, again, everything in our world—that which we can see and that which we cannot see—is, at its essence, energy, and it is vibrating at a particular frequency or wavelength.

If everything is energy, then that means that there is nothing that is *not* energy. And *that* means that nothing exists in isolation; there is no separation between things. Everything exists in what my colleague the biophysics researcher Dr. James Oschman, in his book *Energy Medicine: The Scientific Basis*, calls a living matrix—in layers of interconnectedness. On the most real and true level, everything is connected to everything else in one big unified field.

What I find *most* amazing is that, because these individual layers of energy are connected by communication pathways, every layer knows what every other layer is "doing." We are one unified system of energies, and in this book we will learn to tap their common frequency beneath the surface and awaken to the magnificent fact that we are connected to, and part of, an entire universe that is made of that same subtle energy.

Too often we view ourselves and our activity as isolated, believing that what we think or do has no effect on anything or anyone else—when the truth is that, through this matrix, web, or unified field, *everything is connected* and *everything affects everything else*. At the most fundamental level of our being, we are all one. That means that what each of us does *matters*—that what we do in one area of our life affects *every* area of our life, and everything we do has some impact on everyone and everything else. It also means that, although the mind likes to believe itself separate and alone, our resources are far more outreaching than we previously imagined.

Science has been verifying this interconnectedness for years. One of the most pivotal experiences for my own understanding of this subject was viewing a research video by Dr. Valerie Hunt, emeritus professor of physiological science at UCLA, at one of my father's seminars. Using Kirlian or electrophotography, it showed that a person's biofield—the energy field in and around that person's body—moved into different patterns and frequencies in response to the individual's thoughts and actions. If, for example, someone ate vibrant, whole, healthy foods such as fruits and vegetables, his field was large and robust; with junk foods, his field became nearly undetectable. When a subject's dog came into the room, his field grew and tracked along with the dog as the dog ran around him. When a person chanted "*Om*," her field grew tenfold. This film showed that our personal energy field is flowing at a certain vibrational frequency, and that the frequency changes based on our own internal activity (thoughts, feelings, behaviors, etc.) as well as what we come into contact with in our external environment. These findings have been validated and enhanced today with continued research and the development of technologies such as electromagnetic field therapy devices like the EEG and SQUID (super-conducting quantum interference device), among others, which monitor and measure in even greater detail this substance called energy that we are made of and swimming in.

The energetic influence or exchange works both ways—our energy, our presence, has an effect on the world both around and within us. My friends and colleagues at the HeartMath Institute share research that demonstrates that we can change our DNA (one aspect or vibrational frequency of our system) with emotion (a different vibrational frequency within our system). With anger, rage, and hate, the DNA molecule compresses in length. With love, compassion, and joy, it expands. Thus, the vibrational frequency of our emotions will have a direct impact on our physical body or health.

Another example comes from Russian physicist Vladimir Poponin, who demonstrated in the 1990s that our DNA has an effect on its surrounding environment simply by being. A vacuum was created by taking a glass tube and removing all the air until nothing was left within it except a few randomly placed photons (among the tiniest particles of matter/energy in our physical world). When a specimen of human DNA was placed within the vacuum, the photons responded by changing placement in accordance with the DNA molecule. Even when the DNA was subsequently removed from the vacuum, the photons remained in the same positions—revealing that we have an effect on our world just by being here. It is in this way that humanity has created "reality"—through photon arrangement over the millennia.

So, energies are always affecting each other in a constant exchange. The vibration of a given energy field affects all things that vibrate at that level. Here's an example: If you have two guitars at opposite ends of a room that are tuned to each other and you pluck the G string on one of the guitars, the G string on the other will vibrate. This same dynamic happens physically between human beings. And it also happens between different aspects, or frequencies, within us. The Energy Codes will help you learn how to allow these aspects to work together in a collective genius, with each system supporting the others for your greatest well-being.

Dr. Valerie Hunt at UCLA was the first to discover the relationship between changes in our biofield and our health, and she determined that problems in the body actually start in the energy field. "Until now," she said, "many human diseases have been characterized as 'etiology unknown.' In other words, the cause of the disease could not be determined, and therefore the only possible treatment was alleviation of symptoms. But physiological symptoms appear because of the field disturbance. If we correct the disturbance in the field, the symptoms disappear and we have been healed. If we treat the symptoms directly, then when a stressful situation once more aggravates the incoherent energy that is the source of the problem, the disease condition returns."

The bioenergy field is actually an energetic template that determines what happens in the physical body. There is even evidence that an interference in the energy field precedes and even predicts an injury—meaning that there could be a disruption in a person's energy field and *then* the person would, for example, step off a curb and fracture his ankle—and that even "accidents" aren't just random events. All of this science taps into the deep knowing that I have carried all of my life—a knowing that you carry within you as well.

So, to summarize: everything is connected energetically. The thoughts and emotions we choose have a direct impact on our own DNA and cellular function. Our DNA affects the world around us; therefore we have an impact on the reality that we live in. We *create* this reality by shaping its expression through the vibratory frequencies emitted by our thoughts and emotions. Pretty amazing, right? And yet, when you tap into your deepest knowing, it makes perfect sense.

Truth #2: Your Life Is a Reflection of Your Energy

Life is a reflection of our own consciousness. In other words, we find what we are looking for. When I was working with patients and their symptom patterns and attitudes, I could see this in profound ways.

Now that I could actively perceive the subtle, energetic reality going on below the surface, I was fascinated to observe that people's energy fields would vibrate in different ways as they went about their daily routines. I watched my patients to see if their symptoms coincided with the disturbances I noticed in their energy fields. I was seeing between fifty and sixty patients in a ten-hour day, so I was able to methodically gather quite a lot of meaningful information.

Everything I saw and felt affirmed that we are intelligent, responsive energy that vibrates in different ways, depending on our thoughts and emotions. I could see, for example, that when someone was inspired by what we were discussing, her energy vibrated vital and bright. If someone was talking about doing something he "had to do," his energy became insignificant and small. I could also tell if someone was nervous or saying something different from how he really felt, because his energy field would "wobble." Rather than gathering all of this from body language or voice tone and fluctuation, I literally *saw* it as vibrational shifts in the person's energy field, where colors and wave patterns changed.

As my experience grew, I noticed distinct patterns in the energy. For example, the energy field of a "victimized" person caught up in his circumstances, who held the perspective that he was unable to change his life or relationships, would present as thin and dispersed about two feet off the surface of his body. This was in stark contrast to the thick and robust energy field several feet wide around an individual who felt authentically confident and had decided to step into her power and take initiative. A third pattern I noticed, albeit less frequently, was the huge and powerfully circulating energy system that occurred with someone who seemed happy, joyful, openhearted, and inspired. Centered on the core of their body, these people's energy fields would sometimes extend higher than the room's ceiling and overlap with other people around them. It was as if I could see through people's physical selves into their true essence, and actually see the perspective they applied to their own lives.

In observing these three general patterns again and again, I became aware of a spectrum of energy patterns and the life perspectives to which they corresponded. This is how I came to discover the Model of Awakening. Whether a person's energy was dispersed and on the surface of his field—or, in contrast, whether it was integrated, flowing, and core-centered—seemed to directly reflect (and I later realized would even *determine*) whether that person lived from the Back Side of the Model or the Front Side. In other words, the more unified their energy field was in their core, the more awakened they were to their true nature and power.

This was an exciting breakthrough in my understanding of what it takes to make the shift from the Protective Personality to the Soulful Self. If we could *consciously* shift our energy pattern from dispersed to unified, I thought, we could *consciously* build the circuits to experience ourselves as the Soulful Self.

Dispersed energy is energy that is not flowing smoothly or powerfully. Think of what would happen if we plopped a bunch of stones into a fast-flowing stream. The water would "splat" in all directions. There might even be standing pools left outside the main stream. This dispersal would generate weakness in the overall momentum of the water; some of it would flow sluggishly around the obstacles, which would act like a dam in the stream, instead of moving swiftly. The interfering stones are like "stuckness," "density," "blockage," or "gunk" in your energy field. Collectively these create "interference," which is a by-product of slowed, sluggish energy flow, which cannot maintain enough momentum to sustain health and vitality in our bodies and in our lives. This is also an example of a lack of circuitry through the blocked flow area. If the circuits were there, the energy would flow.

In turning this around, we have nature on our side. Our energy is more like mercury, a liquid metal, than like water. Imagine that you're back in chemistry class and you dropped a little vial of mercury. The mercury would splat in every direction and form little beads and globs. However, when you roll the mercury beads toward one another, they immediately merge into one larger pool of mercury. Like mercury, our energy *wants* to find itself again, and cooperates readily with our attempts to "get ourselves together."

Now imagine that liquid mercury flowing in a thick, robust, re-collected flow. Our energy system is designed to do the same thing, but—just as the mercury droplets require a push in the right direction—our energy requires some semblance of a pathway to follow. You will learn to create those pathways or circuitry and sense and direct your energy field back into one unified flow. (We'll talk more about this in chapter 3, when we take a tour of the body's energy system.)

The "splatting" or dispersal of our energy occurs when we experience traumas, fears, and judgments, as well as rejection. We feel rejection consciously or subconsciously when we don't like events or results or other things about life. Whenever we are exposed to something greater than what we can comprehend—something overwhelming, tremendously upsetting, or frightening—or when we can't accept, process, and flow with life as it happens, we splat. Like the stream suddenly filled with stones, our processes can't continue. Our mind stops, and energy no longer flows. These resistant, rejecting responses, usually in the form of thoughts and emotions, create energetic densities of lower vibration within our system. Then, because our energy is the template for our life, these densities create stuckness and dysfunction in our consciousness and in our physical world. These densities may present as "stones" in the energy stream, the impetus for a splat (and it's easy to understand them that way), but really they are blind spots in our consciousness where we are not yet awakened to our Soulful Self. When we put our attention on these blind spots, using the tools in the Energy Codes, we bring those dispersed parts of ourselves back into integration with the whole field.

My simple Energy Man drawing demonstrates the energy field as I see it when I am working with patients. I believe it will help to explain this concept further.

ENERGY MAN

The human system is made up of many variations of energy bandwidths. For our purposes here, we'll discuss five primary levels or layers, starting from the outside and working inward toward the physical body. They are:

1. The spiritual body, our basic nature or pure energy
2. The mental body, comprising our thoughts and beliefs, etc.
3. The emotional/feeling body, the frequency within which we sense and feel
4. The etheric template, where the chakra system resides; and
5. The physical body, our vehicle here on earth

In the philosophy of yoga, these layers correspond (in reverse order) to the *koshas* or "sheaths" described in the Taittiriya Upanishad. I was unaware of this traditional structure when I began to work with these energies, but delighted, years later, to find that the ancient texts validated each of my findings and the practices I developed.

These energies become increasingly denser (or more concentrated), and their wavelengths shorten; each layer has an impact on the layer beneath. Note that the first layer—the spiritual or pure energy body—resides underneath and throughout all of the other layers, and ultimately has influence over the entire system. Even the dense physical body is just a compressed version of the spiritual body; therefore, when we begin to wake up the spiritual body energies, the entire system is affected. This activates the spontaneous remission and miraculous healings that we've heard and read about and is the purpose and focus of learning to work directly with our subtle energy anatomy.

In the diagram, we see that the goal here is for the outer layer, the higher vibration of conscious energy—our true essence as the Soulful Self—to come into our physical body fully awake, creating the presence of conscious energy in our core. This is embodiment, where we fully compress our essence, our divinity, into a more compacted form, until it becomes physical and we *live as* the Soulful Self. Energetic interferences, blockages, or gunk—which can occur in the mental and/or the emotional

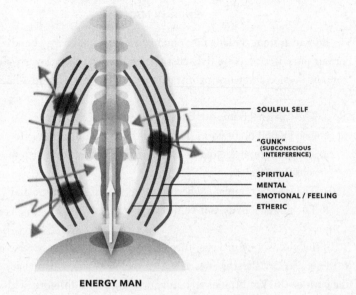

ENERGY MAN

layers due to rejection, resistance to what is happening, or lack of ability to process life circumstances—prevent that pure foundational energy from completing its journey. This gunk (blockages made of dense energies) occurs where the mind can't perceive our true nature.

Blockages represent where we are unawakened as the Soulful Self. This "splattedness" *is* the Protective Personality. The more dispersed our energy is, and the more densities in our system, the more we will look externally for our sense of self and wholeness. This only produces fear and stress. On the other hand, the more unified and integrated the energy is within your system—when you simply embrace what is happening in your life, for example—the more you inherently experience your wholeness and live in peace, harmony, and grace, regardless of your external circumstances.

A SURPRISE IN INDIA

My first trip to India showed me this truth in an unexpected way. Soon after I experienced my first awakening, I shared some of the multidimensional experiences with the personal steward to the teacher of the meditation group I'd just found. I explained how I'd seen other worlds in colors not seen in our own, seen the tissues "inside" my own body and brain become illuminated and visible, and experienced a depth of field with my external vision that made things appear to be nearly see-through when I looked at them, as if something in the air around objects was dancing off their surface. I'd also experienced what I since have learned is known as the Blue Pearl, a view of reality through the lens of a highly elevated state of consciousness. As a result, I was among a small contingent invited by the group's leader to visit her at her home in India, in the small town of Puttaparthi, one of the homes and ashrams of the guru Sathya Sai Baba. I joyfully accepted. I knew there was something big awaiting me in this adventure halfway around the world.

I left for the trip thinking I would be able to put some of my own healing knowledge to use helping those I would meet, while also learning all I could about the new realm that was opening up for me. Yet, much to my surprise, the people I thought I was there to help had something I didn't yet fully have. Most of the villagers in Puttaparthi had nothing of material value. And they also seemed to *want nothing*. But each had a deeply open soul.

The people who worked in the small shops or walked the streets on their way to visit others or to purchase food and other basic goods radiated an essence so beautiful, warm, and present, it was exquisite to experience. The heart-to-heart connection that came through their direct and unwavering eye contact was more than I might encounter over days or even weeks back home in the States, and yet there it was, everywhere I looked. They were connected to what mattered most: living from the true self. Because of this, and even though they had reason to feel otherwise, they were not bogged down with gunk in their energy fields. They were living their lives as spiritual beings, still vibrating with nature. Regardless of the ostensible lack in their outer world, they were at peace. I recognized their presence as a great gift, modeling the vibration I'd experienced in my exalted state and one that we can all experience once we remember how.

In the Soulful Self, there is no energetic gunk or stuckness. In our true state, the mind is fully aware that we are perfect, whole, and complete. And when our energy is in the pattern of the Soulful Self, we have a continuous experience of that wholeness on the mental, emotional, and physical levels; we know this as absolute well-being.

Wherever interference or gunk resides is the layer at which we'll have "problems" or feel stuck in life. If the gunk is in the mental or the emotional layer, for instance, we'll interpret motivations and events as if we're on the Back Side of the Model. We'll find ourselves in arguments, feeling as if we are "right," which can prevent intimate connection. We'll be perplexed at why the world is so unkind and insensitive; we'll feel hurt, disappointed, or disillusioned to exhaustion. We'll be in pain. Since interference in one layer affects all the layers beneath, gunk on the mental and emotional levels can lead to problems in the physical body layer, such as physical injury, disorder, or disease. This is what Dr. Hunt was talking about in her research, and it confirms the reality of the mind-body connection.

Recognizing *where* our energy is dispersed is key to healing any "problem" area we may have. In part 2, I'll provide you with the tools for discovering this and for integrating that dispersed energy so that you experience the absolute well-being that is available to you.

For now, though, I'd just really like you to get the idea that the more dispersed your energy, the more troubled, confusing, and painful your life experience will be. Conversely, the more integrated or unified your energy, the more in charge, at ease, and joyful you will be. And the closer to the core you can move that dispersed energy, the more personal power you will have.

I also want you to know that you unequivocally have the ability to integrate—to heal—what is disrupted within your system, which brings us to our next truth . . .

Truth #3: You Are the Creator of Your Life

Karen, a patient of mine, and I were talking prior to her treatment session in my office one day. She told me that she'd recently been in an auto accident and had excruciating neck and shoulder pain as a result. She was a stressed personality type to begin with, and this, in her words, "was putting her over the top." As she talked, I saw her energy disperse out beyond her body, seemingly untethered to anything at all. She cried as she told me how frightened she'd been when she saw that the truck was about to hit her. I put my hand gently on her shoulder—and, as I touched her, her energy field began to settle a little. Seeing this, I stopped her consultation and asked her to lie down on the treatment table.

Seeing where her energy was not flowing—where it was dispersed or stuck—I put my hands on her heart and her stomach. The energy there began to shift. When she followed my hands with her attention, the energy further intensified in those spots. She reported that she felt calmer, and I witnessed her system settling in. As I removed my hands and again asked her about the accident, her energy instantly dispersed in a splatting pattern. I then asked her to remember my putting my hands on her heart and stomach and to now re-create that feeling for herself. In doing so, she was able to pull her own energy back into her core.

We all have this ability to steward, or manage, the energy flowing through our system and to make it more unified. That's what the Energy Codes teach you how to do. We all also have the ability to unconsciously disperse our energy with the foods we eat, the thoughts we think, the way we treat others, the relationships we have. Our experiences also affect our energy, which, in turn, creates our next experience. Through the feedback loop, we create our own reality; and we are the creators of our own lives. This is one of the most important ideas we can ever embrace about ourselves. When we do, it gives us tremendous freedom and power.

How does this dynamic work? To understand it, we need to look at one simple aspect of our energy system: the photon, one of the smallest known particles in our quantum world, so small, in fact, that it is considered to have *no* mass. Think of the photon as the powerful threshold between energy and matter. It is literally thought of as energy, but can be measured as a particle of quantum energy. When tested to see if it is physical mass, it tests as though it is. When tested to see if it is energy, it behaves as such. It responds to our expectations and thoughts, both conscious and subconscious.

PHOTON DENSITY AND THE QUANTUM CORE

When we talk about our energy pattern, what we're really talking about is the arrangement of photons within our human system or biofield. And when we say that we have the ability to steward or manage our energy, we're referring to our ability to move photons and the electrons they influence—to change their arrangement—within our field. Our physical body becomes a reflection of our photon and electron pattern.

One of the ways we do this is with the mind's attention. You may have heard that focus creates reality. Well, here's the dynamic behind that: that which we focus on increases in *photon density*. In other words, when we put the mind's attention or awareness on something, our attention rearranges photons on the energetic level. Our intentions become more "real" or present in the physical world as the photons and other subatomic particles arrange in accordance with that focused thought. Therefore, where we place our attention determines where we gather and collect energy—in other words, where we place our creative power. If we gather more energy in the outer world, we become dependent on the outer world for feedback and our sense of self; if we nurture more at our deep core space, we can sense and feel ourselves there with a greater sense of safety and well-being.

This, by the way, is the phenomenon behind the Law of Attraction—the metaphysical principle that states that the energies of your thoughts, emotions, words, and actions attract like energies into your life. The often-overlooked key to manifesting in this manner is that photon and electron arrangement—what we create—is determined not only by our conscious focus (what we're aware of thinking about or paying attention to) but also what is going on in the subconscious mind (which we are, by definition, unaware of). We'll look at this more closely later in the book.

For now, think of it this way: if we don't have a sense of our wholeness, true nature, and well-being, our focus moves outward for orientation and protection. We build the ability to perceive what is out there, but we're dispersed. To gain a sense of our wholeness, true nature, and well-being, we must direct our attention inward to the core in order to draw more focus and conceivably a denser quantum pattern there. By concentrating our energy in such a manner that the sensory nervous system can begin to pick up on our true presence at the place of our deep core wisdom, we can feel ourselves as whole again.

The story I told you about my patient Karen is a good example. When she focused on the memory of her accident and relived the terror she had felt, her energy fragmented and dispersed to the outer edges of her field. When I put my hands on her and asked her to pull her focus there, it was as if the photon density increased in the core of her body. Her sensory nervous system could perceive her energy coming "back home," which caused her to calm down. Once she knew where to put her attention, she was able to do this on her own.

This again shows us the main difference in the patterns of energy between the Protective Personality and the Soulful Self. As the Protective Personality, we can't sense or know our wholeness; because the Protective Personality is based in partialness, we don't feel complete or safe. The mind in this perspective is fearful, and it scans the outside world for slights or threats. The mind is externally focused, so our energy disperses outward, away from our core. When living in the Soulful Self, our energy is focused inward and concentrated in our core, where we perceive ourselves as energy beings, whole and complete.

To increase awareness of our Soulful Self in our *life*, we need to increase our awareness of it in our *body and biofield*. Therefore we want to increase the photon density of the Soulful Self by putting our mind's attention on our core. We want to go from being externally focused to internally focused—from looking outside of ourselves to sense how others perceive us, to looking within ourselves to sense and *feel* who we really are. Only then do we awaken to and *become* who we really are.

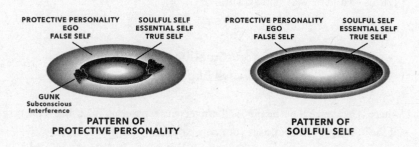

Here's another simple diagram to help illustrate. Think of it as a cross section of a human biofield, with an exterior layer containing varying amounts of energetic gunk and an interior core that is our true essence. The more our focus is exterior—the more we move our essential energy to the surface of our being—the more gunk or densities we allow, and the thicker that exterior layer will become. As our exterior layer becomes thicker, our core—the seat of the Soulful Self—becomes smaller. Our goal then is twofold: both to resolve the gunk or densities in the exterior layer, and to thicken or increase the density at our core.

This is another way of seeing the progression along the Model of Awakening: from the fearful, symptomatic state of the Protective Personality to the graceful, pain-free life of the Soulful Self. The more dispersal or gunk we have, the less we know and identify with our true nature and the more we struggle in life. The greater the presence of our true nature energetically, the less dispersed our energy and the fewer symptoms of dysfunction and pain we will have.

With the Energy Codes, we will increase the density at the core of our being and generate a greater sense of certainty and authenticity—the Soulful Self—to integrate the splatted energy of the Protective Personality. By changing our biofield in this way, we change our perspective, our physiology, and our physical experience of life.

We are all in the process of becoming more awakened to our true nature as the Soulful Self. That means that, energetically, we are always becoming more integrated and unified, or less dispersed. I know that life can sometimes seem to contradict this notion! Yet, I assure you, it is true. Truths #4 and #5 will help explain.

Truth #4: Your Creation—Your Life— Is Always Expanding

There is evidence that the physical universe is expanding. Your life is part of the universal creation, as is your consciousness, and they too are always expanding. Some scientists, myself included, interpret this to mean that we are constantly evolving. We are always waking up. This means that everything that happens in your life is serving that expansion. Therefore everything that happens in your life is in your favor; it is *good*. I know it doesn't always appear or feel that way, but as you apply the practices in part 2, you will begin to sense this truth.

We would never consciously choose many of the things that happen to us, and we struggle to come to terms with and make sense of them. But when we say that we are struggling, we are talking about a place of stuckness within us—about where our vital life energy is being dispersed and lacks enough momentum to continue flowing. Using the Energy Codes can help your mind stop struggling with or rejecting what has happened in your life (and thus keeping that energy stuck). This happens in part by giving it a new context for understanding what has occurred. I call this new context the Bus Stop Conversation.

ELLIE DISCOVERS HER BIGNESS

A student of mine named Ellie was a lovely, smart, and strong forty-year-old who thought she could keep her past from affecting her life. When I met her, she suffered from severe migraines and other health concerns. During childhood she'd been hospitalized for stomach and digestive disorders, such as nausea, constipation, and diarrhea. These issues continued throughout her adult life. She also had gained weight, and had difficulty being intimate and authentic in her relationships.

In her twenties and thirties, Ellie felt she was doing everything necessary to live a "normal life." She was an overachiever at work, chasing success in order to not feel so bad about herself. She would often flirt with men just to feel connection and then sometimes find herself in compromising situations around sex. When I inquired about why it took so much effort to generate love and belonging in her life, she shared with me that when she was about age four, her father started molesting her. Her pediatrician attributed her injuries to playing too roughly on her bicycle. As a result of these experiences, she grew up not knowing how to make distinctions between what was true and what was not. Her Protective Personality was well versed in how to hide the guilt and shame that had built up over the years in her attempts to keep secret a self-image that felt, in her words, like "a person lower than the dirt beneath a snake."

At age twenty, unmarried, she became pregnant by a young man she was dating. She felt that in order to keep her father away from her child, and also to protect her siblings' kids from him, she needed to tell her family the truth about his repeated molestations. Her fears that her family would not be supportive of her proved accurate, as her mother and siblings didn't believe her. They threatened to have Ellie institutionalized for making such disturbing accusations.

Ellie lived with her parents during her pregnancy, feeling completely alone. She chose to put her daughter up for adoption in order to get her away from her father. She entered therapy and worked hard to be okay. Ultimately a criminal court case was brought against her father by Child Protective Services when Ellie's nieces admitted to a school counselor that they too had been molested, and her father went to jail. But Ellie continued to feel the pain of her past and her present inner conflicts. At forty, suffering physically, emotionally suppressed, and having endured a series of unhealthy relationships, she was a perfect example of what happens when we live from the Protective Personality. Ellie needed a new perspective on her life.

Once, in a class I was teaching, a gentleman asked me, "How can all things be 'good' when I've witnessed so much trauma and abandonment?" In that moment, an explanation came out of my mouth that reflected a series of impressions I'd received in meditation. It was the Bus Stop Conversation. Its perspective helped Ellie and it has helped other students of mine. Here's why it works:

Energy cannot be created or destroyed. Therefore, since we are pure energy ourselves, we know that *we have always been* and *will always be*. Right now, though we're in the physical, earthly dimension having a physical experience, our physicality is not the whole of us. Our energy—our spirit—is our true self; when we leave our body and this plane, we'll still be who we really are. Looking at ourselves in this cosmic context raises a question: *What if our being here on this planet in this body isn't some random event, but rather a purposeful means to experience our larger reality of being the Soulful Self?* If this is the case, how does it explain our experience of life to date? That's where the Bus Stop Conversation comes in.

THE BUS STOP CONVERSATION

Imagine yourself at a Cosmic Bus Stop, where you and others pause between trips to this physical plane. As you wait, you get to chatting with the other souls at the bus stop, talking about your plans and agendas for life on Earth. You speak about what you desire to learn, how you wish to grow, and what you'd like to experience as a means of revealing to yourself your own true, divine nature as a being of energy and the creator of your own life.

"I want to learn about my wisdom," one of the other souls says.

"I'm going to learn courage," declares another.

"I want to experience being unconditionally loving," says a third.

"What are *you* going there to do?" someone asks you.

"Well," you might say, "I'm going to have a bunch of experiences of waking myself up. I want to know my ability to forgive. Yes, I'm choosing a Level Ten experience of forgiveness. Not just a Level Three or Level Four. I'm really going for it this time!"

"A Level Ten forgiveness . . . wow! Okay, how are you going to do that?" another soul asks.

"Well, I'm not exactly sure. I suppose someone is going to have to do something that is . . . nearly unforgivable."

One of your companions asks the obvious question: "What would that take?"

You reply, "Well, someone would have to do something like drink too much at happy hour, get behind the wheel, cross the center line on the road, and hit my car head-on. To take it over the top, they might take the lives of my family, or cripple me. It could have been avoided, and would be completely irresponsible.

"Then, after many years of hurt and anger and suffering even more because of my unforgiveness, I will reach way down inside my heart and find a deeper layer of myself than I would ever have known under any other set of circumstances—and forgive them."

You pause for a moment, remembering that the Bus Stop offers an opportunity to enlist others to help you achieve what you want out of your Earth-life.

"Who wants to be the driver for me?" you ask. No one raises a hand.

"Come on," you plead. "I've waited forever to have this chance to evolve myself. I'm asking with all that I have. Will someone please help me catch this opportunity?"

Someone finally chimes in: "I'll do it. I can see how much it means to you. Plus, it will help me with my own mission of self-forgiveness."

"Wonderful! Thank you so much. I'm so moved that you would do that for me. Well, I guess I'll see you on Earth!" And off you go, ready to take on the biggest task of your being thus far.

———

The Bus Stop Conversation is a metaphor, of course, for seeing your own energy as working to dissolve the illusions that you are a separate self. We get to heal our tendency to interrupt the natural flow of life by looking at our circumstances less personally and more as a project of allowing connection again. Looking at our lives through this larger perspective, we see that we are actually quite amazing for having created exactly what we need for our own desired expansion and the discovery of our own depths of beauty, strength, kindness, courage, loving, and so on—in other words, the many facets of our magnificence.

Can you see how this gives us a very empowering way of looking at the things that happen in our life? How it removes any sense of victimhood and Back Side of the Model thinking from our experiences? I have chosen a rather intense example here because that is the way that thousands of people have been transformed in my classes around the world. Energetically, it will hold a space for you to allow your own heart to open into your own Bus Stop Conversation for healing.

We can start to look at our lives in a new way: "Okay, I'm not just making the best of this bad situation. What if I actually *generated* that situation to awaken myself to something? Something more about who I really am? What if on some higher level I *requested* this experience so that I could explore a beautiful, powerful, and magnificent part of me that I wasn't aware of before?"

This is an incredibly freeing and empowering insight. I invite you to take a breath here, and then we'll explore the inspiring Energy Codes Truth #5.

Truth #5: The Purpose of Your Life Is to Discover Your Creatorship

Seeing yourself as a creator and stepping into your true nature as the Soulful Self doesn't mean that what happens to you won't be difficult or that you won't experience some painful emotions over it. However, when you see your life from this perspective and recognize how you are being served by what has happened in it, you discover that you don't need to engage in unnecessary suffering on top of the pain. You no longer take what happened personally to mean something negative or limiting about yourself, others, or the world. You don't create the energetic densities and blockages that cause you to be stymied, stuck, or operating from the view that you are anything less than a powerful creator for whom life is benevolent and unfolding perfectly and according to plan. Simply choosing to believe in the Bus Stop Conversation helps you put your experiences—both the painful and the joyous—in the most empowering context possible and frees you to move forward in the most positive way.

Ellie is a great example of this shift in understanding. Knowing that her difficult life circumstances and the challenges she faced to find her own true voice had been of perfect service to her soulful evolution, Ellie not only became grateful for the unfolding as it had occurred, but also began to see her "bigness of being." She now saw herself as the creator of her entire life experience and thereby found herself on the Front Side of the Model regarding the very things that had previously plagued her with pain. What we think of as forgiveness—letting go of our angry and resentful feelings toward another who we perceive has harmed us—happened seamlessly and automatically as she saw the purpose the events in her life had served, and therefore was no longer even necessary as a conscious process.

After having this epiphany, Ellie was highly motivated to use the Energy Codes practices (which you'll learn in part 2) to dissolve any residue from her past experiences and to live more and more as her Soulful Self. The result was healing in every area of her life: her headaches and digestive symptoms stopped, she's lost nearly fifty pounds and counting, and she now enjoys loving, trusting relationships with her family and others.

Having myself been sexually abused as a child by an extended family member over a period of years, I knew specifically how to direct Ellie into the work of the Energy Codes. Those early experiences confused me about trust, love, and connection with the outside world, and, because my perpetrator threatened that it would be very bad for me if I ever told anyone, I lost my ability to speak my truth about many things in my life for decades. Later I applied the principles of the Codes to embody for myself the gifts and teaching of those events, which is, in part, why I can say with such conviction that I know the Codes work. I actually am grateful for my family member's horrible behavior, as it has taught me my capacity for forgiveness and revealed to me my deep interest in seeing the good. It also served as one of the main aspects of my life that pushed me to seek answers beyond what my previous life and surroundings had to offer me. It sent me on my quest and ultimately contributed to the development of the Codes and the writing of this book.

As I look back at my whole life from my current place of integration on the Front Side of the Model, I can see the different perspectives from which I have lived in my life—from moments of being completely victimized by my circumstances to being completely free and empowered. From this new place, I am no longer controlled by the outer world bringing experiences *to* me; it's now obvious that the experiences in my life have all come *through* me, and ultimately *from* me, and for my own benefit. It's obvious to me that I put them there, as bread crumbs, to lead the smaller, separate me to the discovery of my own magnificent greater self as a creator.

My understanding of the Bus Stop Conversation also enabled me to forgive my father for his choice regarding his will—and to move on from that lovingly, which allowed me to make a further contribution to his work. Despite how painful it seemed initially, the whole experience turned out to be one of my greatest learnings about my own capability and personal power. I discovered that I don't need any external validation to sense, and live as, the greatest version of myself. My Soulful Self is powerfully present in every layer of my being, no matter what happens on the outside. I loved and continue to love my father deeply, and even his action of exclusion could not shake my certainty in my own worth, power, and creatorship. Knowing this, and truly living it, is beyond profound.

When we can forgive our perpetrators because we know that they played a role in our ultimate liberation and expansion and that we—as our life's creators—requested our relationships with them at the Bus Stop, we're viewing life from the Front Side of the Model. This does not imply that we should blame ourselves for what may be a significant amount of pain or trauma; rather, it points to our true greatness. If the support that you were looking for wasn't there, perhaps it was because you didn't need it. If you didn't receive something you wanted, or something that would have made life easier for you, perhaps it was because you are powerful enough to create it on your own. Or if something occurred that was painful beyond belief, perhaps it was to show you your bigness, since nothing can occur that is larger than you, for you are the universe. Perhaps you came here to awaken to that.

I invite you to consider this for just a moment. When I did, it changed my life forever.

It's important to recognize that requests at the Bus Stop are generated without specificity: we cannot know the exact details of how the opportunity we seek will manifest for us. Even our sample Bus Stop Conversation about seeking Level Ten forgiveness was only theoretical; we talked about how it *could* happen, not how it *would* happen. But rest assured, we, as pure awareness itself, will always be provided with what we need to grow in the way we intended when we came here—and, nearly always, it will be something that we would not seemingly consciously choose. Important for Ellie's growth at the time she came to me was to realize that she did not ask for or create her abuse at the Bus Stop. Rather, she asked for/or created the opportunity for a Level Ten experience of forgiveness, and for the discovery of her power to love herself and others unconditionally.

Sometimes the Bus Stop Conversation is more intense than being about an unsupportive family or a difficult boss. Why do some of us have such huge experiences of loss, abuse, and illness? Because *big beings take on really big projects, and they get started right away.* Big beings ask for big happenings at the Bus Stop because smaller life circumstances simply will not budge the "bigness" of an old soul. Rather, it takes a real challenge, something of magnitude, to rock the foundations of a being who already has a lot of earthly experience under his or her belt. Because smaller issues can be handled without hesitation, big beings request big "stories" such as Ellie's to dig deeply enough to find their full magnificence.

WORKING AT THE LEVEL OF ENERGY RATHER THAN STORY

Until we understand the spiritual, energetic dimension of our physical life experience, we simply go about life on the story route—buying into the dramas happening at the exterior/surface of life, unaware of our cosmic agenda that lies underneath. I call the story route the bumper-car way of living. While life is always expanding, serving our awakening, we grow through *friction*—psychological pain and hard-learned lessons—as the means of discovering who we are. We spend a lot of time experiencing what isn't true about ourselves in order to discover what is. Like bumper cars at an amusement park, we bump into something, then back up and turn the wheel, then we go bump into something else. By the process of elimination, we figure out what's true.

But once we really get the Bus Stop Conversation, we become empowered to work with life in an astounding new way. By recognizing that you are your life's creator and consciously assuming that role, you move into a new place of power and authority—from sitting in the backseat of the car or awkwardly trying to drive from the roof to being square in the driver's seat. This helps you work consciously to evolve toward wholeness rather than unconsciously trying to work things out at the story level—which takes months or years of wading through stuckness and pain—and go right to working on the energy level, which takes only minutes, hours, or days. As we'll continue to see, it's at the energy level that we have the power to make quick, effective, and sustainable change.

When you yourself have the experience of "getting" the Bus Stop Conversation, you will find that in the moment of acceptance and realization, you begin the process of truly setting yourself free from fear and unawareness and consciously accomplishing your life's purpose. You'll get to work resolving the densities that these traumas and other difficulties create and begin gleaning what they reveal to you about your true self. Most significantly, you'll be placing yourself in the vibrational neighborhood where true illumination can occur. You will lift yourself from the confines of a three-dimensional viewpoint and set yourself up for accessing and experiencing the multidimensional space of the Divine.

Remembering that the story level is the level of the symptom, and the level of the actual *cause* of what's happening in our life is the energy flowing underneath, we begin to really get that it's on the energy level that we have the greatest ability to make change. The story route will always be harder. Why? Because once the mind writes a story, it becomes attached to it—giving the mind a false sense of orientation or groundedness. The mind then makes that story "right" or "wrong," which attaches another level of energy to it and gives us an additional process to work through on our way to resolution. Without the story, we are free to make efficient and sustainable changes in the energy flow, which in turn will produce new and rejuvenating energies to live by.

We'll get to how to do that soon enough. For now, your job is to start seeing your life as being without problems to survive and react to. Instead, view any "problem" as a project. Any trouble spots are not "broken" things that need to be healed or fixed, but rather questions whose answers need to be set free from deep inside you and allowed to rise into your conscious awareness. Each density within your system is a piece of your magnificence, pocketed away. Each has within it a special part of your wholeness that will make you more at home within yourself and in the world. Ultimately, when these pockets are opened and reconnected to the flow within your system, your deepest abundance will rise up into the consciousness of your life, revealing inspiration, exaltation, creativity, wonder, awe, and a life most magical.

Before you can begin working at the energy level to change your life, you'll need to know a little more about your energy system—what it looks like, how it functions, and what tools you have for working with it to make positive, sustainable change. Therefore, in chapter 3, I'm going to take you on a quick tour of some bioenergetic basics. Then we'll launch into the Energy Codes Program in part 2, and move beyond theory to start embodying your true essence as the Soulful Self.

THE INVISIBLE YOU:

BIOENERGY BASICS

Imagine that you are coming into this world as an energy being. You've just completed your conversations at the Cosmic Bus Stop and boarded the bus. The next thing you know, you land hard and just kind of splat. Your energy disperses in all directions and you become a fragmented version of your original self, losing all bearings for navigating your new world. You have a case of "cosmic amnesia"—you don't know who you really are. Without a sense of your true identity, you can only orient yourself by what you encounter here on the physical plane, so you develop a new or false self. In an attempt to make sense of your life as you are now experiencing it, your mind writes stories about why you feel lost, who made you that way, and what your circumstances mean about you, others, and the world. These stories, which become the mind's beliefs, are limiting compared with the truth of your essential nature.

All of humanity goes through this splatting or loss of identity. It is our collective destiny to integrate or put back together our dispersed energy and to awaken from our cosmic amnesia, to "re-member" who we really are.

This is why I refer to life as Project Awakening. The purpose of living is to continue to enliven the higher-frequency energy of the Soulful Self—to continue to come into the body with *all* of our spirit self—so we can know and experience our wholeness here on Earth. As we integrate each dispersed aspect of energy within our system, we build new circuitry, and we expand into a greater experience of ourselves. Once our energy is unified, we know who we really are, and there is no more existential pain of feeling wrong, broken, or like something is missing within us. We feel completely complete.

Your System Was Designed to Heal

The good news is that you are already headed for this place of completeness. Your system was designed to move toward this integration and has been providing you with clues about your dispersal through symptoms that call for your attention. Your mind may think of these symptoms as troubles, problems, or patterns of unhealthy behavior such as sabotaging relationships, denying your responsibility in disagreements, and pushing away intimacy. Repeated job loss, ongoing financial issues, and recurring physical pain patterns can all be nudging you to become aware of imbalances. Other symptoms can be chronic or persistent headaches, back pain, or digestive issues. All hint that there is more available to you than you've accepted for yourself.

Symptoms like these continue to create pain until we somehow resolve or come to peace with them, which usually occurs only if we see what purpose they serve. When we resolve them, we gain access to higher-frequency qualities of our true nature, such as courage, forgiveness, compassion, love, creativity, acceptance, and joy. It's by going through difficult situations that we progressively express more as the true spirit being.

At the internal energy level, we have signs or symptoms too. Perhaps unknowingly, you've been experiencing them your whole life. These present as energy shifts that create bodily sensations—a knot in your stomach, a lump in your throat, or a tightening in your jaw in reaction to a criticism, an upcoming event, or a thought about something or someone from your past. They are the chill up your spine, the goose bumps on your arms, and the shaking in your legs when asked to perform something you didn't feel prepared for.

While we are a lot less familiar with addressing life at this body-sensation/energy level of our being, doing so is actually the easiest, quickest route to healing and wholeness. At the energy level, we don't have to figure out what it takes to resolve our problems before they begin to shift. Here, a higher intelligence than the logical, rational, strategizing, thinking mind is at work and guides us to healing and wholeness. And the truth is that the mind doesn't have to consciously know how our system does what it does.

Let me share with you a couple of other experiences of mine to help you see what I mean.

OTHER SURPRISES IN PUTTAPARTHI

In Puttaparthi—the small village that was home to the guru Sai Baba and one of his ashrams—I had several other dramatic surprises. Every day my travel companions and I would go to the ashram and sit for hours on a hard marble floor, meditating among the ten thousand others who were gathered awaiting Sai Baba's arrival. This was quite uncomfortable, as I was new to this world of meditation and spiritual study. The streets and the people were dusty and dirty, the food unfamiliar, and the smells pungent and stinging to my senses. If not for the great distance from home and the magnificent experiences I'd had in meditation prior to being invited to go to India, I'd most likely have left within a few days. But something kept me there.

One day, rather than going into the ashram to sit, my companions and I stayed in our teacher's apartment, which was located just above the wall of the ashram, its windows overlooking the courtyard through which Sai Baba would slowly walk every morning on his way into the hall. This particular day was a celebration for the women of the ashram, and rather than taking his usual path, Sai Baba turned and walked to the area just beneath where we stood watching from the third floor. Nearing the end of the red carpet that had been laid out for him, he stopped in front of a section of thousands of women and raised his hands in a blessing motion.

A bit skeptical at all the extravagant adoration and worship, I just watched. Then the strangest thing happened. As Sai Baba's hands went up in front of his body, my hands went up too! They were lifted by something other than my mind or my will. All at once, my chest was on fire. A glorious sense of fullness lit up inside of me, and I felt light as a feather. One second later, a wave of energy pushed against my chest so forcefully that it knocked me backward, off-balance. Julia, another woman in our group, a powerful energy healer herself, had the same response. As we both stumbled backward, we looked at each other in disbelief.

Suddenly I felt hot and flushed. Julia helped me sit down near the side wall of the apartment. A few moments later the entire room became a brilliant red, as if a giant floodlight had been turned on that blinded me to everything else. It then changed to orange, yellow, green, blue, indigo, violet, and finally white. Later I realized that each time I experienced a new color, an emotional sensation also occurred within me. With the red coloring in the room, I felt a deep sense of belonging. When things were infused with orange all around me, the sensation became comforting, wise, connecting, and knowing. This was followed by a sense of quickening and clarity as the room went yellow.

Everything I perceived then melted into the loveliest sense of warmth and wonder as the space around me glowed in a combination of these colors. A "loving" pinkish-orange shimmered its way into a golden and then green hue, and the next thing I knew I felt as though love had engulfed me in a warm embrace. As my surroundings settled into this loving presence, the light became more intense. Like looking through the reverse side of binoculars, there was a concentration, an exaggerated focusing of my internal view, and a sense of "causation," generating, or creating filled my being. It was a quickening. And it felt as if I had done this a million times before. Then brilliant cobalt blue lit up the space. The center of my head felt cold and hot at the same time, and as if the space within it spanned light-years. Then I couldn't find the boundary of my being. A violet light then flashed and I sat in a great void for a while. Finally I disappeared into a vast whiteness for what seemed like quite some time, vibrating in such an all-encompassing blissful state that I could have stayed there forever. It felt like something was breathing me into wholeness.

When I opened my eyes, the room was empty. My companions had all graciously left me there to allow the process. This event made it apparent to me, and to some of the others, that the very profound realm within me that had started opening back home was continuing to do so. I was now in this awe-inspiring world of energy in a whole new way. The energy was moving and my consciousness was following it as though that was all there was. Indeed, it was as though I was the energy itself. I would later learn that I could open to this state intentionally, and I could also connect with others through this amazing hidden matrix at the foundation of our being. Still later, I would realize that we can all do this.

This was an instantaneous happening, however, not one I'd tried to create or practice. This and the other openings were spontaneous—they happened without my mind's efforts. While this lack of mental trying would eventually become an important part of my work in helping thousands of people, in that moment I simply enjoyed the ride.

NIGHTTIME YOGA

When I returned home from India, my journey into the energetic realm accelerated. I had a continuous stream of new "happenings," both by day and by night. I found myself actually living life from an energetic level all the time—seeing and feeling energy move, prior to my own thoughts being obvious to me. I wasn't trying to do this. I was simply observing it; it was entirely outside the normal use of my rational, thinking mind. For example, I would wake up in the middle of the night with my body in strange positions that I would later be unable to re-create. I felt like I was inside some unknown energy pattern or shape, and that in my sleep my own energy system was aligning to it. This was mysterious, but it was also wonderful, because my body was healing itself spontaneously of the scoliosis I'd had since birth and the migraine headaches that were related to stress and the structural issues of spinal misalignments.

As these nighttime episodes continued, I recognized the energy patterns as expressions of the sacred geometries known as yoga poses. I became able to re-create during the day what my body had done naturally at night. I wasn't unfamiliar with yoga, but this spontaneity was taking it a giant step further into a new realm of healing and integration. In fact, I was rediscovering and retranslating the tremendous healing wisdom embedded in the ancient practice of yoga, much of which had been lost in translation over the centuries. My new understanding of yoga's true purpose and potency inspired me to develop a teaching system called Body-

Awake Yoga. This system has since led thousands of people to miracles and revelations, both on and off the yoga mat. Since yoga practice is a perfect complement to the Energy Code practices, I offer a basic pose (asana) in each of the chapters in part 2 for you to ground yourself further into your body and awaken your consciousness there.

In addition to this nighttime yoga, I found myself perceiving an entire world of experiences from inside my body while sleeping. Actually, I was in a half-asleep, lucid dream state much like meditation, which happened automatically for me in the middle of the night. I could feel my energy "working things out" in my body, as if something was unwinding or untangling itself. The energy was drawn in from beyond my physical body, from above my head, and it moved through the full length of my body and out my feet in a palpable way, causing a shift structurally on the inside as it went. My muscles relaxed, and it felt like I could slip into areas of my body that I had never experienced before, like I could breathe my Self into every part, opening and relaxing as I did so. The joints of my spine would move, the tissues in my gut and torso would release, and my body would stretch itself from the inside out as I learned to participate with and follow this deep internal movement of energy. (The ancients called these awakenings *kundalini* energy and *samadhi*, a state of intense inward concentration.)

The more I followed the sensations with my awareness and "collaborated" with what was happening—gently squeezing the area that was being affected *as* it was being affected—the more I could feel and trace the path of it and allow the tissues to align to it, settle, and calm. Sometimes, the shifts in energy were accompanied by emotional states, where I would suddenly have an outpouring of tears or feel great joy for seemingly no reason at all. It was both phenomenal and sacred.

Somatic psychology has found that when trauma or emotional overload happens and we cannot fully process an experience, the unprocessed parts of the event get split within the mind and recorded in the body—in the energy field. In order to release the trauma from our mind-body system and reintegrate the split parts that reside in the mind, we must become consciously aware of what has been split off and regain a complete "story" of ourselves. I had worked successfully with this belief in my clinic over the years, but something different was happening to me. I wasn't working through the "story" of my life and its events, trying to resolve my unresolved wounding at the level of my mind. In fact, I wasn't using my thinking mind at all; my mind was simply observing and following the energy. In this way, I was working *underneath* the story at the level of raw energy, deep within. In this experience, all that existed was my *awareness,* the *energy* moving through my body, and the *effect* that energy was having—the changes that were occurring—as it moved. In fact, the more I softened into what was happening, the more I began to sense that I *was* the energy making my way through the tissues of my body and unwinding the blockages from the inside out. This was completely transformational.

Energy was flowing, I was seeing and feeling it, and it was untangling old emotional patterns that I hadn't been conscious of before. The results were tangible, for me and for those with whom I was sharing this work: Des shaved record-breaking times off her adventure racing scores; Jenny overcame her reproductive issues and had multiple children after being told she would not be able to become pregnant; and David emerged from depression that had begun after losing his wife ten years earlier. This world of energy is real, and it is our pathway to freedom and happiness.

It's at *this* level of our being—the level beyond the thoughts and feelings of the mental and emotional bodies—that I invite you to work out what is showing up as symptoms or problems in your life, because this is the level at which those things originate, the level at which the energy splats and fragments and disperses. Healing our lives at the energy level requires relinquishing control with the logical mind. We have to *let our energy lead and the mind follow.* Our energy is the real us, and it will never fail. To do this we'll be looking inward, to the energy flowing within the body, for direction and answers, rather than referencing the external world. Self-referencing our own energy in this way is the foundation for building the awareness of and living as the Soulful Self.

The Vedic principles of the ancient East state that one of the eight most important things we will ever learn to do is to withdraw our senses from the outer to the inner world—to shift our awareness from the relative reality of our stories to the absolute reality of the energy beneath. I found the same to be true, without even knowing this information beforehand, in my own embodiment process. If we ever want to awaken, if we ever want to become truly masterful, we have to teach the mind to merge with the truth of who we are—the energy-wisdom deep within—and become self-referencing. The goal is not to learn how to respond better to the outer world, but rather to be creative and generative in our thinking, actions, and expressions. We want to act from a place of truth, from our truest self. Only then can we experience a life of true happiness, radiant health, and total well-being.

The Energy Codes give you a systematic way to become self-referencing and to live as the energy that is your core. In order to best use them, though, you'll benefit greatly from understanding a bit more about what your energy system looks like, how it functions, and how integration—our goal—actually occurs.

It's All About the Flow

As any practitioner of an energy-healing modality will tell you, our energy system is dynamic, yet it flows in structured ways. My Torus Man illustration on page 72 shows the movement of energy throughout our system, along certain pathways within and surrounding the physical body, as well as through naturally occurring hubs or centers called *chakras*. A torus is a lens that refracts light and power, and the one around Torus Man shows the equilateral, three-dimensional power of energy circling around the body.

TORUS MAN

In this graphic, a person stands on Earth and energy flows through his system and around him in a doughnut-shaped grid or torus field. A smaller field is centered in the heart area, where there is an astounding concentration of energy. The arrow coming down into the crown of this individual's head represents high-frequency universal or cosmic energy from beyond the physical body that rushes all the way down through a central channel within this person, out of his feet, and deep into the earth. This energy

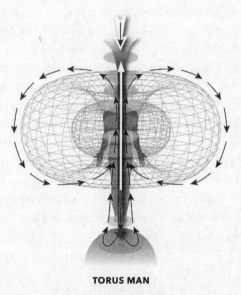

TORUS MAN

passing down through Torus Man's body is our true nature or essence; it's pure Spirit energy, pure consciousness. It's the real *you*. *You* are pouring down straight into the earth and then reflecting back up, creating an energetic flow known as your physical body.

As this cosmic energy hits the earth and is grounded, the high-frequency energy of the Soulful Self gets stepped down and is available for human consumption, meaning it becomes possible for us in our human form to perceive and work with it for our conscious evolution. It rises upward through the body's central channel, activating the various energy centers along the way. Despite our inability to remember (until we can) our true nature because of the Great Splat that we undergo when we arrive in this physical world, this energy is pure essential truth and clarity. It's the soul, who we really are. And it not only builds and regenerates the body, but also creates *everything* we experience as our physical life.

Key components in the dynamic of our energy and reality creation are the chakras, an ancient Sanskrit term for "wheels." Seven revolving centers of energy occur along our main energetic channel, the spine.

THE CHAKRAS

Much like radio stations, each of the energy centers of our body has a unique vibrational frequency—and each, being at a different frequency of the light spectrum, has a specific color associated with it. The colors I saw in that apartment above Sai Baba were the result of my essential energy moving up through—and waking up—the energy centers within that central channel of my system. As the energy passed through each of my chakras, one at a time, I experienced each chakra's unique frequency, qualities, and capacity awakening.

The torus field flows as the arrows in our diagram demonstrate. We see from the arrows below the feet that once our essential energy passes down through the central channel of the body and into the earth, it circles and rises back up through our central channel. As it's rising, it encounters the chakras or rotating energy vortices in the body's electromagnetic field. These wheels move high-frequency light energy—or photons—into distinctive subdivisions of our body. How well we integrate these energies ultimately determines our level of consciousness.

When these energy centers are open and flowing optimally, energy rises up through the body without any interference. In the illustration, the energy rises all the way up through the central channel and shoots out the crown chakra at the top of the head. Then it fountains down in all directions and comes back into the root chakra at the base of the spine. The energy continuously cycles in this pattern, creating the torus flow, and it is constantly being replenished from overhead. Again, that energy is *you*. It's the way the system was designed to operate and illustrates perfect health and wellness. And because we *are* the energy flowing through the body—the intelligent, pure creative energy or Spirit—the flow needs to be unimpeded in order for wholeness and total integration in our physical life to occur. Anything less than this optimal flow means that we will experience ourselves in some way as splatted, dispersed, or distorted in our thinking.

If any of our chakras are bogged down or blocked with energetic gunk, a disturbance or wobble interrupts the flow, since energy must now move around the blockage rather than traveling through the central channel in a pure, straight line. As the energy wobbles, it distorts the energy field and our perception of reality—which we misperceive as empty of possibility, love, or abundance. Below is an image of Torus Man with a wobble, causing a distortion in his field.

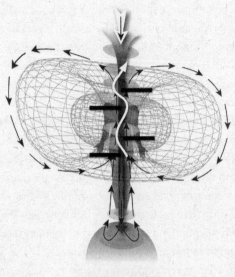

**DISTORTED / WOBBLE
TORUS MAN**

Going back to Energy Codes Truth #2—*Your life is a reflection of your energy*—we see that the torus field creates our reality. When you look out into the world, your perceptions follow how this field operates. Any gunk, interference, or gap in the circuitry between those chakra radio stations creates a wobble in the energy field, causing you to see through a distorted filter. The Protective Personality sees life as unkind or it misperceives itself as inadequate in some way.

Energy becomes physical reality in large part through the chakras, as they directly correlate to aspects of our consciousness. The state of our energy in a given chakra determines how we perceive the area of life that chakra relates to and how we function there. A lack of flow or other disturbance in any chakra will become a dysfunction in the aspect of our life that chakra rules. Each chakra is also associated with an endocrine gland, so the balanced, free flow through the chakras also affects our body chemistry by the glandular secretions it ignites along the way. (In chapter 9, we will explore other ways that new science is tying together light, energy, and chemistry to paint additional pictures of the amazing creation that we are.)

For example, lack of flow through the root chakra at the base of the spine results in a lack of groundedness and a feeling of not belonging in this life as an equal, with gifts and power and the right to live a wonderful life. This wobble at the root might set up a further problem with the chakras above it as the energy rises. The second chakra, now compromised, might create challenging relationships, subdued creativity, or imbalance in sexual energy. The third chakra would reveal reduced personal esteem and clarity in the world, setting up defensiveness and pain.

Following is a compilation of the various energies of the chakra system and the levels of consciousness they represent. We'll look further at each chakra's effect on our reality in the Energy Codes in part 2.

To make the Quantum Flip to embodying the Soulful Self and experiencing a more peaceful, flowing, and joyous life, we must eliminate gaps, densities, or interferences in the energy field and return it to its optimum flow. As I always say, "If it isn't flowing in your life, it's because it isn't flowing in your body!" And, "If it isn't flowing in your body, it won't be flowing in your life!"

As we get energy flowing again, we activate that chakra. The more activated our chakras are, with energy flowing through and between them along the central channel, the more of our true power and potential we can express. For instance, a person who has a healthy flow in her third or solar plexus chakra, which governs mental activity, among other things, will have a sense of personal power, confidence, and assertiveness. A person with an unimpeded, healthy flow in his fourth or heart chakra will be authentically loving and kind. A person with a healthy flow between these two chakras will be able to assert personal power in a loving way.

So, again, the more of our system that is flowing and integrated, the more we can embody the expression of the Soulful Self. Therefore facilitating a healthy flow throughout this central channel will be a major part of our work. We're going to work with this full spectrum of vital energies

The Chakras

	BODY AREAS AFFECTED	"BACK SIDE" SYMPTOMS	"FRONT SIDE" CHARACTERISTICS
7 - CROWN *Musical Note: B* **Light / Violet, White** *Top of the head*	Upper skull, skin, cerebral cortex, right eye, right brain, central nervous system, *pineal gland*	Depression, obsessive thinking, confusion, sensitivity to pollutants, chronic exhaustion, epilepsy, Alzheimer's	Divine Personality, magnetism, miraculous achievement, transcendence, peace with self, collaboration with higher purpose, inner vision. "I am a divine being." "I am that." "Life is a reflection of all that I am."
6 - THIRD EYE *Musical Note: A* **Consciousness / Indigo** *Inward from the center of forehead toward the middle of the brain, above and between the eyebrows*	Eyes, base of skull, ears, nose, left eye, left brain, sinuses, *pituitary gland, and pineal gland*	Nightmares, hallucinations, headaches, learning difficulties, poor vision, neurological issues, glaucoma	Charisma, high intuition, healthy perspective, freedom from attachment, generating insightful creations, perceiving beyond the five senses, seeing the meaning "behind the scenes." "I am the one behind the eyes."
5 - THROAT *Musical Note: G* **Sound / Blue** *Halfway between the heart and the throat, centrally at the base of the neck*	Mouth, throat, ears, neck, voice, lungs, chest, jaw, airways, nape of neck, arms, *thyroid and parathyroid glands*	Perfectionism, inability to express emotions, blocked creativity, sore throat, thyroid issues, neck ache, tinnitus, asthma	Good communicator, ease with meditation, artistic inspiration, can listen. "I hear and speak the truth with love and compassion." "I manifest myself here fully." "My life is a reflection of my inner world."
4 - HEART *Musical Note: F* **Air / Green, Pink** *In the center of the chest, beneath the breastbone*	Heart, chest, circulation, arms, hands, lower lungs, rib cage, skin, upper back, *thymus gland*	Fear of betrayal, codependency, melancholy, shallow breathing, high blood pressure, heart disease, cancer, inability to perceive or receive love	Compassion, unconditional love, conscious lovemaking. "There is more than enough for all." "There is only one of us here—we are one." "Everything is a reflection of the Divine, and is in my favor."
3 - SOLAR PLEXUS *Musical Note: E* **Fire / Yellow** *About three inches above the navel, at the base of the sternum*	Digestive system, muscles, stomach, liver, diaphragm, gall bladder, lower back, trapdoor of the autonomic nervous system, spleen, *pancreas*	Oversensitivity to criticism, need to control, low self-esteem, stomach ulcers, digestive issues, chronic fatigue, allergies, diabetes	Respect for self and others, personal power, flexibility, high self-esteem, spontaneity, uninhibited. "I allow my own way, and allow you yours." "I open my mind to possibility."
2 - SACRAL *Musical Note: D* **Water / Orange** *Just below the navel*	Bladder, prostate, womb, pelvis, nervous system, lower back, fluid function, *adrenal glands, sex organs*	Unbalanced sex drive, emotional instability, feelings of isolation, impotence, frigidity, bladder and prostate issues, low back pain	Inner knowing, trust, expression, attuned to feelings, creativity. "I sense and feel my way through life." "I need nothing from you, and I am simply here to share." "I follow my gut."
1 - ROOT *Musical Note: C* **Earth / Red** *Base of the spine*	Bone, skeletal structure, hips, legs, feet, genitals, base of spine, kidneys, body's life force, teeth, nails, blood, building of cells, *adrenal glands*	Mental lethargy and spaciness, incapacity for inner stillness, osteoarthritis, poor general health, lacking vital energy	Self-mastery, high physical energy, groundedness, vibrant health. A recognition that "I am here as Source." "This is my gig." "I belong." "I bring what I choose to experience."

PRACTICES	BREATHWORK	YOGA POSES FOR GREATER INTEGRATION
• Discovering Your Meditation Style • Walking in Nature Using Central Channel Breath • Mindful and Thinkless Presence • Blending Patterns to Engage the Soulful Self	Central Channel Breath	• Corpse Pose *(savasana)* • Headstand *(sirsasana)* • Rabbit Pose *(sasangasana)* • Wide Angle Forward Fold *(prasarita padottanasana)*
• Alkaline Ash Nutrition Program • Conscious Exercise • Chemistry Through Thought • Energy Codes Brain Yoga	Visionary Breath	• Downward Dog *(adho mukha svanasana)* • Shoulderstand *(salamba sarvangasana)* • Child's Pose *(balasana)* • Exalted Warrior *(viparita virabhadrasana)*, also called Warrior 4 • Balancing Poses
• Breaths for Chakras 1–7 • Thousand Tiny Straws Breath • Fern Frond Breath • Breath Patterns for Healing	Manifesting Breath	• Cobra Pose *(bhujangasana)* • Plow Pose *(halasana)* • Bridge Pose *(setu bandhasana)* • Toning with Sound *(Om, Ma, Ha)*
• Generating Loving Presence • Choosing to Be Loved • Loving Triage • Seeing Everything as Love (aka "It's All in My Favor")	Heart Coherence Breath	• Triangle Pose *(trikonasana)* • Thread the Needle *(sucirandhrasana)* • Fish Pose *(matsyasana)* • Reclined Spinal Twist *(supta matsyendrasana)*
• Morter March • mPower Step • B.E.S.T. Release	Solar Plexus Breath	• Camel Pose *(ustrasana)* • Bow Pose *(dhanurasana)* • Reverse Table Top *(purvottanasana)* • Crescent Warrior *(anjanayasana)* • Breath of Fire *(kapalabhati pranayama)*
• Take It to the Body • Don't Name It – FEEL It • One Eye on the Inside • Don't Want It, Have It	Vessel Breath *(Buddha Belly Breath)*	• Boat Pose *(navasana)* • Pigeon Pose *(eka pada rajakapotasana)* • Yogic bicycle *(dwichakrikasana)* • Seated Spinal Twist *(ardha matsyendrasana)* • Breath of Fire *(kapalabhati pranayama)*
• Subject – Object – Subject • Central Channel Anchor Points • Central Channel Breathing • Drop In, Drop Through	Central Channel Breath	• Chair Pose *(utkatasana)* • Warrior 1 *(virabhadrasana I)* • Pyramid Pose *(parsvottanasana)* • Tree Pose *(vrksasana)* • Standing Forward Fold *(uttanasana)*

to clear the interferences that are keeping us from living as our whole, true selves.

Before I move on to how to clear those densities, I want to offer one other way to view the dynamics of energy flow: I want you to consider blockages as *gaps* rather than as obstructions.

Building the Circuitry to Perceive the Soulful Self

We usually think of an impediment as a blockage. We say, "I need to find what's in my way and get rid of it."

In fact, there is no such thing as a "block." That's a misperception. A more powerful way of understanding a blockage, density, interference, or piece of energetic gunk is as an *absence* of conscious vital life force. If everything is energy—and it is—then where energy *isn't* flowing is a spot that lacks the *ability* to have energy flowing! It's a spot that doesn't have animation or consciousness moving through it. Spirit isn't alive and active in that place, but . . . it's not because it isn't already there; it's only because *the mind* hasn't awakened to or perceived it there yet. In other words, the mind doesn't yet have awareness of our true nature—our essence or magnificence—in that particular place.

Embodiment is really about *awakening*—awakening our mind or consciousness to the presence within the body of the Soulful Self. That's how we bring the Soulful Self to life in physical form. We "turn it on" or "bring it online." The easiest way to think about this is with the analogy of circuitry. We touched on this briefly, but we'll go a bit deeper now.

The Soulful Self has electromagnetic circuitry. Eastern traditions describe this as a network of *nadis* or meridians that run throughout the body and, when activated or turned on, bring into the body (and our physical life) the energy and perspective of the Soulful Self. This circuitry enlivens our central nervous system. We can develop the central nervous system's capacity to perceive the subtle energy of the Soulful Self through *bioenergetics*—where the energetic layers of our biology connect with the energetic layers of the soul to create our life on Earth.

I will continue at times to use the terms *barriers* and *blockages* to describe those places in the energy field where the circuitry is offline. I do so only because people are used to thinking in that way; in truth, there is no blockage or barrier, only a lack of the circuitry of the Soulful Self.

How do places in the body go offline or splat? Usually this happens because we come up against a situation we don't know how to deal with mentally and emotionally, so we sidestep it instead—we do whatever we can think of in order to survive or cope in those circumstances; we don't go straight through the situation with an intact sense of our true self. When the direct circuitry is active, we are fully aware of or awakened to our true nature. Conversely, if areas on the circuit are not powered up, we cannot perceive our true nature. Our energy field wobbles, a distortion happens, our perception blurs, our physical health declines, and other areas of our lives are shaken. We simply don't have the active circuits in that area that would allow us to perceive ourselves accurately and move right through a situation—through intimacy challenges, mental or emotional confrontation, or chronic physical pain.

Angela's story illustrates this point. Raised in a family involved in a cult, Angela had been traumatically abused—mentally, emotionally, and sexually—her entire life until, at age sixteen, she found ways to not come home. She worked three jobs, volunteered at school, took a job out of state for the summer, all as a means to survive. Both of her parents were mentally ill, and she'd had no one to talk to about her horrific traumas and nowhere to go for help. Before I met her, she had not shared the details of it with anyone. She had shut down her circuitry to survive. She was terrified of opening herself to trust and love, terrified of life itself. Working with the Energy Codes, she completely transformed her self-image and the ability to reveal her deep truth. She has greatly diminished lifelong battles with anemia, chronic sinus infections, broken eardrums, bladder infections, deep depression, extreme physical pain, seizures, and PTSD. She had been diagnosed with breast cancer, but credits her use of the Energy Codes and other natural modalities for her remission. Today Angela is happy and living an inspired life—painting, gardening, traveling, and enjoying close relationships. She continues to develop her circuitry to engage *with* her life experiences rather than circumventing them for safety.

When we do turn on or activate circuits that have been offline, we awaken our conscious awareness of Spirit in that chakra. Healing—physical, mental, and emotional—happens in the aspect of our life that that chakra correlates to. In remembering the wholeness of our being as we, piece by piece, bring the life force back into each dormant place, a return to vibrant health happens automatically. Though we often think of healing as "fixing a problem"—curing a dysfunction or disease—it's actually not that. When we truly heal, the problem simply goes away because we've created a healthy state that is all-encompassing. Having the presence of essential life force is by definition a state of perfect health; dysfunction and disease cannot coexist with it.

Sara's experience demonstrates the success of circuits coming online. When she started taking my live Level 1 course, she had great difficulty expressing her innermost truth to others. She experienced tremendous emotional anxiety and shutdown and had to leave the training room for hours at a time. Sara discovered that she felt "shaken to the core" by the thought of allowing the truth of her being to shine or speaking her truth out loud, having never before experienced feeling invited, safe, or comfortable to do so. This resistance affected her entire system energetically.

Through our work together, she learned to "turn on" the energy of each of her chakras and began to embody her true self. She's healed in numerous and exceptional ways. As she explains, "Regenerated the S1 disc that appeared totally gone (it was bone-on-bone). Severe IBS is gone! Psoriasis (below knees and on hands and face) is gone! Severe joint pain in ankles, feet, wrists, and hands is gone! Abnormal precancerous mammograms and pap smears now normal. Migraines are gone. Plantar fasciitis is gone. Deep fear and sadness are gone, gone, gone!" She now joyfully teaches the Energy Codes to help others heal too.

The big-picture goal of the Energy Codes, therefore, is not to fix problems the way even some energy medicine approaches (both ancient and current) can, but rather to embody your truest, fullest self, which creates healing in every area of life as a by-product. Spirit is the healing force in our life; that is, because healing happens when the energy being (the *real us*) becomes activated in all of its circuitry, the energy being or Spirit *is* the healer within.

So how do we turn on or activate the circuitry of the sensory nervous system to perceive the subtle energy within our body that is the Soulful Self? How do we "re-member" (literally, put back together) ourselves on the energetic level and reconnect our energy flow so that we can heal from the inside out rather than from the outside in? It takes more than just thinking differently or using the mind in a brand-new way. It takes a holistic approach, involving the collaboration of mind, body, and spirit.

Integration by Unifying Mind, Body, and Spirit (or Breath)

A full integration of our system, where we get it flowing optimally like the Torus Man, happens in a twofold way: We'll integrate the energy of unresolved issues and subconscious interferences that are keeping us fragmented and operating from the Protective Personality. And we will activate more of the untapped, built-in circuitry of high-frequency energy that is the Soulful Self. These are really two sides of the same coin, since we are dealing with the whole self—the body, the mind, and the breath.

Let's look in general at the role the body plays in all of this.

THE ROLE OF THE BODY

When we're fragmented and in the Protective Personality, we identify as the rational mind, believing we *have* a body and (if we're spiritually inclined) *have* a spirit or soul. But actually, as we've learned, we *are* the soul—the energy being—who *has* a body and *has* a mind. The body and mind are merely tools to help us have our best, most heavenly, life here on Earth. But we haven't been using them the way they were designed or intended to be used.

We are not just spiritual beings having a physical or earthly experience; we are spiritual beings having a *spiritual* experience at the physical end of the energy spectrum. The difference between the two is huge—it's the difference between living as the Protective Personality and living as the Soulful Self. The body plays a key role in this difference.

Often we think of our body as being the vehicle for experiencing a physical life. But while the body places us in three dimensions and enables us to be physical and interact with matter, it's also our tool for engaging with spiritual dimensions. In fact, it's *the* primary communication device of the soul, which uses it as an intermediary or translator to "talk" to the conscious mind.

Anything that is happening in the physical body is happening on the energetic level first. Bodily sensations are energy shifts that occur in the energy body and are felt in the physical body. Therefore the body is an important gateway into the energetic realm of our life. It's through the body that the mind can sense the subtle energy shifts that reveal the state of our energy field, and it's through the body that the mind can interact with that field, changing its pattern by stewarding our energy so that we may get different results in our life.

This brings us to the role of the mind.

THE ROLE OF THE MIND

In the Protective Personality, the mind focuses on protecting us—keeping safe both our physical body and our personal identity or sense of self. Here, the thinking mind is in charge, and it employs the more ancient, reactive part of our brain and physiology. Always on guard, constantly looking into the past for comparisons and the future for possible threats, it continually sends stress chemicals through the body as it engages varying levels of the fight-flight-or-fright response.

To become awake as the Soulful Self, we must put the observing, witnessing mind to use to sense what's happening in the energy body, discover any dispersal, and direct energy integration. The older, reactive part of the brain can't do this. It's a job for the higher, more evolved creative and intuitive centers—the anatomy of the Soulful Self. The sensory capability of the central nervous system must be put in charge. These are tools we've had all along but have underutilized. Albert Einstein was referencing this when he reportedly said, "The intuitive mind is a sacred gift and the rational mind is a faithful servant. We have created a society that honors the servant and has forgotten the gift."

Put another way, your thinking, reactive mind is like a rapidly spinning ceiling fan. You would never stick your finger through it to feel what's on the other side, because you might get bruised or cut. The same is true of the thinking mind; its rapid motion stops the smooth, natural flow of your essential energy as it's rising toward your awakening full potential. There sits your Soulful Self, your essential energy, limited by the false beliefs and knee-jerk reactions of your Protective Personality.

There is a version of life beyond the spinning blades of the thinking mind that we *must* contact to experience our full potential. In order to glimpse it—let alone actually touch it—we need to slow down the whirring blades enough to let us pass through to the other side. The Energy Codes have a powerful way of doing this, using the mind, body, and breath. When we tether the mind to the body, as we will do with the Codes—when we put the mind to its highest use as an observer and guide—it slows down. This is because the body vibrates at a slower frequency than the mind alone. Once the mind connects through awareness to the body, it begins to slow to a rate more closely associated with nature and the earth. (This is the alpha frequency state of the brain, which you may have heard of.) Suddenly we (as the pure awareness that we are) are able to perceive life from a different, more grace-filled perspective.

Connecting the mind to the body helps us slow down our thinking process and check its constant search for safety. The Energy Codes practices restore the mind to its intended role: to use its focus, attention, intention, and will to sense, anchor, and activate our essential energy within our physical body. We will actually retrain our mind, forging and strengthening the neural pathways, to keep us in touch with the deeper version of ourselves, the Soulful Self. Driven not by fear and protectiveness, but rather by wisdom and love, the Soulful Self's messages and directions will move us forward quickly and painlessly in our evolution.

Fundamental to making the mind-body connection and to slowing down the ceiling fan is the breath.

THE ROLE OF THE BREATH

We all know the importance of breathing; it's our body's most crucial function. While we can go without water or food for days and even weeks, only minutes without breath causes us to lose our connection with the body and leave this physical plane. Breathing is a major part of most meditation practices. When the breath is shallow and rapid, the primitive survival aspect of the brain takes over, causing the mind to function reactively and defensively (speeding up the whirring of the fan blades) and triggering the body's fight-flight-or-fright response. This is different from when the breath is slow, deliberate, and deep in the lower lobes of the lungs, which activates the numerous parasympathetic nerve endings there and immediately helps to calm both the mind and the body, shifting it out of survival mode and into a more creative state. Conscious, intentional, deep breathing draws us away from the surface of our life and into its interior.

You can see this for yourself. Right now, just begin slowing and deepening your breath through the nose as you continue to read. You'll find that your breath brings you more into the moment and allows you to capture more of this message. Short and shallow breathing agitates your system and disperses your energy, particularly when you are in stressful conditions.

The breath has a life-changing capacity in addition to its vital purposes. The breath is actually spirit in "physical" form. It *is* the vital life force. When the breath stops, it's because the spirit has left the body completely and for the last time. It makes sense that the breath would be key in bringing that vital life force to areas where it is lacking, to enlivening the *nadis*, or energy pathways, and in activating circuitry within our system that is not yet online.

This is how the breath helps to integrate the dispersed energy within us: it infuses the high-frequency energy of the Soulful Self into the lower-frequency densities within our system, raising the vibration and awakening our consciousness in those areas, and bringing those circuits online. It literally breathes the intelligent energy that is the source of all creation through our energy body and into our physical body—through the empty spaces between the particles that make up the atoms that make up the molecules that build the cells and ultimately all of the tissues of our body.

Unification happens as a dance between these three vital parts—body, mind, and spirit or breath. In part 2, you will learn that unification's specific dance steps. It's actually quite simple: the soul speaks to the body, and the body translates for the mind. Disconnection happens when the mind isn't listening when the body speaks! We will teach the mind how to listen so that it becomes easy and natural to slow the fan blades enough to hear and feel the body speak as the Soulful Self, and to follow those messages to awakening.

Using Your Imagination in Doing This Work

Working with your energy system involves some imagination. Quantum science tells us that everything happens at the energy level *before* it happens at the physical level—we start to manifest whatever we think about consciously through arranging subatomic particles into a specific pattern. The imagination is the tool for shifting energy patterns, but that doesn't mean that what we'll be doing isn't "real"! It only means that your thoughts will be generative, original, and inspired rather than habitual, reactionary, or conditioned. I call this alpha thinking, since it uses the alpha frequency of the brain. Your imagination puts you back in touch with the rest of who you truly are.

Now I'd like to share with you a story of the actual results one of my students got from applying the same methods you will learn in this book.

THE MUSIC RETURNS TO JERALYN'S LIFE

I had just finished leading a meditation for the opening of one of my JourneyAwake excursions in Cuzco, Peru, when a woman approached me holding a small photo.

She knelt in front of me, hands trembling, and handed me the picture.

"This is my son, Dylan. He always wanted to go to Machu Picchu. But he's gone now, so I told him I would take the trip for him."

I nodded and let her continue.

"I went online to search for 'sacred journeys to Machu Picchu.' Your picture came up. I was expecting a Peruvian shaman, but Dylan told me to come with you, so . . . here we are."

Dylan had taken his own life just three months before this excursion, and Jeralyn's heart was broken. I assured her that we were here to help her find a sense of peace—but I also knew, given the intensity of the energy around her story, she would likely discover even more than that.

I tucked the photo into my backpack, and over the next couple of days, I learned more about Jeralyn. She had divorced an abusive spouse; while she was still caught up in a legal battle over money, Dylan had left the planet. In the days after our meeting, she walked about the temples in the Sacred Valley of Peru with a distant look in her eyes; even as people in our group embraced her and cared for her along the way, she held herself apart. Seeing this, I was not surprised when she told me that she wouldn't be joining the smaller group for the hike up the mountain to the peak of Huayna Picchu as planned. She was overwhelmed.

I told her that I understood, and that we'd be thinking of her.

At the top of the peak, I performed a ceremony for staying in the Spirit of Life, "showing" Dylan the view that he'd have seen from our vantage point. Greg, a member of our community, took a picture of me holding Dylan's photo, so that we could share it with his mother when we got back down the mountain.

On the ride back to our hotel that evening, Greg sat next to me on the train. Tears were in his eyes as he showed me the photo he had taken on the mountaintop. A ray of light shone from the heavens on the center of Dylan's face, as though it were an arrow straight from the Divine to his lips. Tears burst from my own eyes as Greg and I looked at each other; we knew that something profound had just taken place. Dylan was delivering a message to his mother to let her know he was still there for her.

After seeing that unmistakable sign, Jeralyn dived into the fundamental offerings of the Energy Codes and began to pierce the immobility of her grief with her breath. Immediately she experienced mental and emotional relief. Over the next months, she committed to learning everything that she could about living as the Soulful Self. She came to see me at various events around the world, saying, "I know there are answers here for me. I can feel them working in me every day."

Jeralyn was a professionally trained opera singer and had a deep and extraordinary love and appreciation for music. Because part of the focus of the Energy Codes work is to tap into our true essence, I thought that music might be an avenue, in part, for her recovery—but it turned out to be far more than that.

Through the Energy Codes practices, and her integration of the Bus Stop Conversation, Jeralyn began to realize that there were tremendous gifts seated within her greatest pain. She found her breath, and she found her core presence. She also found a new expression of her exquisite talent and began to use her music for healing, as it had helped to heal her. She had been trained to perform, but now singing, toning, and creating music came from a different place within. The sounds were different—but more importantly, the feeling was different. She began to sense new life once again as she learned to anchor herself in her core, breathe in her belly where her comforting rhythms resided, and use the practices she learned in our courses; with these tools, she could feel into her grief, pain, and disillusionment, and dissolve them.

By bringing the offline parts of herself back online, Jeralyn was able to pierce the pain and confusion that surrounded her and find a new sense of absolute clarity and certainty that she had not had before. Seated in this new peace and strength, she began to speak to other parents who'd lost children. She also held sound healing concerts for cancer patients, who experienced profound reduction in pain and a restoration of vitality and joy, and began to help other people find their way through their grief, as she had.

All of this awakening happened within the first year of her loss; no one outside of our community had seen such a change take place so completely. The CEO of Compassionate Friends, an international organization for families who have lost a child, stated that, in his fifteen-year tenure as CEO, he had never seen anyone do as well as Jeralyn in such a short time. "What was she doing?" he asked.

Because of her Quantum Flip, Jeralyn feels her son with her every day. He even guides her, in a type of divine collaboration. She knows this, because she can drop into her core and live from the anchored and grounded place of her Soulful Self. There she experiences a place of no-separation between the worlds, a personal HeavenEarth. Naturally, sometimes she still feels the loss of Dylan in his physical form. When she does, she turns to her Energy Codes practices and lands deep in her core as her Soulful

Self; in that place, she doesn't have to miss him, because she can feel him beside her, connected to her through the eternal energy of their divine selves.

OTHER STORIES FROM STUDENTS AND PATIENTS

Following are additional real-life examples that illustrate the transformations that come about through the use of the Codes.

Mike scheduled a session with me to address his depression and extreme anxiety. He was on seven medications for those two issues and hadn't slept through the night in seven years. He'd been diagnosed with a schizophrenic break and was in great mental, emotional, and physical pain. Within a few months of working with the Energy Codes and bioenergetics, he was functioning well with only one prescription medication, and soon thereafter his prescribing doctor was able to wean him off that one as well.

Colleen's childhood had been challenging. Her father died when she was eleven, and a controlling and overbearing grandmother interfered with her mother's attempts to raise her on her own. Colleen had some verbal, cognitive, and physical developmental issues and was diagnosed with diabetes at age nineteen and placed on insulin. She had a highly antagonistic and abrasive relationship with her grandmother, and had trouble engaging in relationships of any kind. After working with the Energy Codes, Colleen experienced dramatic shifts in her health and emotional well-being. In addition to being able to engage compassionately with her grandmother and navigate her passing, she formed meaningful friendships for the first time. For six years now, she has tested free of diabetes, and has not needed any pharmaceuticals to regulate her blood sugar levels. She's even seen significant changes in her eyesight, eliminating an astigmatism (and reducing her refractive correction for nearsightedness in her eyeglasses from a 7 to a 3.25). She feels she's living life from an entirely different perspective and credits the Energy Codes for her newfound abilities and skills.

I've also witnessed numerous improvements in and even healing of allergies, asthma, chronic injuries, and all kinds of other pain and illness patterns once the underlying energetic issue was addressed and resolved. I'll be sharing other real-life stories of healing and whole-life wellness that have come about through the use of the Energy Codes throughout the book.

The Seven Energy Codes

The seven Energy Codes are the road map for living as the Soulful Self. You can practice the principles and methods on your own by following the guidance in part 2. They will help you to heal mental, emotional, and physical dysfunctions; create balance and well-being in every area of your life; and live your true nature and divine purpose.

Each of the seven Codes corresponds to a chakra, a major energy center of the body, from the base of the spine to the crown of your head. The Codes build on one another, so ideally you'll want to approach them in the order they have been laid out.

Here's a brief overview of the seven Energy Codes:

1. *The Anchoring Code: Getting Back in Your Body.* We live identified as the mind, believing that's all there is. As a result, we try to think our way to a better life. But the raw energy moving in the body shows us a very different reality about our true nature. By turning our attention inward to the body and grounding our awareness there, the Anchoring Code takes us the first step in shifting our focus from the external world to the energetic core that is our true essence, and thus in identifying as that essence—the Soulful Self.

2. *The Feeling Code: The Language of the Soul.* Having anchored our attention in the body's core, we now continue awakening our sensory nervous system and training it on what it can perceive. As we sense and feel the energy shifts taking place within the body, we begin a divine dialogue between our true self—the soul—and our mind. This gives us a revolutionary new way of

understanding and responding to what happens in our life and simultaneously builds our presence as the Soulful Self.

3. *The Clearing Code: The Healing Power of the Subconscious.* For most of us, communication between the conscious and subconscious levels of the mind has been shut down due to emotional overload during key life experiences. This means we can't get traction creating what we want in life because unresolved issues that lie outside of our awareness are holding us back. In the Clearing Code, we learn how to open the door to our subconscious, resolve the residue of the experiences that are trapped there, and reintegrate the energy that has been tied up with this into the flow of our system—simultaneously giving us the energetic potency and coherence we need to manifest our wishes and bringing us ever closer to living in our wholeness as the Soulful Self.

4. *The Heart Code: The Universal Solvent.* The vibrational frequency we experience as love *is* the energy of the Soulful Self. This energy is our true nature and the highest vibration we can experience here in physical form. It's also a universal solvent—able to resolve all stuckness, transmute all interferences, and heal all wounds. In the Heart Code, we intentionally generate this awe-inspiring vibration within ourselves, which—despite what we've believed before now about needing to get or find love from others—is where we experience it most powerfully. We then use it to dissolve lower-frequency energetic densities of the Protective Personality and to create more sensory neurocircuitry for perceiving, activating, and animating the Soulful Self.

5. *The Breath Code: The Power of Life Itself.* To manifest means to bring into physical reality. Here we learn the most powerful tool we have for manifesting spirit or energy in physical form—the breath. Breath *is* energy, vitality, or life force; it is life itself.

When we systematically breathe our essential energy into our energetic densities—the places where we're stuck—we lighten and lessen the Protective Personality; when we breathe into the core of the body, we energize and enliven the Soulful Self. While we've been doing this throughout the previous Codes, in the Breath Code we'll learn additional, more advanced breathwork techniques to heal specific physical issues as well as to continue awakening to our highest consciousness and full potential.

6. *The Chemistry Code: The Alchemy of Embodiment.* We're often more accustomed to responding reactively to our external environment than proactively generating—from within—the life we would love. Consequently, our perspective and body are in survival mode, creating the stress-based chemistry of the fight-flight-or-fright response. The Chemistry Code gives us the keys for swiftly and effectively shifting our physiology from "threatened" to "safe," further facilitating our transformation from the Protective Personality to the Soulful Self. It teaches us how to create an optimal physical environment or "home" for increasing the presence of the Soulful Self.

7. *The Spirit Code: Where the Many Become One.* Identifying as the mind, we hold ourselves separate from everything: from each other, from nature, and even from our own energy—our true, spiritual Self. Yet our system is designed for us to experience the connection and oneness that, at the level of energy, is our truth. By the time we reach this Code, having integrated enough of our previously dispersed energy and activated the higher-brain centers that allow us to live "above" the fight-flight-or-fright response, we automatically see life from a different perspective. In the Spirit Code, we focus on stilling the thinking mind and becoming truly present so we can readily perceive the soulful communications that are constantly rising up within our body and act according to them, without hesitation or doubt. This is Creatorship. It is living as the Soulful Self.

———

The Energy Codes represent a whole new approach to healing. In general, our culture has looked at well-being from the outside in, upside down, and backward. We must change this if we are ever to create the life we want—or, more importantly, become our destiny as true creators.

In order to get the most out of this work and create the level of integration and embodiment that the Energy Codes promise, we must make the following shifts in our mental perception of health, healing, and our identity.

1. What harms (and heals) us does not come from the outer world. We must stop thinking that only viruses, bacteria, and other microorganisms make us "sick," and medicine and surgery make us "well." We must understand that true wholeness, healing, and integration come from within, because they begin in our energy field.

2. We are more than "merely human." When we study traditional spirituality (or even less conventional modalities such as yoga), we tend to see ourselves as mere human beings in search of God or Spirit, which will save us from our lot in life. The truth is, we are that which we are seeking. We are energy beings—and, because everything in the universe is interconnected, we are one with the divine energy that is Source. We are rooted in Heaven, and our final frontier is to fully embody our divine Self here on Earth.

3. There is nothing "wrong" in your life. There are no problems to overcome, and no obstacles to be victorious over. When we make the Quantum Flip and begin to view life from the Front Side of the Model, we see that there was never anything wrong, because all of our life experiences are happening for our ultimate benefit. It's all in our favor, and it has been all along.

In the Energy Codes program, you will find detailed information about each Code, instructions for doing the practices, descriptions of the results you can expect from each practice, and more. You'll learn everything you need to know to make your own Quantum Flip and begin living fully as your Soulful Self. Your understanding of the above truths will only increase as you immerse yourself in the work of bringing online your whole, divine, energetic self and integrating all the multiple layers of your being.

With that, let's get started using the Energy Codes!

Part II

A New Way of Being—
The Energy Codes Program

Chapter 4

THE ANCHORING CODE:

GETTING BACK IN YOUR BODY

I was sitting at my dining room table one afternoon, writing a description for a course I'd been invited to teach, when all of a sudden I felt a vibration in my head. It was so strong that I shook my head a couple of times to try to shake off the feeling and get my bearings. It stopped, and I returned to typing. Moments later it began again. I shook my head once more. It persisted, and in a few moments became so pronounced that I had to leave my work and lie down.

The instant I rested my head on the pillows, I experienced a glowing and vibrating sensation in and around my head and what felt like a shaft of golden light running up and down through the core of my body, from the center of my head to the tip of my spine. It drew my attention inward by its very presence. As with my initial exalted experience, I knew I was again waking up to a different version of what it meant to be "me"—only this time, rather than being a boundless ray of light, I was experiencing it in my body. Heaven and Earth were merging as the spiritual aspect of my nature tangibly came alive within my physical form. Without really trying, I found myself feeling and sensing deep within my body in a way I hadn't known was possible. It felt as though I could *see inside* of my own chest, neck, and head. Images of places, some of them otherworldly, filled my mind. They felt so familiar, yet they were not places I had ever been, at least not that I could recall. Still, with each of them, I felt like I belonged there, as if I'd been there hundreds of times.

In the weeks and months following, I continued to have these vibration sensations; I noticed that, if I brought my attention to the core of my body, I could manage them without having to stop what I was doing—instead, I could allow the process to happen without it taking me out of my day. Simply squeezing the muscles at the core of my body and breathing into those vibrating areas allowed me to direct and focus this immense amount of energy. As I did, I could feel the energy collect and intensify at my core. All the while, I felt as if I was remembering something from deep within.

A dramatic shift in my thoughts, my emotions, and the feelings within my body would accompany the change. The more concentrated my energy became at my core, the more freedom and ease I felt. Rather than highly vulnerable, anxious, and fragmented as I'd felt for so much of my life, I felt noticeably more collected and grounded in my body and in the world. It was from this state that my life began to truly unfold—to heal and flow. Every area of my life experience changed radically as this energy increased in presence inside me—as what I came to know as the Soulful Self took hold.

I had experienced similar vibratory sensations in my body and life previously; we all do, to one degree or another. But if we don't recognize them as something that serves—as something that's calling out for our attention—we often let them pass by. At the time I'm describing, the feeling was too pronounced in me to ignore, but it wasn't a new phenomenon, or solely a result of my exalted experience. My awakening simply turned up the volume.

Years later I would learn that this act of bringing my attention to the core of my body is a practice called *pratyahara*, taught by masters of consciousness in the East as a way to "inhabit" our wholeness. But during this energetic growth spurt, I was finding my way into my body on my own, using the guidance I was receiving from my own system as a compass. It was from the practices I developed at that time that the Energy Codes began to emerge—starting with this, the Anchoring Code. As the name implies, this Code empowers us to anchor the essential, energetic part of our nature to our physical form—the body. This is the first step toward living as the Soulful Self.

What Is the Anchoring Code?

As energy beings, we choose our physical destination at the Bus Stop, and we choose to come into this world in a way that's perfect for our growth. But *after* the Bus Stop, we land here in the three-dimensional plane and *disperse* on contact. It's as if our mind goes one way, our body goes another, and our soul or breath yet another, and we don't remember who we truly are and where we came from. (It's all part of the fun.) We try to figure out who we are, where we are, whether we're safe, how to fit in, how to follow the rules, how to please the people who seem to matter the most to our survival, and so on. We try to get our bearings, and with all of that figuring out, we end up using our mind disproportionately to our whole being— living almost entirely from our head, out of touch with our body, our energy, and the rest of our true nature instead of internally referencing our own inherent knowing and truth. Our culture teaches and reinforces this way of being, as most everyone around us is stuck doing the same thing.

The problem with living from our head, however, is that we never quite feel like our whole selves or like we're at home here. We don't feel comfortable, complete, or safe. We spend all of our time and energy trying to either fix or deny our sense of incompleteness, but nothing we do solves the problem, which is that we don't know ourselves as whole, as the Soulful Self. The key to being grounded in our wholeness resides within our own living, breathing, physical body.

In order to experience being at home in this world and operate at our true capacity for wellness, happiness, and creativity, we must *anchor ourselves*—meaning, our true selves as energy beings—to this Earth plane and to the physical body. We must live not just in our head, but rather in our whole system: mind, body, and breath combined. We need to become *embodied*. After all, the body is the most concentrated layer of our energy; it is not separate from us. If we're not in the body at all, we leave the Earth plane altogether—so clearly, the body has everything to do with why we are here!

Embodiment happens when we recognize that we *are* the Spirit and we *have* a mind and a body. We use our mind and body for our profound experience on Earth, but we should not confuse them with our actual identity. To integrate our spirit with our mind and body, we have to stop looking outside of ourselves to get our bearings and identity, and instead attune our senses to the Soulful Self's vibration.

How do we do this?

We need to place our attention on the central channel of energy in the core of the body, where the chakras reside in their most concentrated state. The central channel is the home of the Soulful Self. Through the practices offered in this Code, we will begin constructing this home so that we can perceive the Soulful Self, and wholeness can prevail.

The Anchoring Code grounds you in the body. It supports your efforts to stop identifying as the mind. It is the first step in shifting your attention and focus from the external world to the energetic core that is our true essence. You'll still be using your mind and five senses; you'll just be using them differently than you ever have before: directing them inward rather than outward, with the goal of bringing your mind, body, and soul into true relationship with one another. This unity will, in turn, give you the energetic clout to integrate your dispersed energy and create structure out of chaos. This awakens the healer within and also provides more kinetic energy for your daily experience, peace of mind, and overall sense of well-being. Your life then becomes your chosen adventure, rather than something to survive and endure.

The Anchoring Code practices powerfully enhance our ability to perceive the clues and cues that our Soulful Self is constantly signaling to the mind about how to unfold into our true magnificence. While this Code is the first step in a larger, more powerful process, doing just these practices will create noticeable energy shifts within you. As you align and create greater flow within the central channel, those shifts will translate into significant improvements in your physical, mental, and emotional life.

The Anchoring Code practices have their roots in ancient traditions (such as the yogic teaching of *pratyahara*), but I've refined and streamlined them so that they are accessible and available to every one of us, without exception, right now. It is not necessary to travel to India or Tibet, or to spend years in silent contemplation in order to be "ready" to receive this knowledge. In fact, you don't need any life interruption at all! You can do these practices anywhere, at any time, throughout the day, in just a few minutes.

Before we launch into the Energy Codes practices, I want to remind you of one key point: these practices *cannot* be done solely with your mind. You can't simply imagine yourself doing them. You have to experience them physically, *in the body*. You have to use your entire human system to build the circuitry: body, mind, and breath/energy/spirit.

Working with the body, we can bypass the thinking/story phase of the mind, with its dramas and perceptions of suffering, and move directly to the source of the problem and solution. The Energy Code practices are your "operations manual" for training the mind, the body, and the breath to live as the Soulful Self.

Let's get to the practices themselves.

The Anchoring Code Practices

PRACTICE 1: SUBJECT-OBJECT-SUBJECT

Have you ever watched a movie that was so intense that it pulled you in completely? Perhaps you found yourself talking to the screen, or flooring an imaginary gas pedal during the big chase scene. Or perhaps you were so immersed in the painful dialogue that you found yourself in tears. Then suddenly, often for no reason, you found yourself again in the theater with all the other onlookers, just watching a movie . . . and something dramatically shifted inside you as you dropped back into your reality. Even though it briefly felt like you were there in that other world, you were only watching it.

We go through our own lives in much the same way. We focus on and are absorbed in things outside of ourselves, to the point that we forget that we are in charge of the experiences within our own body. We throw our energy out onto the object of our attention and anchor it there, instead of inside ourselves. When our energy is hooked into all these outside entities, we can never quite relax, as we don't feel strong, safe, or complete. Dispersal weakens our system and can lead to the breakdown of our immunity and our ability to heal.

This dispersal happens even if we're throwing energy at someone we love or something we take great joy in experiencing. When we disembody, even in a positive situation, it actually has a disempowering effect, because we lose our sense of self. This is the dynamic at play when people "lose themselves" in relationships. Instead of being centered, they—the subject—get caught up in the object of their affections.

Conversely, when we pull our focus and awareness into our own central channel, we remain concentrated energetically even as we engage in the world. We also have a lot more power at our disposal, because we're coming from a place that is anchored and grounded.

To help people consciously move into this empowered place, I use a practice called Subject-Object-Subject. Here's how you can experience it:

1. Look at something external to you that's about five feet away. It can be a person, an object, anything.
2. Put all of your focus and attention on it; really study it. Feel as if you're throwing your energy into it. You can even focus on it with love.
3. Now pull your awareness back into yourself, back to your core. Feel that you're now in your body, looking out through your own eyes.
4. Notice what this feels like. Your peripheral vision expands. You might even be able to see your own nose or cheeks. More, you can feel yourself inhabiting your body again.
5. Hold this awareness of self as you take several breaths in and out.

OBJECT   SUBJECT

SMALL PERSONAL ENERGY FIELD

LARGE PERSONAL ENERGY FIELD

SUBJECT - OBJECT - SUBJECT

I often demonstrate this practice with the groups I speak to. Standing in front of the audience, I'll say, "Throw all your power onto me. Just disempower yourself and give me all your power." Then, once they've done that, I'll say, "Now, claim all your power back. Just call your energy back into yourself—back home."

When the audience throws all their power onto me, it literally pushes my body backward, away from them, as if I've been hit by a big wave. Then, when they pull their energy back into themselves, I am drawn toward them. This happens with every group, every time—and everyone in the room observes it.

The irony of this is that, when we throw all our energy and attention onto something or someone, it actually pushes them away. This can result in all kinds of complications in relationships, including confusion, mixed messages, and control issues. Instead of trying to figure out the story of why someone is playing hard to get or backing away from our love, if we anchor in our core, we can express love and invite the object of our love closer, simply because we aren't overpowering or "overtrying" with our energy. Overall, it allows us to be responsible and response-able. (I'll elaborate on the Soulful Self in relationships later in the book.)

Shifting our focus from outside ourselves to inside ourselves—from object to subject—makes all the difference in the results we get in relationships, and in creative endeavors. We're so used to dispersing our energy by throwing it out into the world that we may not even know we're doing it, but this behavior keeps us living in the Protective Personality, with all its attendant dramas.

It takes only a simple shift in awareness—grounding back into your body—to begin living as the Soulful Self. The rest of the Anchoring Code practices will give you the additional tools you need to begin that shift. Every tool in each of the Codes will be more effective when you "stay on Self" as you do them. And realize that staying on Self does not render you less available for your life. You become less conditional. You actually enhance your true availability as you become less dependent on the outer world for your sense of okay-ness.

PRACTICE 2: CENTRAL CHANNEL ANCHOR POINTS

Anchoring your consciousness inside your body in a structured way is the first step in embodying the Soulful Self. The Central Channel Anchor Points are a primary tool for doing this, since the central channel (or core) is the home base of the Soulful Self.

In this practice, we use four main "locks" or anchor points for tethering our essential energy in the channel. The root chakra is the gateway through which we connect with the earth—and fully exist and participate in this physical world. So we will place our attention there first, using a version of an ancient practice called *mūla bandha*, which in Sanskrit means "root lock."

Mūla bandha or "Root Lock"

I get countless e-mails and thank-yous for this next practice. It locks us into the body immediately. But beware: it might keep you from being able to get a good "upset" going! People constantly tell me about how they get "un-mad" as soon as they utilize *mūla bandha*.

To do this amazing energy shift, you will focus your awareness on the base of the spine. This instantly triggers the gathering of dispersed pockets of energy throughout your system and tethers them there.

Imagine a bunch of helium balloons scattered all around a room. With *mūla bandha*, we're grabbing all the strings, pulling them together, and tying them to one little sandbag that then drops (anchors) to the earth. Boom! What was chaotic just settled and became more organized. Our awareness was suddenly redirected from the outer, surface layers of our system to the core of the body, making the first small shift from the perspective of the Protective Personality to that of the Soulful Self.

The result is an immediate sense of deep groundedness and well-being, of feeling as though you belong here and that this life is "your gig." As you continue to gather those energetic balloons and organize yourself out of that splatted, dispersed state, you'll start to feel your strength and presence in the body. You'll no longer view yourself as a victim of any happening or circumstance, but rather will begin living as the creator of your life. *Mūla bandha* is how we begin to build the sensory neurocircuitry to establish this new identity. It seems simple, moving from living in our head to living in our core, but it's rather big stuff!

Here's how you do it:

1. Contract the muscles at the base of your pelvic bowl and lift them toward your navel, as if drawing energy up into the body from the earth below. (You may know this as a Kegel exercise or by how it feels to stop midstream when urinating.) Don't worry if it takes you a few days or even weeks to master this. It will come!

2. Once you've practiced contracting those muscles a few times and gotten a feel for it, squeeze them as tight as you can and then release by one-half. Hold in this place while taking several breaths in and out of the belly—not the chest. (Breathing in the chest activates the fight-flight-or-fright response, due to the type of [sympathetic] nerve endings located in the upper lobes of the lungs. Belly breathing activates healing and creativity, due to the calming of [parasympathetic] nerve endings, as well as increasing the blood supply in the lungs' lower lobes.)

3. Now release by one-half again and hold there for several more belly breaths until you begin to feel a sense of "being in there" without clenching or expending too much effort. Our goal is to create awareness in tissues that we typically aren't conscious of, and then to develop our sensory perception in that area to a finer and finer degree. Ultimately, as you progress in this practice and tone the tissues, only a small amount of tension in the musculature will be needed to focus the energy—but for now, give it all you've got!

4. Practice multiple times per day, as much as you can and would like. You cannot overdo this!

With practice, this variation of *mūla bandha* allows the energy field to be tethered succinctly and consistently enough at the root of the spine that the tissues there can start to wake up. A new vibration will establish itself, and this will let the tissues know that the Soulful Self is moving in!

Squeeze the Heart

For our next anchor point, we will move up the central channel into the heart center, called *anāhata chakra*, in the middle of the chest. Here, as with *mūla bandha*, we're going to squeeze the muscles in order to bring our conscious attention to the area and "lock in" our energy there.

Here's how to work with the heart center anchor point:

1. Contract inside the heart center space by squeezing or tightening the muscles in the center of the chest—not off to the left where the heart muscle is, but rather in the chakra area, centered over the spine. Pull your pectoralis muscles together and back toward your spine. Pull your shoulder blades together and down. Pull your deltoid muscles (around the caps of your shoulders) down and tighten them. Then go inside the chest from there. (If you find the specifics confusing, just imagine that you're lying on your back doing a bench press and pushing heavy weights up toward the ceiling. Or practice by picking up or pushing something very heavy and noticing where the active muscles are.)

2. Squeeze and hold for a few belly breaths. Then, as we did with *mūla bandha*, relax the tension by one-half, and take a few more breaths into the belly.

3. Relax by half again and continue to breathe. As you grow more comfortable with this exercise, allow your awareness to penetrate deeper into the chest. Try to contract the tiny muscles around the spine and behind the heart, deep within the core of the body.

4. Practice multiple times per day, as much as you can and would like, ultimately allowing the front side of the heart center to be open while contracting all around both sides and behind. There is a connective tissue that physically anchors your heart to your spine; visualize this as you relax into its support as you engage in this practice. It will feel wonderful as you do!

Squeezing the heart in this way creates the same tethering of our consciousness, our essential energy, to the body that we did at the root chakra through *mūla bandha,* giving us one more point of contact for anchoring the awareness of the Soulful Self. This further shifts the awareness from outside to inside, physically drawing conscious energy to the heart center to activate calmness, relaxation, healing, and love. Your mind will begin to experience how fantastic it feels to activate this loving presence of the Soul.

Constrict the Throat

Our next stop up the central channel is the throat. Here we want to squeeze the throat to the point that we're breathing like Darth Vader—constricting the air passages and allowing the breath to be felt and heard as it passes through. Your breathing should make a noticeable sound both on the inhale and the exhale. In yoga, this is known as *ujjayi pranayama,* or "victorious breath." It allows us to "follow" the sound into where we should be living all of the time—the victory of the Quantum Flip into the Soulful Self.

Here's how to do it:

1. Let your lower jaw open slightly, lips closed, and gently tighten the muscles of your throat as you draw the back of your tongue up and posterior, constricting the opening. Draw your chin subtly back (don't clench your teeth) and feel the back and crown of your head lift toward the ceiling.

2. Take several deep belly breaths in and out through your nose. Allow the breath to make a hissing sound, like waves on sand, as

it passes in and out. It's almost like a snore. You have permission
to breathe as loudly as you want!

When you've constricted the throat just enough that you can hear the
breath, you know your essential energy is anchored through the central
channel up to this point. When you follow the sound with your mind into
the central channel of the body, it further draws the consciousness into the
core of the body. This is important to the overall success of embodiment—
it will center your confidence and clarity tremendously.

Be the One Behind the Eyes

Our last stop along the central channel is in the center of the head. As the
energy flows up from the throat, we want to direct it up through the mid-
brain, to just underneath and between the two brain hemispheres. This
area is home to the very important pineal gland.

The pineal gland contains light receptor cells called rods and cones,
which are similar to those found in our eyes. Part of its function may be to
"see" and receive the high-frequency, subtle, invisible energy of the inner
world, whereas our eyes receive and transmit the visible light energy. In
other words, this is the home of your inner or sixth sense. I have personally
experienced this since I developed the extraordinary sensory perception
and circuitry of my own embodiment.

Here's how we do this practice:

1. With your eyes open or closed, put your attention on the center
   of your forehead, between your eyebrows, on the area known
   as the third eye. Bring your attention onto the Self (subject), and
   feel the sensation as you focus your attention on that spot.

2. If you need more sensation to really feel that you're tethered
   there, roll your eyes upward until you feel a tension behind them.

3. Hold this tension temporarily as you breathe in and out from
   the belly several times.

Similar to our Subject-Object-Subject exercise, the goal of this anchor point is to recognize yourself as the "one behind the eyes." This dramatically shifts your focus from external to internal, from "out there" to "home" inside your core. To be anchored in the body, you need to *be* the consciousness looking out through your body's eyes.

––––––

Now that you're familiar with the four anchor points along the central channel, you want to start viewing and experiencing the channel as a vital, flowing energetic pathway—the superhighway of your whole energy system. Eventually, when you're able to do the work without the extra guidance the anchor points provide, you will relax them and allow a feeling of falling into the body. More on that later. In the meantime, squeeze away!

Start contracting the anchor points one at a time: root lock, heart center, throat, and third eye. Hold this tension as you breathe audibly in and out through your nose. Once you've worked your way up the channel, connect the four areas as if there's a plumb line dropping down through the channel—from the tension behind your eyes, to the throat where you're constricting and hearing your breath, to the heart that you're squeezing, down into *mūla bandha*, and from there all the way down into the earth like the roots of a tree.

Practice feeling that alignment, sensing it, imagining it—making it up, if you have to. The more you do this, the more you will start to build sensory perception in this area, and the increased circuitry of the sensory system will increase both the awareness of the Soulful Self and its energetic flow.

Remember that quote often attributed to Albert Einstein: "The intuitive mind is a sacred gift and the rational mind is a faithful servant. We have created a society that honors the servant and has forgotten the gift." This sensing ability is how we should use the rational mind—as a servant to the intuitive mind. You're employing the mind to direct and use your senses differently than you have ever used them before. The result is that you become awake in your true essence in a way you have not been awake before.

Besides the four anchor points, the other powerful ingredient that

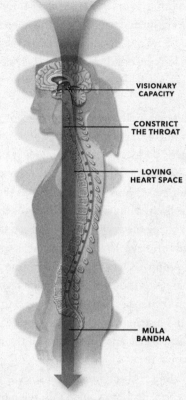

VISIONARY
CAPACITY

CONSTRICT
THE THROAT

LOVING
HEART SPACE

MŪLA
BANDHA

CENTRAL CHANNEL ANCHOR POINTS

helps to bring this true essence fully online within the central channel is the following unique breathing pattern.

PRACTICE 3: CENTRAL CHANNEL BREATHING

If there's one thing I see that keeps people from living into their fullness, it's that they barely breathe! Breath is energy—so when we draw breath into and exhale it from our body, we move energy into and out of our personal energy field as well. Breathing while maintaining a conscious connection to our anchor points and the earth is an efficient way to activate our energy centers (chakras) and solidify the energy in our central channel, the seat of embodiment for the Soulful Self.

Central Channel Breathing is a fundamental practice of the Energy Codes. Breathing through the core of the body gives you the tangible experience of your multidimensional reality (body-mind-spirit), and swiftly shifts you out of survival and reactivity mode and into a perspective based in a sense of higher purpose instead.

As with the other practices, here you'll be doing belly breathing—meaning that, with each breath, you will extend the belly on the inhale and compress it for the exhale, rather than breathing shallowly in the chest. As you breathe through the central channel according to the instructions below, you want to take special care to have your concentration travel up and down through each energy center in the core of the body, like going up and down *inside* the elevator within an elevator shaft, *without skipping any portion of the central channel*. This is key to igniting all of your electro-magnetic and eventually neurological circuitry.

Here's how to do Central Channel Breathing:

1. Start with your anchor points—lifting the pelvic floor in *mūla bandha*, squeezing the heart as if doing a bench press, Darth Vader–style in-the-throat breath, and momentary tension behind the eyes.

2. Take your attention up above your head—about six inches—and inhale from there. Initially, it may help to visualize a white or golden ball of light with the breath, so feel free to give that a try. (Ultimately, though, you want to realize that you *are* the ball of light, so you can feel *yourself* moving down through the top of your head and through your own central channel—as if you are in the elevator going down to the basement floor—rather than seeing it from an external focal point.)

3. Inhale all the way down through the channel, into your belly, keeping your anchor points squeezed as best you can. Extend your belly on the inhale.

4. Exhale from the belly, straight down through *mūla bandha* and into the earth, still squeezing your four anchor points. Retract your belly toward the spine on the exhale.

5. Now reverse the action: draw a breath from within the earth up through *mūla bandha* into the belly. As you exhale, feel yourself as the energy flows up through the shaft of the central channel and out the top of the head.

Repeat the whole cycle. Note that a complete cycle includes two full breaths: one inhale starting from the top, six inches above your head into the heart/belly/core space, followed by an exhale down into the earth; and one inhale into the heart/belly/core space from the earth, followed by an exhale out the top of the head.

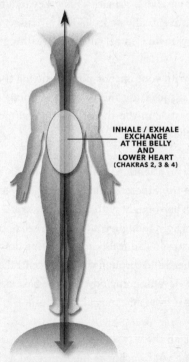

INHALE / EXHALE
EXCHANGE
AT THE BELLY
AND
LOWER HEART
(CHAKRAS 2, 3 & 4)

CENTRAL CHANNEL BREATH
1ST & 7TH CHAKRAS

When you first start this practice, breathe at a comfortable rate. This will allow you to concentrate on maintaining the tension in your anchor points and moving (as the breath) up and down your central channel. Once you become proficient and holding the anchor points starts to feel natural, you can deliberately speed up or slow down your breath to create specific outcomes. More active or fierce versions of this practice—where you breathe more quickly, powerfully, and audibly—serve to pierce through densities within tissues and veils between chakras, whereas slow, gentle, and deep versions are for the intricate details of circuitry building and integrating subtle energies. Slower breathing also promotes relaxation and eases the effects of stress and prolonged mental concentration. I'll provide more details on mastering these specifics as we progress through the book.

To engage in a more active version of Central Channel Breathing, breathe to a count of four: inhale for two counts, and exhale for two counts. You will notice that the exhale here happens in a "whoosh." You can imagine that forceful breath piercing any thicknesses or densities you observe along your central channel.

To employ a gentler version of this practice, slow the breath to a count of six, eight, or ten, maintaining equal lengths of inhale and exhale.

With any form of Central Channel Breathing, the most important thing is to consciously follow the breath (and, ideally, to *be* the breath) up and down the system, activating all the circuits along the path. Don't skip over any of the anchor points or any area along the channel in between.

You will progress quickly if you do this practice several times throughout the day—especially every night when you go to bed, making it the last thing you do before you fall asleep, and every morning as soon as you awaken, before your feet hit the floor. These times, on either side of sleep, are when the subconscious and conscious minds talk to each other the most, and so are the best times to create and establish a new reality for yourself.

For maximum benefit, make *every* breath, every day, a central channel breath! Each time you breathe in from beyond the body, and through the body, and then exhale out to beyond the body again, you are activating the subconscious awareness of being more than just a physical being, and you draw from your multidimensionality, rejuvenating yourself constantly. This is how I accomplish so much in a week's time and feel as if I'm getting younger every year.

PRACTICE 4: DROP IN, DROP THROUGH

Drop In, Drop Through is a more free-flowing version of Central Channel Breathing and has a slightly different purpose and use. Like Subject-Object-Subject, it works to pull all of our energy into the center of our body from where it might otherwise be hanging out—in our head, around the surface of our shoulders, and up above the body. In this practice, we're going to let the energy drop in and fall all the way down through the body like a rushing waterfall, gathering densities with it as it goes and flushing them down into the earth in a powerful release.

This "flushing" has huge value for us. It keeps us from holding on to stagnant energies like old thought patterns, stories, or other habits, and from trying to control circumstances and situations. We hold on to these unhelpful energies not because they feel good, but because they are what we know. They're familiar. Yet if we don't let these things go, their dispersed densities will continue to weaken our energy field and flow and create painful friction in our lives as they clamor to be released.

If, however, we can energetically familiarize ourselves with change and letting go—by letting energy flush down through us, as we will in this exercise—and get familiar with what that flushing feels like in the body, it becomes easier and easier for the mind to let go of thoughts and ideas that no longer serve us. That's because letting go energetically, through the body, replicates the energetic pattern we would experience if we truly released something mentally and emotionally. Since letting go is harder for the mind at the level of story, we can do it much more easily and quickly at the level of the energy, where the density actually resides. We are then able to turn our mind to more creative and productive pursuits.

Imagine, for instance, that you're having a conflict with someone, and you really want the other person to see and agree with your point of view. Now imagine that this person suddenly gets what you're trying to say, and agrees with all of it. Suddenly all of the effort you've been expending to convince them will release. You'll no longer be holding an agenda, because your mission is complete. That change in your outer world—the release of friction due to the other person's shift—then causes a change in your inner world, and a rush of energy will pour down through your body as your desire comes to fruition.

Of course, this example is change from the outside in, which we can't ultimately control—but we *can* do the reverse, and create change from the inside out. We can practice what it would feel like if we were *already* understood, *before* the other person gets what we're trying to say. This would allow us to drop our agenda and stop the friction in its tracks before it creates conflict. Exercises like this one are powerful for releasing the stuck energy and conditions of the Protective Personality.

Here's how to practice Drop In, Drop Through:

1. Notice the energy around your head and shoulders right now. (It's likely more pronounced than in your belly, hip, and leg areas.)

2. Drop all of the tension that you can, all at once, into the center of your head as you take a deep breath into your core. Just let go of everything in the upper half of your body.

3. Then squeeze all four anchor points to center yourself in your core.

4. Now, as you exhale, drop this energy all the way through the central channel and into the ground beneath where you're sitting or standing. Then release all anchor points, but stay in the core. Dropping In allows you to feel more energy in the creative centers in the middle of the brain, and Dropping Through allows you to drop everything else and anchor in your rootedness. Feels so good!

5. Consistently, in between *mūla bandha* (realizing that this will actually only be intermittent), Drop In, Drop Through all day

long. Drop the pelvic floor, drop the belly, drop the shoulders, open the bottoms of the feet, and drop into the earth as you walk. Feel a waterfall of loving support fall through you with every step.

Whenever we have an attachment to something, we hold our energy. We keep it stuck. This doesn't allow for anything to move, change, or flow. It keeps us arrested at the mental body layer of the Energy Man drawing, preventing us from dropping into our core. It doesn't allow for revelations to occur. Proactively moving stuck energy is just part of the self-mastery we're going for with the Energy Codes. We want to get used to *moving* energy, not holding on to it, so we can be in a state of flow and nonattachment while remaining anchored in our body. This optimal state creates greater space for creativity, love, and a sense of well-being that is not reliant on external circumstance or validation. Later, in additional Code chapters, you will learn that the power of love acts as a bonfire, transmuting these dense and stuck energies into creativity to be used proactively for enhancing your life experience.

The Anchoring Code Chakra Correlation: Root Chakra

While the work of this Code affects your whole system in important ways, it has a particular influence on the root chakra, focused at the base of the spine. Because the chakras each govern a specific aspect of consciousness, an area of life, and a region of the physical body, improving the function and flow of a chakra will have a specific, positive impact on your health, your experiences, and the way you view and approach life.

The root chakra, also known as the base chakra or *mūlādhāra chakra* (literally, "root support" in Sanskrit), is the energy center associated with our most primal level of being. It represents physical survival and security. People with an inactive root chakra are not very grounded in their body or in their physical life and tend to feel anxious, unstable, and unsafe, constantly beset by survival-related issues. They may act materialistic, flighty, or flippant, or simply be externally focused. They often have big challenges with communication, feelings, and self-esteem, and so have serial marriages or jobs. Or they may "stuff" these tendencies deep into their bodies and experience tremendous internal conflict while appearing on the outside to be happy and strong. At some point, their bodies can no longer hold up under this energy drain and they fail to outrun their fears.

Many people with first-chakra issues also suffer from a strong sense that they don't belong. It's as though they have one sense of reality internally—behind their eyes—that doesn't match the reality they're operating in. As a result, they tend to doubt themselves, feel crazy, or simply withdraw in order to cope. Because this chakra, and its level of our consciousness, governs our physical presence and well-being at a general level, physical body symptoms can include poor general health, compromised immunity, and low vitality, as well as problems in the body's structural system, such as osteoporosis, joint pain and weakness, and instability in the legs and feet.

If you're not in your root chakra, you're not in your body. And if you're not here fully, you suffer. The Anchoring Code practices can help!

The following chart offers a summary of some of the key characteristics of the root chakra. Notice how the energetic properties of the chakra mirror the physical body areas.

The Anchoring Code Chakra Correlation: Root Chakra

NAME(S)	First chakra, base chakra, *mūlādhāra chakra*
LOCATION	Base of the spine
COLOR	Red
MUSICAL NOTE	C
BODY AREAS AFFECTED	Bone, skeletal structure, hips, legs, feet, genitals, base of spine, kidneys, body's life force, teeth, nails, blood, building of cells, **adrenal glands**
"BACK SIDE" SYMPTOMS	Mental lethargy and spaciness, incapacity for inner stillness, osteoarthritis, poor general health, lacking vital energy
"FRONT SIDE" CHARACTERISTICS	Self-mastery, high physical energy, groundedness, vibrant health. A recognition that "I am here as Source." "This is my gig." "I belong." "I *bring* what I choose to experience."
PRACTICES	• Subject – Object – Subject • Central Channel Anchor Points • Central Channel Breathing • Drop In, Drop Through
BREATHWORK (as explained in Chapter 8)	Central Channel Breath
YOGA POSES FOR GREATER INTEGRATION	• Chair Pose (*utkaṭāsana*) • Warrior 1 (*vīrabhadrāsana I*) • Pyramid Pose (*pārśvottānāsana*) • Tree Pose (*vṛkṣāsana*) • Standing Forward Fold (*uttānāsana*)

Due to its location at the base of the central channel—the place where energy (the real us) enters our body from the earth—a wobble or impairment in this chakra can cause a ripple-effect wobble up the rest of the channel, not allowing the ultimate activation of the high-brain centers of creativity. If this is the case, we never get to experience our true destiny. Rather we continue to try to make life work the best we can, from the Back Side of the Model, in survival mode. Therefore, having our essential energy activated in and flowing optimally through our root chakra is fundamental to our well-being.

The Anchoring Code gives us the tools to do that. Using the practices in this Code, you can establish the strong sense of safety, belonging, and well-being that results from integration of the root chakra. You begin to recognize that "this world is my gig" and "I can handle this." You can cultivate, and sustain, lifelong vitality. Rather than perceiving the world as something you're trying to fit into, you see that this life is yours to play with, to express into creatively as an adventure, and to experience with strong physical health, vitality, and self-mastery.

Yoga for the Anchoring Code

To help facilitate your ability to do the Energy Codes practices and reinforce their benefits, at this point I'd like to add a bit of specialized yoga to the mix. Done with focus and presence, yoga is the perfect blend of mind, body, and soul or breath. It focuses the mind on an area of the body that you simultaneously move and breathe through. This is the collaboration you need to truly land and anchor your essential energy in the body, and thereby gain the ability to steer and manage that energy's pattern and flow.

My personal teaching practice, BodyAwake Yoga, builds circuits of *conscious* communication in the body during each pose. If yoga hasn't been your thing before now, don't worry. Even if you've never done yoga, you will likely be able to do the basic practices suggested here. But don't let their apparent simplicity fool you; though simple, they provide powerful cumulative benefits, even to the seasoned yoga student or teacher. Many long-term yoga teachers (thirty years and more) have been astounded at the differences made by these additional instructions. I'm certain they will also help you!

Now, on to the poses for the Anchoring Code.

Chair Pose (*utkatāsana*), which is simple and accessible to just about everyone, can help powerfully integrate the root chakra and ground your energy at the base of the central channel so you can begin building your presence as the Soulful Self. If standing or balance is a challenge for you, you can also practice Chair Pose by sitting on the very edge of . . . you guessed it, a chair!

CHAIR POSE (*UTKATĀSANA*)

In Chair Pose, the body mimics the act of sitting back onto a chair. Here's how to do it:

1. Stand with your feet hip-width distance apart. Plant your heels and the ball mounds of your feet down into the earth. Feel the connection between you and the ground you're standing on.

2. Bend your knees and sit your hips back as if you're going to sit in a chair. Push your sitting bones back so your knees don't go forward past your toes. Keep your knees parallel; don't let them splay outward. If you need more support, touch the knees together.

3. If your shoulder flexibility allows, raise your arms over your head; otherwise, simply raise them as high as possible as you hold the pose.

4. Hold for three to ten breaths, then release by straightening the legs. Bring the hands back down by your sides.

Now let's integrate our Anchoring Code practices and BodyAwake principles with Chair Pose to increase the benefits of all.

1. While holding Chair Pose, focus on a space two feet beneath your feet, within the earth. Feel yourself anchor into that energy.

2. Lift your toes, and then set them back down. Lean back on your heels and feel the central channel open up. Then lean forward on your toes and feel it close down. (This is a great practice to help find the sensations of the central channel.) When you're ready, lean back again and stay there with a focus on the central channel.

3. Press into your right foot, then your left, with toes relaxed. Roll the ankles around, pressing into the ankle joints so you can "feel yourself in there." Gently rise and drop a little, emphasizing the knees. Contract the thigh and hip muscles, squeezing the hip joint on the front, back, inner, and outer aspects—all while taking deep breaths up and down along the central channel as we've practiced. If your knees are touching for support, squeeze them together now to feel the circuitry building there.

4. Squeeze *mūla bandha*. Squeeze the back of the heart space by drawing the shoulder blades together and down. Stretch the arms fully upward while energetically "plugging" them back into the shoulder sockets, and tuck the chin. Raise the eyes and feel the tension behind them. Feel yourself align down the entire channel and front aspect of the spine—and past it, down the legs into the feet, and ultimately down into the earth.

5. Take a couple of breaths up and down the channel. Begin by pulling the energy up from the earth two feet below where you are standing, inhaling upward through the whole channel of the legs and into the central channel. Collect the breath in the core, then exhale upward through the heart, the throat, the third eye, and out through the top of the head. On the next inhale, draw the breath down from overhead, through the head, throat, heart,

belly, and *mūla bandha*; then exhale down through the legs and into the earth. Ideally, you will eventually *be* the breath as it passes through the body.

ADDITIONAL YOGA POSES TO INTEGRATE THE ROOT CHAKRA

You can use the following asanas along with Chair Pose to enhance your work with the Anchoring Code. (For additional resources regarding yoga poses recommended for use with each of the seven Energy Codes, visit drsuemorter.com/energycodesbook.)

Once you feel steady and grounded in each posture, begin to integrate Central Channel Breathing, pulling the energy and breath from beneath the feet, through the central channel, and exhaling out through the top of the head, then inhaling through the top of the head and down the channel, and exhaling out through *mūla bandha* and down through the soles of the feet into the earth.

- Warrior 1 (*vīrabhadrāsana I*)
- Pyramid Pose (*pārśvottānāsana*)
- Tree Pose (*vṛkṣāsana*)
- Standing Forward Fold (*uttānāsana*)

Common Obstacles with the Anchoring Code

When I teach the Anchoring Code to a group at a live event, a few common challenges inevitably arise. These are easy to work through and typically resolve with practice.

Challenge #1: You can't squeeze and breathe at the same time. Oftentimes when people find it difficult to breathe into the belly and squeeze/lift the belly and pelvic floor at the same time, they get confused about which one they should be doing. "Do I squeeze or breathe deeply?" they ask. My answer is always, "Yes!" You have to try to do both at the same time so that you can feel the resistance—the friction—that this creates.

Remember that we create friction in order to figure out a path toward knowing who we truly are. The internal friction of squeezing and breathing at the same time is an internal alternative to the story-based, bumper-cars approach to evolving our consciousness. One way we learn in this world is through *resistance*. For example, when we debate with someone, we come to know more of who we are because of the distinctions that are being made—the differences. Likewise, when we generate resistance internally by simultaneously squeezing inwardly and stretching outwardly as the breath is filling the belly and the muscles are tightening, the resistance makes the distinction between pressing in versus pushing out. We can feel it with our sensory system and find where we are supposed to be "living" inside the body in a manner that we might not have noticed before. We learn, through the resistance, "who and where" we are. *By creating this resistance internally, we don't have to create it in our outer world relationships.* The mind relaxes, as does our body's fight-flight-or-fright response, and we create an environment more conducive for the Soulful Self to emerge. Afterward, we relax the pelvic floor and maintain our sense of Self.

Challenge #2: You can't feel or sense any of these areas when squeezing. Many of us have been living in our head for so many years that we've lost the ability to feel the subtle sensations of our body. That's really okay! If, as you practice squeezing on the inside, you can't really feel it, place a hand on the outside of the area and gently press until you feel sensation there. To help bring your focus to the base of the spine for *mūla bandha*, for example, press on the low belly, just above your pubic bone, or even sit on one of your hands or feet. For the heart, press your fingers into the breastbone, "go inside," and press back out against your hand, or else lie on your back and lift something heavy as if doing a bench press. For the throat, use your palm or fingers to apply a light pressure on your neck (front or back), again "go inside," and press out. And for the pineal gland in the center of the head, press between the eyebrows as you rotate your eyes upward. You really don't need to worry about doing it "right." In the next chapter, you will gain more understanding of what to do in this situation, but for now use these suggestions. The goal here is to bring your focus and conscious awareness to the area you're working with, so you can begin to build the photon density—the presence—of the Soulful Self there. Your ability to sense it will return and build!

Challenge #3: It feels like too much to do all at once. When people start to do these practices, especially Central Channel Breathing, it can feel like a lot to concentrate on at the same time. But that's true for many things we become proficient at in life, such as coordinating hands and feet when learning to drive, or cooking a meal with multiple dishes that all need to finish at the same time, or perfecting that golf swing—geez! I invite you to go into these, and all of the Energy Codes tools, knowing that they might feel a bit awkward and mechanical at first, but that, like anything else you've ever learned to do, they will get much easier with practice. In fact, you may begin to feel more ease with them in as little as a few days. Stay in a place of love and compassion for yourself, and it will happen even faster.

If you can't squeeze all the anchor points and breathe up and down through the central channel at the same time, start by practicing *mūla bandha* alone. As you go about your day, take a moment to lift the pelvic floor and feel your own energetic presence there. Breathe several times in and out, and then release it. Repeat this as frequently as you remember to throughout the day. Then build on it by squeezing the heart, and practice having your awareness in those two centers as you take deep belly breaths. Then add the throat, and finally the attention behind the eyes. You'll be breathing up and down the channel in no time!

Most important is that you don't give up. *Mūla bandha* is something anyone can do, and even this sole, small effort will have a big impact as it begins to steer the mind toward the Quantum Flip we're striving to create with the Energy Codes. So start small, and take it step by step, building your awareness within the central channel and breathing through each piece of the practice until it becomes more accessible. The same is true for all of the other Codes' practices: break them down into smaller bites if you need to, but stay at it. The benefits are too tremendous to give up.

———

Once you've established an anchoring of your conscious attention inside the core of the body, you're ready to further engage and identify with the Soulful Self. You do this by sensing and feeling the specific energy patterns happening within you that are associated with your life experiences. You'll develop a whole new method for understanding and responding to what's

Chapter 5

THE FEELING CODE:
THE LANGUAGE OF THE SOUL

A few years ago, I ended an eight-year relationship that I thought was going to be for the rest of my life. And while I had begun to build new circuits and integrate much of what had opened within me from my ray-of-light experience, this was new territory.

It wasn't pleasant. I had just lost my mother the year before; now this relationship was dissolving too. We had agreements about how the disentanglement would unfold, but things didn't exactly go as discussed. One Sunday night, I arrived home from the airport to a half-empty house. The dogs—who were supposed to remain with me—were also gone. I was devastated.

This pain was something that I never dreamed I could experience. It was soul-piercing—and all the worse for being so unexpected. I simply *didn't have* those kinds of exchanges in the world. And during this unraveling, I had started to travel and speak to public audiences, which I knew was my true life path—but I also had the responsibility of a clinic, other doctors and staff, and patients to care for and guide. Canceled flights and travel issues often kept me from meeting my commitments to my patients and team. Stress like I had never known was building up inside me.

One day I was just leaving my house to go to the office when I realized that I'd forgotten something. I walked back through my bedroom toward my closet . . . and collapsed onto my bed. My broken heart imploded, and I dissolved into a full-body cry. The tears felt like they were rising up from beneath my bones, carried on waves of despair up through my throat and out of my mouth and eyes, even through my skin.

I had been putting so much energy into staying the course, determined to keep going, stay strong, make things happen. "Just don't think about it," I told myself. I couldn't imagine having one more thing to have to *feel*. But in my emotionally exhausted state, it just came bursting out like water breaching a cracked dam.

Sprawled on that bed in a puddle of tears, I let go of everything. I gave myself permission to just fall into the pain. Maybe I was tired of fighting, of hanging on; maybe it was simply time for me to awaken. Whatever the case, in those moments my internal experience of *who I am* changed forever.

Sobbing, I grabbed hold of my chest, my belly, clutching my core. Then these words came into my head: "If it all goes away, at least I'll have *me*."

In that moment, in the midst of my tears, I felt the greatest sense of joy that I have ever felt. It was so confusing: I was more upset than I had been in years, and I was overjoyed at the same time.

Letting go of trying to *make* it better is what allowed it to *be* better. I had been acting like a warrior on a march, but I got maxed out to the point that I simply couldn't be that anymore. When I dropped my armor and allowed myself to feel, all was revealed. I was able to release the idea that I was supposed to be strong and make everything work. All of my Protective Personality efforts melted in an instant, and all of my unresolved emotion flooded up and out in joyful release.

There on my bed, my thinking mind and its Protective Personality surrendered to my Soulful Self. Until that day, I hadn't known that I was in warrior mode. My drive to protect myself, to "fix" what was "wrong," remained subconscious until I became overwhelmed, which brought me to my core, and I let go and dropped in. In this moment my exalted experience from years prior landed in my body more deeply than ever before.

Today I don't wait until the dam is ready to break before I drop in. Now I mostly *live* in. But if something pulls me back from my core, I drop in and allow myself to *feel* what's really happening as soon as I sense something creating a charge in my energy field. I save myself the pain of trying to run things with my mind and my Protective Personality, and let my body—my feeling—tell my mind what to do.

In this, the Feeling Code, I share these practices with you.

What Is the Feeling Code?

With the Anchoring Code, we began tethering the energy of the Soulful Self to the physical body—giving it a home to inhabit. We focused the mind in the body to make this happen and established a relationship between the mind, the body, and the Soulful Self. That new connection paves the way for increasing the presence of the Soulful Self and beginning to receive its invaluable communications—and to fully experience what life is all about.

Life is Project Awakening—awakening to the Soulful Self so we can engage with our world from our highest, true nature and experience a divinely guided, magical life. This awakening happens through friction— bumping up against the places where we're not yet awakened to our magnificence or where our circuits are not yet turned on. Without friction, we can't gain awareness about which parts of ourselves are still in the dark; we need to be jostled out of our status quo in order to see where we need to redirect our energy and reintegrate the fragmented and dispersed parts of ourselves.

We cannot avoid friction. We have no choice in the matter; until we are fully living as our Soulful Self, friction will show us the places where we need to build our circuitry and awaken to our greatness. However, we *do* have a choice about where our friction occurs: in our inner world at the energy level or in our outer world at the level of story.

Here's an example of how this works. Let's suppose someone in your life says something you don't like, and you get upset about it. You have a mental and emotional reaction to his or her words, and tell yourself a story about what those words mean about you, your relationships with others, and the world in general. Your mind says things like, "Why is this happening?" "He shouldn't have done that," and "How am I ever going to get okay with life now that this has happened?" After a while, you might ask yourself, "Why can't I just get over this?" or "Why can't I forgive this?"

The reason you can't "get over it" is that the mind is operating on the level of story. The mind's inability to process your feelings is an effort by your whole system to keep you from moving on until you glean what you need from the experience—to bring certain circuits online and reintegrate energy that is dispersed. Many times this reintegration shows up as an "epiphany" or an "ah-ha moment." Once your energy has shifted and those circuits fire up, the story changes, and so does the mind's relationship to the event that caused the friction.

From the Protective Personality's perspective, friction looks like: "This is crazy. I can't let go of this. I can't get out of it!" From the Soulful Self's view, friction is saying: "We're going to hold this right here and keep doing this until you focus on it and actually surrender to it—even if it exhausts you." Because, whether you're surrendering intentionally or from exhaustion, surrender is surrender, as far as the Soulful Self is concerned. It's like, "It's okay. I'll be right here, waiting for you to discover me when you're ready—whatever that takes."

Friction certainly gets our attention. It undeniably helps us to grow. But we can grow through friction in ways other than the story route—and that's what the Feeling Code will help us to do. Generally, we tell ourselves a painful story and try to figure out "why" an experience has occurred. Instead, we can simply notice the energy shifts that accompany what's happening, work with what they reveal, and manage the energy. The body acts as the intermediary or translator in the ongoing dialogue between the Soulful Self and the mind. This conversation is what the Feeling Code is all about, and it allows us to have more conscious choice about what our reality looks like.

Shifting your orientation from the mind to the body, from *thinking* to *feeling,* from *rationalizing* to *sensing*, will initiate a drastic shift in perception. It will increase your intuitive capacity, enhance your energetic flow, and allow your physical body to heal because it is no longer mired in stress and a "survivalist" story line. It will open the channel to direct communication among the mind, the body, and the Soulful Self. But in order to work with the Feeling Code effectively, we need to learn the difference between *feeling* and *emotion.*

In traditional psychology, when we talk about "feeling our feelings," we mean that we allow ourselves to fully experience our emotional states so we can get the stuck energy of denied or unprocessed emotions flowing once again. But there is a difference between *feeling our feelings* and *feeling our emotions*. Both reside within the same bandwidth in our system—but if our attention is in our mind, we experience an "emotion"; if we are focused in our body, we experience a visceral, cellular sensation instead—a "feeling." The Feeling Code recognizes the difference between the feeling layer and the emotional layer of our energy field.

Once thought to be in charge of the output from the central nervous system (the brain) to the organs of our body, the vagus nerve is now recognized to be responsible for 80 to 90 percent of the *sensory* input from the gut to the brain—reporting to us the nudge from our core. Sensing from within our deep essential self is subtle but imperative for awakening to our greater reality within. The sensory nervous system is ten to one hundred to a thousand times more abundant in nerve count than our motor nervous system, demonstrating the greater importance of sensing what is actually happening in our inner realm compared to the actions that we subsequently take in our outer world.

The vagus nerve's ability to transport information from the gut level of our being is part of the magic of the enteric nervous system, considered the body's "second brain." It enables us to integrate information, metabolize it, and generate responses within our core without ever having to check in with the brain in our head—generating what I believe to be our deep sense of truth and knowing. The Energy Codes teach us how to perceive on a subtler energy level in order to manifest more easily and effectively.

When friction happens in your world, you have three reactions to it: a mental reaction, an emotional reaction, and a physical reaction or bodily sensation. With what you now know about energy, we will look not to the emotions (which are tied to the story), but instead to the physical feelings, which are generated by shifts in our energy field.

Even if a situation (such as the ending of a relationship or the loss of a job) happened a year ago, or ten, or twenty, if the friction it generated in our energy field has not been resolved, it will still cause a sensation in the body, such as a knot in our stomach. There's a reason it's still affecting us where it's affecting us; when we notice it and learn to work with it, we build the circuitry needed for energy to pass through that area. If we stay on the story level, the energy has to detour and creates a wobble in the central channel and a corresponding dysfunction in our external life. In other words, when we go straight to the source, it makes our life easier across the board.

We have to expend much more effort emotionally when most of our circuits are asleep. We get exhausted emotionally. We are less pliable. We break instead of bend and crash instead of soar. When more circuits come online, it's easy to be courageous, forgiving, joyful, and resilient. That's because these are the qualities of our true nature, and when more of that nature is awake, we engage with life with the full use of our inherent capabilities.

The Feeling Code provides you with a new energetic language I call body-talk. This is the key to receiving the communications of the Soulful Self and translating them for the mind so that you can begin to uncover the lessons and revelations in every life scenario. In later Codes, we'll master ways to work even more effectively with that communication, integrate the learning that friction demands, and become more whole, integrated, and fully online versions of ourselves.

The Feeling Code Practices

PRACTICE 1: TAKE IT TO THE BODY

In Take It to the Body, we interrupt the old pattern of focusing on the story and focus attention instead onto the body. In this way, we can integrate the energy beneath the story rather than continue to loop in the mind through "story-writing." This practice is revolutionary because it's an evolutionary shortcut—a total game-changer that eliminates years of work on the mental and emotional levels by going directly to the source of the issue—the energy—and resolving it then and there.

Here's how you do this simple but life-changing exercise:

Whenever friction happens in your life and you have an emotional or "charged" reaction, immediately ask "Where?" rather than "Why?"—as in, "*Where* in the body do I feel this?" rather than "*Why* is this happening to me?"

1. Turn your attention inward and focus within your body. Sense and feel the energy shifts that accompany your emotional reaction. There will be a "charge" somewhere. It may feel like tightness or tension, vibrating or buzzing sensations, jittering or quivering, dull or sharp pain, heat or cold, bursts of movement, etc. A shift will occur.

2. Answer these questions about what you feel:

   - Where in your body is the sensation? Is it in your heart, your throat, your head, your gut, your thighs? It can be off the central line of your body, too, in shoulders, arms, etc. Does it travel from one place to another?
   - What does the sensation feel like? (Again, there are any number of characteristics the sensation can have. Don't try to judge or explain them. Just observe, then *feel* and *experience* them.)
   - What energy center, or chakra, and area of consciousness does the location of the sensation most closely correspond to? To answer this, you may need to refer to the chart on page 76 for help. The hands, for example, correspond to the heart chakra; the legs to the root chakra.

3. Next, communicate with this cutoff part of your consciousness to let it know that you're making contact with it. You do this by *internally squeezing* the area where you feel the sensation. This lets your body know, "I hear you, and I'm getting the mind to pay attention to you now."

4. As you squeeze the muscles in that area, do the Central Channel Breathing you learned in the Anchoring Code and include the

specific area of sensation in the exercise. Start your breathing pattern from the end of the channel nearest the area you're squeezing, then "grab" that area along the way with the mind, and bring it into the flow of energy. For example, if the sensation is a jitteriness in your thighs, start your Central Channel Breathing from within the earth below your feet, draw the breath up through the channel to the thighs while squeezing them, then "grab" them and bring them into the flow of the channel, with *mūla bandha* and the other three anchor points. Continue inhaling as the energy rises into the belly and heart, then exhale from the belly/heart up the central channel and out the top of your head. Then reverse the direction: inhale from overhead down through the anchor points of the central channel into the heart/belly, squeezing the thigh muscles on the exhale as you push the energy down into the earth. Imagine that the *centers* of the thighs and lower legs are hollow and the energy runs straight through.

5. Repeat, making at least two complete cycles through the channel. (As a reminder, a cycle is one trip up and one trip down the channel, regardless of which direction you started with.) Continue until you feel a shift in the energy, or six to eight times if you are not feeling much of this energy yet. It will come!

Take It to the Body is one of the most powerful practices for expediting your evolution in consciousness and embodiment. Instead of wasting time and energetic resources writing stories about the "rightness" or "wrongness" of what's happened, or blaming yourself or others, or avoiding the situation, you simply find out where in your body you are activated in that moment and get to work resolving the issue in the spot that's calling out for your attention. Remember, that spot isn't just a twinge or a jitter; it's a laser pointer showing you where you need to build the communication flow of energy and the circuits in the sensory nervous system to eventually perceive yourself more fully inside and awaken to more of your wholeness and magnificence. It's the soul energy speaking through the body to the mind, showing it where there is a gap in information and energy flow.

It may feel foreign and challenging at first to engage your mind in this way and avoid the story—but doing anything else is unproductive, because the story is not why you came here. The stories we tell ourselves have nothing to do with our divinity, except that we're meant to untie them. In our most efficient efforts, we don't shift our reality through story. We do so by working with the raw, real, eternal energy that is the purest version of ourselves. Your energy follows your consciousness. By consciously breathing our way through the central channel with this new circuit-building practice, we more fully embody our wholeness.

I do want to make the point here that I am by no means asking you to deny any emotion that has already arisen. As I tell people in my workshops, always "have what you have" first. Always feel what is there to be felt and do the work of Take It to the Body at the same time. You must be *consciously present* with everything if you want to truly process it. But I believe that you will eventually find it faster and more comprehensive just to work with the energy underneath. Most people ultimately find that they can go straight to this causal level without the need to linger in the emotional body of energies.

As you'll discover, Take It to the Body requires us to be vulnerable. But, as I always tell my students at this point in our coursework, *your vulnerability is your power.* Your willingness to sense and feel what's really there in your body, and to let yourself experience it and work with it, *is* vulnerable, because it's acknowledging the real, true you. You have to let go of all the defensive strategies the Protective Personality employs to shield you from getting hurt, and connect, through sensation, with the very places inside you that feel painful, stuck, and wounded.

Ironically, working with wounds, stuckness, and hurt at the level of energy is far less difficult and threatening than working with them at the level of story. Rather than getting caught up in right and wrong, emotion and judgment, we can simply get the fragmented energy flowing back into our system until, ultimately, it's all integrated. Then, miraculously, the emotional charge around the situation suddenly disappears. Where fear and conflict once were, we suddenly have the inner resources of wisdom, resilience, and joy.

PRACTICE 2: DON'T NAME IT—FEEL IT

Another powerful practice for decreasing the time and effort spent on story-writing is to *stop naming our symptoms.* Naming and labeling a stuck energy only makes it more stuck, because it makes it more "real." Remember, anything we put our attention on increases in presence!

When you encounter a situation that causes friction and it brings up an emotion, you may name that emotion while you're having it. You may notice that this intensifies the named emotion. Why? Because now you're not only experiencing the emotion, you're simultaneously creating a mental story about that emotion. For example, if you are sitting in traffic and start to feel anxious, parts of your body may feel restless, jittery, or tingly. If you go straight to the source, do your Central Channel Breathing while "grabbing" the body part and sensation, and immediately reintegrate, you will feel better almost at once. However, if you think, *I feel anxious,* suddenly you are not only feeling these bodily sensations, you are emotionally reacting to your own story about what it means to be anxious.

The moment you name what you're feeling—especially if these are emotions that you've labeled as negative, such as anxiety, fear, anger, or sadness—you almost *have* to go into story, because you have biases and judgments about those feelings and what they mean about and to you. You don't want to be anxious, afraid, angry, or sad, so you resist or avoid how you feel, which in turn makes it even harder to let go and resolve the issue. However, if you can stay out of the mind-set of judgment and storytelling, you can set yourself free more rapidly.

All Emotions Are Created Equal

All energies, and therefore all emotions, are created equal. Understanding this can help the mind make the paradigm shift from operating at the story level to operating at the energy level. When we make certain emotions undesirable—when we consider joy and contentment "good," but fear, anger, sadness, shame, and guilt "bad"—we have a harder time not naming them. This in turn makes it harder to work with them energetically. But since *all* emotions are just energies of differing frequencies, none is better or worse than the rest. All serve their unique roles in the universal energy pulse that is expanding and anchoring, expanding and anchoring—in the natural cycle that we, and all of nature, go through. The so-called positive emotions are efforts to expand, while the negative emotions are efforts to anchor. Anger and fear, for example, keep us from losing our connection to what is vital to us, and they are heavier energies with a lower vibration. Conversely, love, hope, and inspiration break down our boundaries and help us expand through higher-vibration energy frequencies.

Think of it like this: a jellyfish swims through the water by contracting and expanding its body. It is the actual *contraction* that causes it to move forward, before it expands again. Every experience serves a purpose, and all possible human experiences are needed. Anger, for example, is the default way your system keeps you more contracted and closer to being "in the body" rather than further dispersing—until, that is, you learn to drop in intentionally, which relieves the need for the energetic vibration of anger altogether.

So, right now, conjure up some anger. Think of something or someone that really gets to you. There will be a tightening or an "anchoring" in your energy field both within and around your physical body. Notice how that feels so you can recognize it again later. Then think of something that brings you great joy. You'll likely experience an "expansion."

When we are operating at the story level, the emotions that go along with these energetic contractions and expansions are just a reflection or by-product of the energy itself. Both are needed, but if we can learn to work with the energy instead of waiting for it to default to the emotional state, we will master our life before it masters us!

If we can start to think of emotions as energies—as efforts to anchor or expand—we won't be afraid of sadness. We won't deflect our shame. Instead, we'll realize that each of these emotions is playing a role in the tides of the ever-expanding universe, acting as a placeholder to direct our attention to a spot where our energy is dispersed or fragmented—an aspect of our Soulful Self that we've not yet awakened to. It's a beautifully orchestrated dynamic that keeps us on the path of circuit-building toward full integration.

Disease as a Placeholder

Physical disease is also energy. Many people are terrified of getting ill, but there's another way to look at sickness: it helps bring our attention to an area in our energy field that needs to be activated. When we look at disease this way, we can more swiftly grasp the lesson behind the problem and move through it, rather than beating ourselves up if we think we have "caused" this horrible situation. Many of my students are relieved to hear this and interpret it as another nudge from the universe to become more conscious of our greatness in an additional way—like an ever-abiding friend who will not let up until we see our magnificence.

You can work with stuck energy that manifests as physical symptoms in the body in a similar way to working with emotions. The truth is that the disease process is merely a by-product of our dispersal; in other words, it's a circuitry issue! We're splatted in some way, but not yet aware of it. When we keep our attention focused almost entirely on the outer world, we forget to pay attention to what's happening within us. We don't sense the nuances—the little nudges—of the fluctuations in our subtle energy flow, so the energy needs to "speak" louder to get our attention. We get wake-up calls in the form of disharmony in life and/or in the body.

Unless and until we retract our senses and draw them into the inner realm, until we honor and give attention to what's going on in there, and make decisions accordingly, the call to wake up and become the Soulful Self just keeps growing louder. The call *has* to grow louder. The energy is bumping up against a lack of circuitry—that stuck place where our awareness isn't yet turned on—and creating friction there. Unable to flow through the system, the energy has to go somewhere, so it starts to overstimulate the surrounding tissues. We might experience this as inflammation or irritation, hyperfunction, or even exhaustion. Once those tissues become overactive, they eventually become exhausted, collapse, and break down. This cellular breakdown is what we consider a chronic, degenerative disease—but really, it's all an attempt by the Soulful Self to get the attention of the mind. A trauma or disease is only there to help us find the circuitry we need to turn on in order to keep becoming the greatest version of ourselves. Harnessing this is about more than just healing; it is also about conscious evolution of the soul.

Unfortunately, giving our hurts the attention they need is often the last thing we want to do. When a symptom is severe, we have a tendency to want to move away from it—to disown the situation as something that is outside, something foreign, that's happening *to* us. However, the longer we remain unaware of the places where our energy is not flowing, the more significant the disorder or disease process grows.

Thirty-two-year-old Joan was in severe pain from stomach ulcers and colitis when I met her. She wasn't sleeping due to severe diarrhea and abdominal pain, which continued throughout the night. She was on five medications, but none of them relieved her symptoms. Her doctor was recommending surgery, and she was frightened. She didn't want to have surgery. Her mother had passed away from a surgery-related complication, and she was consumed with imagining a similar possibility for herself. On the other hand, she wanted "to get rid of the bad colon and the nasty part of her stomach." This was *not* her best answer, but it was all she'd known to do.

Western medicine's approach has historically supported this detachment. First it names the disease, giving it more weight, density, and story, and making it harder to resolve. Then it either extracts the problem through surgery or masks it with medication. These strategies, however successful in the short term, ultimately lead us away from the truth and resolution of the real issue.

Joan and I worked with the Energy Codes, and Joan began to find pockets of emotional energy that had been shoved "under the surface" for her entire life. Now this emotional energy was rising up to be released, and it was eating her up inside. Through our work together, Joan recognized that she didn't have to identify the exact story that had created the emotional energy block in order to free it and reset her system to normal function. I'd seen hundreds of cases where something had happened in someone's life that they could not emotionally "digest," which led to them not being able to physically digest either. The body is a reflection of our consciousness. Joan learned how to steward the process of working underneath the story and heal with grace. Using the Energy Codes practices, she was able to heal completely without surgery. She no longer wanted to reject a part of herself that had actually been trying to enhance, even save, her life. Instead she embraced her true self—her Soulful Self—and her body was able to stop calling out for her attention and heal itself.

My invitation to you is to do what at first feels counterintuitive: lean *into* the problem, and into the pain. Come *toward* it with your attention, and then go *into* it with your heartfelt focus and allow your mind to receive the information about what is needed there, because the body *will* reveal that to you, if you are sensing and feeling within. It might not be with words, but now you will know how to interpret the language of the soul with your mind, and how to respond. When you become adept at this, using the practices in this and later Codes, you will be able to detect the friction or charge in your energy and resolve it, enabling you to heal and even prevent disease.

For instance, Marsha brought her distraught eighteen-month-old daughter, Heather, into my office, reporting that Heather had not had a bowel movement larger than the size of an almond in her entire eighteen months. Nor had she slept for more than twenty minutes at a time unless being driven in the car. Marsha, her husband, and her mother had been taking turns twenty-four hours a day to keep the baby as comfortable as possible. I asked two questions: Had there been difficulty during the delivery? Or difficulty in the marriage? These are the two most common neuro-emotional reasons I've seen in infant health challenges. Marsha began to cry. The couple had been planning a divorce when they learned that she was pregnant. They decided to stay together for the baby.

I treated the baby with the bioenergetic work that I used in my office and utilized the Energy Codes with Marsha to *lean into* the reality that she still had unresolved energies to deal with. As Marsha's energy began to move again, she felt renewed. The infant gained normal bowel function and sleep patterns within a matter of days. Years of ear, nose, and throat conditions were likely prevented for this infant, as we established a cleansing and filtering flow in her system, and Marsha was freed in her inner world to allow her life to begin again. She was able to connect with that nudge from within, soliciting greater awareness of her deepest truth—her Soulful Self. Her relationship pulled through and it truly has been a "happily ever after."

When we really understand this, we see just how perfectly designed our system is. Even a chronic disease shows us where we most crucially need to put our focus. And, thank goodness, it's never too late to achieve the healing toward which our life is trying to direct us—which, in itself, is less about healing than it is about *revealing*. Our system, our life as a whole, is designed to show us the wholeness that we inherently are.

I hope that you find this as exciting as I do—not only the tremendous capacity we have for healing, but the built-in guidance that is available and that is always attempting to steward our life for our highest good. The Energy Codes will show you how to preempt traumas and health issues by building circuitry that removes the disturbance in the field before it manifests in the physical world. But I want to reassure you that, if conditions exist in your body already, that's okay! The process to build circuitry where disease already exists and the process to build circuitry to prevent disease are *exactly the same*. It's the same mechanism. When energy is allowed to flow optimally again, health resumes whether disease existed or not, because that optimal flow *is* the energetic state that reflects as health or wellness in the physical world.

As part of this Feeling Code practice of Don't Name It—FEEL It, I'd like to steer you away from naming your ailments. This means no self-diagnosing, and no anxious rushing out to the doctor for the diagnosis either. The reason is the same as for why we won't name our emotions: the moment we name something, we go into the story of it. We look up our diagnosis online and find out what is supposedly going to happen to us now that we have this condition. And while we *absolutely* want to be responsible and seek attention if something's running out of control with our health (we have a symptom that won't resolve, or are repeatedly becoming ill) and we're unable to get a handle on it, we don't want to lose sight of the bigger, underlying truth: that the symptom or condition that is now manifested in our physical world actually started in the energy field—and that if we desire a true, full "curing" of it, the energy field is where we must ultimately resolve it. Therefore, while you never want to put yourself at risk while you are learning these practices, and you always want to seek help if you are concerned, keep in mind one of my father's favorite sayings: "You don't have a headache due to a lack of aspirin in your system!" Let's first look to the cause and address the gifts it is offering us.

I'd like to give you an example from one of my coursework students, Kat.

KAT AWAKENS HER HEALER WITHIN

Fifteen years ago, Kat suffered a rotator cuff injury. It never healed properly, and she had pain and range-of-motion issues over the years. Based on a recommendation I make to all of my students, she had started to take yoga classes and incorporated the Energy Codes breathwork into her practice. To her dismay, after one of her yoga classes, she had significant pain in her injured shoulder. The pain extended down her arm, and even down the side of her body.

When she felt the pain, she immediately started telling herself an old story about her shoulder: "Well, the doctors *did* say that this was always going to be compromised, that it would never be the same and I'd just have to live with it. They said I'd never be able to—" Then, before she finished the sentence, she caught herself. She remembered the examples I'd shared about my own healings of injuries using the Codes and chose a different thought: "What if the energy is shifting in my shoulder and is actually healing?" She decided to rest and fully commit herself to doing the breathing practices she'd learned.

Within three days, not only was the pain from the yoga completely gone, but so were all the previous symptoms from her injury. She was totally pain-free and, for the first time in fifteen years, had full range of motion in her shoulder. All traces of the injury had disappeared after three days of doing the very practices taught in this chapter—starting with her choice not to name what she was sensing, and not to allow someone else's prognosis (aka story) to inhibit her ability to heal. She took all of her mental power and will and used her mind in a new way—sensing the energy disruption, breathing the flow back into the shoulder, and integrating it into the central channel. The result? A completely healed shoulder and greater integration of her Soulful Self.

When we interrupt old belief patterns and allow energy to move underneath our stories, we tap the realm of the miraculous, a world beyond logic, the place of our ultimate creativity. The first step, starting with the Feeling Code, is to teach the mind to sense and support the movement of energy for healing any and all issues that are calling for our attention. If we can drop into this sensing before the mind veers off into storytelling, we allow the Soulful Self to take the wheel and guide us toward complete integration. When this happens, we more than heal; we begin to reveal as our true magnificent self and the creator we actually are.

PRACTICE 3: ONE EYE ON THE INSIDE

With the first two practices, you can see how absolutely fundamental "taking it to the body" is in this work. Therefore, I want to invite you to make Take It to the Body an ongoing practice and, ultimately, a way of life. I call this having "one eye on the inside."

Whereas Take It to the Body is more of a triage tool to use when something upsetting arises (or even when something wonderful occurs and we want to build the circuits for sustaining its benefit—more on that later), One Eye on the Inside is just what it sounds like: a state of continuous attunement to what is happening at the energy level of our body as we go through our everyday waking, walking life.

Besides the calmness and empowerment that come with handling energy shifts swiftly rather than allowing things to escalate into heightened emotion, story, or dis-ease, when we keep one eye on the inside, we also get the huge benefit of being continually in touch with other types of communication from the Soulful Self—the creative impulses, inspirations, and knowings that are constantly rising from deep within our core and up to our conscious mind. When we take action on these soulful communications, we literally give life to ourselves as the Soulful Self in the physical world. The result is a truly magical, inspired way of living. It sets the soul free—and because the soul is the real you, it sets *you* free.

To make having one eye on the inside your new habit, I highly recommend starting every day doing a Central Channel Scan. Here's how to do it:

1. Before you get up for the day, while you're still lying in bed, very slowly bring your attention down through the central channel,

from above the head to the center of the brain and then down to where the skull meets the neck. From there, taking several central channel breaths to do so, go down into the throat, and then inch by inch down into the center of the chest, where the heart center is. Then, from deep within the core, go lower still, down through the solar plexus, then into the stomach and the navel area. Continue beneath the navel into the wisdom center area of the second chakra. From there, go farther down, through the belly and out the tip of the spine.

2. As you scan, go slowly—again, only inch by inch—and thoroughly enough that you can pick up on any surges of energy or areas that your attention seems to skip over. Notice any sensations, or if there seems to be a gap in the flow of energy along the channel. You'll recognize these "blank spots" because you'll be focusing, tracing each inch of the central channel, down through your head, your neck, your upper chest . . . and suddenly your attention is right at your heart, as if it's skipped three inches along the channel, or you find that you're now thinking about your to-do list for the day! When this happens, you know that you couldn't stay focused along every inch of the channel because your energetic circuitry isn't consciously connected in those areas and all the way through.

3. If you notice an area of sensation or one of those blank spots, go back and squeeze it, and breathe through it as you continue up or down the central channel along your way. This will begin to establish the sensory circuits to bring greater awareness to that area, activating the conscious energy there. It will also inform you about the area of life and the aspects of your essential, true self that might be calling for your mind's attention on that particular day.

4. Take note of any feeling, awareness, or information that comes to you as you integrate this area. If you hear your inner wisdom

speaking through a sensation, guide the mind to listen to what it says. Most important, just "be with" what you find. Observe what impact this awareness has as you revisit it throughout the day.

5. To see what domain of life the offline area governs, consult the chakra diagrams in this book. If you find pain or sensation (or lack of sensation) in any particular area, don't name the symptoms as a condition or a "thing" to have to heal. Instead, simply focus on integrating the energy. For example, if you find tightness in your throat that you think might be the beginning of an illness, rather than name it a sore throat, just begin to work with the energy. More often than not, it will dissipate right before your eyes. This happens in my workshops all the time. Once they're back home, people report that they've stopped naming so many things, and consequently they have fewer "things" that need to be healed. We have to remember that we are a *flowing stream of energy*—and our primary focus must be to keep the energy flowing. When the energy gets blocked and we have symptoms, we tend to want to name it a "something" to heal. The invitation here is to first simply try moving the energy in this effective way and see how things change.

6. Remain aware of what arises in your energy field throughout the day—again, not naming the emotions or sensations that you observe, only keeping that eye on the inside to gain awareness of how you need to integrate the next time you work with your Central Channel Breathing and squeezing your points of sensation.

7. Just before you go to sleep at night, while lying in bed, do another scan, paying particular attention to the areas you noticed in the morning. Does anything feel different? Do Central Channel Breathing while squeezing any points of sensation or blank spots. Then relax into sleep.

Many of my personal circuits were built with this practice in the early morning hours from 3:00 to 5:00 a.m. So if you awaken in the middle of the night, rather than reaching for your phone or tablet, or lying there letting the mind tell stories about your sleeplessness, spend your time wisely with these practices and you will not be plagued with that concern again. By the way, in the ancient Eastern traditions, these were the sacred hours when the most important work of conscious evolution could be done.

Although it's easy and beneficial to keep one eye on the inside when you do your scans first thing in the morning and last thing at night, you can use this scanning practice at any time to learn more about how your life experiences have affected—and are still affecting—you. You can, for example, take a few moments to think about a conflict or challenge you're experiencing today, and take it to the body to see where it appears; then squeeze and breathe into that place before going on with your day.

You can also reflect back over your whole life, thinking or journaling about experiences that were clearly part of your Bus Stop Conversation. (You'll know what those are because they're the real doozies in your life.) As you reflect on one of these experiences, take your attention to the body and see what reveals itself to you, following the instructions for that practice earlier in this chapter.

The more you practice, the easier you will find it to decipher your Soulful Self's energetic language expressed in the body. The practices you learn in later Codes will give even more nuance to this, but for now, spend as much time as you can with one eye on the inside, getting familiar with the cadence of your feeling language and allowing it to reveal where you can bring more of your innate magnificence online—until eventually you are living *from* this place on the inside where your true power resides.

PRACTICE 4: DON'T WANT IT, HAVE IT

In this final practice for the Feeling Code, we will compare different energies within your system and get a feel for one that will really help you manifest what you want. For, as much as this book is a guide to healing all areas of your life and health by returning to your Soulful Self, it is also a guide to manifesting your heart's desire by fully embodying the energy that is the essential version of you.

Our physical reality unfolds according to our energy pattern. The dynamic at play is structural rather than personal; it's our energy's vibrational frequency that determines what shows up in our life. In this practice, we're going to go within and feel the contrast between two different energy frequencies. These frequencies play *the* crucial role in whether or not you manifest from the soul's passion. It's an exercise in experiencing—in feeling energetically—the difference between *wanting* something and actually *having* it, and then anchoring the desired energy pattern in order to create what we desire. In my thirty-plus years of working with patients and clients regarding their health and happiness, this has been one of the greatest tools for transformation and healing they have realized for themselves. Now this work allows you to embody that same benefit on your own.

If something is vibrating at one frequency, by definition it's not vibrating at another. *Wanting* has a different frequency than *having* does; so if we're in the vibration of wanting something, we're not going to have it. Again, it's a structural matter, with each energetic pattern setting into motion and creating a particular result. Therefore, to manifest something in your life, you must vibrationally embody *having* it—you must create the feelings in your body that would be created if you already had what you're wishing to manifest. If you keep plugging into the wanting of it, the photon arrangement goes to wanting, not having, and until that vibratory frequency shifts, it's impossible for what you desire to manifest.

The great news is that, once you make that shift from wanting to having, it's impossible for what you desire *not* to manifest!

Give this exercise a try:

1. Close your eyes and go within. Bring to mind something you really *want*. Notice how you feel in your body. Specifically, where are the sensations? What are their qualities?

2. Now imagine that you already *have* your desired result, that it's already manifested and is part of your daily reality. Focus on

how you feel in your body "having" it. Notice where the energy is accentuated, and sense the difference.

3. Next, practice recalling the vibratory frequency of "having" at will and holding it in your consciousness for as long as you can. Whenever your attention goes to the thing you *want,* call up that feeling vibration of *having,* and even connect with *each other* the areas that stood out. This will allow a sort of carving of a new connective pathway in the energy field. Continue this and it will soon become easy, even automatic.

I've watched this practice shift hundreds of patterns for people right in the moment.

Chris was ready for a new relationship. He'd been married before, was heartbroken when he got divorced, and then was ready to begin again. Yet when he described the life he wanted, his yearning appeared rather stressful—such that his energy moved up and almost out of his body as he spoke. As I drew his attention to this fact, and asked him to imagine how it would feel in his body when he already *had* that loving relationship, his energy immediately dropped into his heart area and even grounded more deeply in his core. By feeling it in his body and breathing to build the circuits to sustain it, by imagining *having* the relationship rather than *wanting* it, he felt instant relief.

Geri came to me with a heavy energy field that appeared bogged down and "flat." Her words confirmed that she'd been in a dark place for quite some time. She let me know she'd been having thoughts of suicide. She wanted to feel different, but she just couldn't seem to change the way she felt. I helped Geri with the simple practice of running a different energy through her body while she imagined what it might be like to be through this tough time, and she began to shift. Her energy began to move as she breathed through the central channel while creating the feelings in her body that she would have if she were *already having* a happier life, rather than wanting it to arrive sometime in the future. By building new pathways for the energy to flow from the empowering central channel, Geri felt like a different person before she left her session that day. When she returned a few days later, she reported that she still maintained, in her words, her "open heart and lighter mind." Geri brought the future to the present time and allowed her body to establish a new energetic pattern as though it were already true. When I spoke with her months later, she felt brighter and had "no thoughts of anything harmful or distressing in any way." In fact, she was "actually feeling joy!"

Remember, in order for every step of enlightenment—every step toward living as the Soulful Self—to have staying power, it requires embodiment. If you add this embodiment component to any ritual, any activity you're doing, any affirmation you're saying, or any dream you're dreaming, what you're working to create will manifest in the physical world more quickly. Why? Because ultimately all acceptance, release, creation, and evolution *must* happen inside our body, in our energy field. It must be embodied.

Likewise, you will find your desires changing as more and more communication circuitry is activated between the deep inner core and the mind and you begin to move away from the Protective Personality. You will find that what you "want" is different than it used to be. The impulses that arise from deep within you might surprise your mind, but your heart will sing in delight as they unfold. Remember not to get stuck on *how* things are going to happen; just enhance the vibration in which they can!

Catch It, Don't Miss It!

You can utilize these practices to anchor the fabulous experiences in your life by taking your attention to the body and walking with one eye on the inside while having experiences you love. I call it Catch It, Don't Miss It! and it's implemented the same way as these exercises, only you'll use it when there is a fantastic charge, not an upsetting one. It's as if you are "spreading the good news" throughout the entire subtle energy or chakra system and enlivening the circuits with the high-frequency energies that are being generated in your delight. For instance, whenever my students and I come upon a gorgeous vista while visiting sacred sites around the world in our JourneyAwake excursions, we use this energy practice. As you connect the mind with the Soulful Self on a daily basis, moment by moment, breath by breath, you will begin to find more of these deeply joyful moments in your everyday life as well.

The Feeling Code Chakra Correlation: Second Chakra

The Feeling Code is correlated with the second, or sacral, chakra. Known as *svādhiṣṭhāna chakra* in Sanskrit (which literally translates to "one's own seat"), this chakra governs the emotional/feeling layer or body of the human energy system. That's why integrating the second chakra has a stabilizing effect on the emotions. With a wobble-free second chakra, we drop the story-writing and are much less reactive emotionally and more able to work with the feeling body's energetic level.

Many people with second-chakra issues suffer from emotional and mental health issues such as depression or anxiety. They may be overemotional or engage in escapist behaviors to try to deal with repressed feelings. They may have trouble trusting themselves and others. They may have lower digestive tract issues, issues with the elimination system (including the kidneys and bladder), or reproductive organ issues.

Below is a chart showing key characteristics of the second chakra.

The Feeling Code Chakra Correlation: Sacral Chakra

NAME(S)	Second chakra, *svādhiṣṭhāna chakra*
LOCATION	Just below the navel
COLOR	Orange
MUSICAL NOTE	D
BODY AREAS AFFECTED	Bladder, prostate, womb, pelvis, nervous system, lower back, fluid function, *adrenal glands, sex organs*
"BACK SIDE" SYMPTOMS	Unbalanced sex drive, emotional instability, feelings of isolation, impotence, frigidity, bladder and prostate issues, low back pain
"FRONT SIDE" CHARACTERISTICS	Inner knowing, trust, expression, attuned to feelings, creativity. "I sense and feel my way through life." "I need nothing from you, and I am simply here to share." "I follow my gut."
PRACTICES	• Take It to the Body • Don't Name It – FEEL It • One Eye on the Inside • Don't Want It, Have It
BREATHWORK (as explained in Chapter 8)	Vessel Breath *(Buddha Belly Breath)*
YOGA POSES FOR GREATER INTEGRATION	• Boat Pose *(navāsana)* • Pigeon Pose *(eka pada rajakapotāsana)* • Yogic Bicycle *(dwichakrikāsana)* • Seated Spinal Twist *(ardha matsyendrāsana)* • Breath of Fire *(kapalabhati prānāyāma)*

By improving the energetic flow and vitality of the second chakra, the Feeling Code also improves creativity, sex drive, and trust in all relationships—interpersonal relationships as well as relationships with money, power, and time.

As with all the chakras, the health of the sacral chakra can be greatly enhanced with particular yoga asanas or poses.

Yoga for the Feeling Code

One of the primary postures to create alignment and flow in this energy center is Boat Pose.

BOAT POSE (*NAVĀSANA*)

Here's how to practice Boat Pose:

1. Sit on a mat or the floor with your feet together and your knees bent toward the ceiling.

2. Place your hands on the back of your thighs to support yourself. Now sit up as tall as you can, engaging *mūla bandha*, lengthening the spine, and keeping the chest open. (Keep your chin at neutral, rather than pointed at the ceiling.)

3. With your hands still holding behind your thighs, lean back until your arms are at full length and your torso is at about a sixty-degree angle to the floor. Don't lean back too far, or your spine will start to curl. If you keep lifting your pelvic floor (*mūla bandha*) and lengthening your spine, you should feel your core muscles engage.

4. Using your core muscles to stabilize yourself, remove your hands from your thighs and extend them toward the front of your mat with your palms facing each other, beside your

thighs. Feel your inner strength as you hover your torso at that sixty-degree angle.

5. If you feel strong and balanced here, lift your feet off the floor until your calves are parallel to the floor, or as an advanced version, even fully extend your lower legs to complete alignment with your thighs. Keep your torso stable and your spine long.

6. Hold for about five breaths, then release your feet to the floor and rest for a breath or two.

7. Repeat two to five times.

Now let's integrate our Feeling Code and BodyAwake practices while in Boat Pose.

1. Holding the pose (with feet on or off the ground), find your grounded center while focusing on the space two feet beneath where your sitting bones touch the mat.

2. Quicken your core by squeezing your central channel muscles at the four anchor points, including rolling your eyes up to feel the tension behind them.

3. Contract all the muscles in your thighs, lower legs, and feet. (This builds thousands of tiny circuits for carrying energy information and activates your connective tissue matrix of communication.)

4. Contract the muscles in your arms and forearms, and extend your fingers.

5. Breathe in through the feet and contracted legs to *mūla bandha*, and then exhale out up through the central channel, squeezing all the way up and out the top of your head. On the next inhale,

breathe in from overhead down through the central channel anchor points to *mūla bandha* and out through your legs and feet.

6. Keep lifting your heart to the sky with a feeling of joyful accomplishment as you breathe with passion in this pose. Big circuit-building is happening here!

ADDITIONAL YOGA POSES TO INTEGRATE THE SACRAL CHAKRA

You can use these asanas along with Boat Pose to enhance your work with the Feeling Code.

Squeezing areas of sensation while holding these poses will help you center yourself in your body's core, encourage the integration of fragmented energy, and build circuitry to sustain your orientation both on the mat and off. Remember, creating resistance in the body allows us to orient ourselves and prevents us from having to generate friction in our outer world.

The contracting enables you to find your true core, but relaxing in these poses (as opposed to squeezing areas where sensation is noted, as in the exercises in this Code) is also beneficial, because it allows your system to experience softening as well. Taking a few additional breaths in these poses while simply *imagining* the same pathway enables the direction of energy while encouraging system-wide relaxation.

- Pigeon Pose (*eka pada rajakapotāsana*)
- Yogic Bicycle (*dwichakrikāsana*)
- Seated Spinal Twist (*ardha matsyendrāsana*)
- Breath of Fire (*kapalabhati prānāyāma*)

Here in the Feeling Code, we became acquainted with the language of the Soulful Self as it communicates through the physical body. We learned to listen to the cues and clues that come as bodily sensations, which indicate the shifts in the energy field of the Soulful Self. These communications tell us what "unfinished business" from our past and present we need to process in order to achieve a greater level of wholeness.

Next, in the Clearing Code, we'll take another huge step toward realizing our true potential, by more fully understanding when unfinished business is causing our circuitry to be offline and then by clearing those blockages of optimal energy flow. We'll look at how the *subconscious mind*, not the *conscious mind*, determines what we manifest in life, and discover how to clear the subconscious in order to accelerate healing and the integration of the Soulful Self.

Chapter 6

THE CLEARING CODE:
THE HEALING POWER OF
THE SUBCONSCIOUS

Many mornings while I was growing up, I would come downstairs at five o'clock to find my father sitting at his desk, lost in thought, with just a single lamp burning over his head.

"How long have you been here?" I'd ask.

"Almost long enough . . . but not quite," he'd reply, smiling. "I'm working on something, and I'm really close to figuring it out."

And figure things out he did! He was ahead of his time, and shared everything he learned with inspiring magnetism. Hundreds of doctors from around the world flocked to his seminars to learn from him; in turn, they used the techniques he developed to help tens of thousands of patients heal from conditions that traditional medical modalities had not cured.

It all started in the early 1970s, when my father—then operating a standard chiropractic practice—became curious as to why, with the same types of treatments, some patients got well and some didn't. In search of answers, he studied every philosophy and technique available in the various modalities of natural healing, looking for a common denominator where successful results were reported.

He found that when the flow of "energy"—specifically the flow of electromagnetic energy through the body—was present, people got well. When that flow was stymied, people didn't heal.

My father's research and understanding were augmented by the new field of quantum science, which focused on energy flow and the energy field that it generates. To his great delight, as he applied what he was learning to his patient cases, he was able to get real-time clinical results in keeping with the theoretical findings in this groundbreaking new field. (Science, of course, continues to evolve. Where we once thought that the movement of electrical nerve impulses created an electromagnetic energy field around the body, for example, we now know that it is the energy field that generates the nervous system in the first place! The energy comes first. This is why we are working with the energy field—the primary, master system of our being.)

At the heart of my father's work was the understanding that nearly 100 percent of the time when pain or dysfunction was present in the body, an unresolved emotional component contributed to the blockage of energy. He found that the energy system functioned similarly to the digestive system, breaking down and assimilating our life experiences. However, when we experience life situations that we don't know how to deal with, we pocket away the unresolved thoughts and emotions instead of processing them—like a meal that doesn't get fully digested and remains in our system too long. Eventually, as more and more unprocessed life events (and the associated thoughts and emotions) accumulate, that pocketed energy builds up and blocks the flow of energy in our system. If we don't deal with it, we have symptoms—sometimes horrible ones.

My father also recognized that most people were not aware of how the thoughts they were thinking influenced their emotions and energy flow—and, therefore, their body's ability to heal. Many of these thoughts were happening *subconsciously*, in a part of the brain that is outside of our conscious awareness yet plays a fundamental role in everything that happens in our body and in our life. He realized that, if we want to heal, we *must* gain access to the thoughts and emotions that have been pocketed away in the subconscious and release them. And he discovered a way to do that.

His research explored the relationship between the conscious and subconscious aspects of the nervous system, and the mechanism that allows or prohibits communication between the two, which I call the "trapdoor."

The techniques he developed open this trapdoor and provide access to the unresolved subconscious interferences—or energetic dispersal—that keep us from being mentally, emotionally, and physically well. Contacting and releasing that stuck energy causes energy to flow through our system again—sustaining, rejuvenating, and healing our body and our life.

My father developed the BioEnergetic Synchronization Technique, or B.E.S.T., which syncs up energy that has been dispersed by stressful experiences and gets it flowing through the body again, allowing self-healing to occur automatically. In essence, it creates connections for communication where disconnection has occurred.

Hundreds of doctors worldwide have been administering B.E.S.T. for more than thirty years to tens of thousands of patients, with amazing results. Seemingly miraculous healings have happened in all kinds of cases. People diagnosed with conditions considered to be chronic and degenerative have healed once the energy flowed freely through their bodies again. There was even a case of regenerating severed tissues, which is unheard of—yet it happened, and happens. Daniel, twenty-three years old, had been running a combine in the field when his equipment locked up. In his attempts to free one of the moving parts, his two last fingers were caught and severed just beyond the distal joint. Through the use of the B.E.S.T. technique to focus on completing the energy flow through the body and hands, the ends of Daniel's fingers regenerated without surgery—he grew new fingertips, including the bone structure and fingerprints. His body was able to heal itself when the communication system was running as it is designed.

While I worked alongside my father, I became aware that an aspect of my life's purpose was to take his work further—to empower people to be *self-healing* and realize the truth of their individual capacity as creators to manage their energy and transform their lives. I wanted people to be able to make a difference for themselves instead of having to rely on a doctor to remove their energy blockages and resolve their energetic interferences. I wanted to put the power of this knowledge in people's own hands. I asked my father to help me develop a self-administered version of B.E.S.T. to do this, and he, my brother, and I worked together to create B.E.S.T. Release. The three of us then presented it to a group of clients at a gathering in

Chicago in 2006. Once again, "miracles" started to happen on the spot as people began to use this self-help version of the work.

I now teach B.E.S.T. Release live to hundreds of people in my course-work every year, and I'm going to teach it to you here. Along with other powerful, related practices, it is the foundation of the Clearing Code.

What Is the Clearing Code?

When something happens that's highly upsetting—to the point that our conscious mind cannot process it fully—the subconscious mind pockets portions of it away so that the conscious mind can move on and keep managing the tasks of daily living.

Think of the conscious mind as a little room in your brain. In the floor of that little room is a trapdoor—and beneath that trapdoor is the subconscious mind. When the upsetting thing happens, the conscious mind's room floods with that upset. Much of the flood also pours through the open trapdoor into the chamber below. If the event is really upsetting, it overwhelms our system: a short-circuiting occurs, and the trapdoor slams shut with the floodwaters still trapped underneath. In this case, the last input or message that got through to the subconscious before the door slammed shut was "upset," which translates to the body as "emergency."

Because the subconscious controls the unconscious functions of the body—including things like your heartbeat, breathing, and digestion—this message of upset sends the body into emergency mode. Because the trapdoor is now shut, no new messages can get into the subconscious mind to turn that emergency command off. After a time, the upsetting situation will likely get resolved on the conscious level, where we understand, forgive, let go, or otherwise become okay with what happened, and where we believe that it's over and we are safe. However, if the trapdoor never gets reopened so that the subconscious can receive the good news that all is well, then the subconscious belief and physiological response will reflect that the problem still exists. The body will continue perpetually in emergency mode and exhaust itself over the issue. Ultimately, this leads to breakdown states like adrenal fatigue, thyroid exhaustion, and hormonal imbalances—and, because the problem is in the subconscious, we don't even know what's happening, or remember why.

The trapdoor is a metaphor, of course; the real players in this drama of communication are two key areas of the brain: the thalamus and the hypothalamus. The thalamus relates to the conscious mind; it's the area of the brain that, among other functions, receives input from our five senses about what's happening in the outer world. The hypothalamus relates to the subconscious mind, where things happen underneath our conscious awareness; it receives input from the thalamus, and relays that input as commands to the inner world—the body—about how to respond. It also plays the very important role within the Energy Codes practices of relaying the information from the inner body up to the conscious mind, allowing us to perceive our deep inner wisdom on a conscious level, in large part via the vagus nerve and the enteric nervous system.

The trapdoor also represents the relationship between our conscious decisions and our subconscious agreement or receptivity to those decisions. For example, at the end of a long day, our thalamus, informed by our senses that it is night and our daily tasks are done, might communicate that it is safe and appropriate to relax and prepare for sleep. But if our hypothalamus can't hear the message, our body and the rest of our brain won't relax, but will keep running full steam ahead, potentially resulting in insomnia, anxiety, or other dysfunctions. If something happens that is so upsetting that the thalamus and hypothalamus stop talking to each other even in part, we lose the ability to consciously control and direct our lives. In this case, whatever is hiding beneath the trapdoor of the subconscious is running us, despite what we do consciously. We experience this as something that is not working the way we (consciously) want it to. This is the beauty of our system: what is hidden seeks to be revealed and drives us to awaken.

The disruptive short-circuiting happens anytime we reject something. When you really get down to it, we either embrace or reject everything in life. When we say or even *think or feel*, "This isn't happening," or "I can't accept this"—when we avoid looking at our reality clearly because we don't like what we see, or when something happens that doesn't live up to our conscious desires and expectations—we are rejecting it. We will not allow ourselves to fully process the energy of it. When we are rejecting, we are disconnecting from our ability to metabolize life: to lean in, to release, to move on. Our resistance then becomes an interference or blockage in that spot in our system, and our flow stops there.

When we reject something, it doesn't just go away. Rather, we send it through the trapdoor into the subconscious, where it, at least in part, becomes hidden to us—unknown. Until we open the trapdoor to look in there and make it known—even if that happens at the energy level and not the story level—it's going to remain there, in charge, driving our thoughts, our decisions, our physiology, and our vibrational frequency, which determines what we attract into our life. Even though we can't "see" it consciously, we are still putting energy (i.e., our power) into it, so it's consuming resources that could be used for healing or creating. It's a dispersal of our focus. It's a continuous splat.

Another way of saying this is that if we don't agree with what is happening, we stop being present with it. We think about how it "should" be, defend ourselves, or write a new story to make ourselves the victim. As a result, we don't build the circuitry to invite the Soulful Self's presence by way of the situation, and we get stuck. The energy—the real us—doesn't stay in flow. Then the physical body (a reflection of the energy body) starts to become stymied too. It stops functioning as effectively as it could. What starts as an energy issue eventually becomes a tissue issue.

Perhaps you have been trying to generate a life of your choosing but haven't been able to create real, sustainable change. Perhaps you've tried self-help techniques, saying affirmations, or creating vision boards. This understanding about the subconscious is your missing piece. What you desire hasn't happened because that trapdoor in your mind has slammed shut. Despite your conscious actions, the energy beneath it all, which you are emitting as a vibration, is one of unresolvedness, unforgiveness, fear, or whatever the results of your life's biggest upsets have been. And, as you know, it's the vibrational frequency you emit that manifests in the physical world.

The good news is, it's never too late to open that trapdoor and give your subconscious mind the good news that things don't have to be this way anymore. In order to create a life you truly love—a life full of vibrant health, joy, and connectedness—you need to start by accepting life as it comes. Use a Front Side of the Model perspective, knowing that everything that happens is truly for your highest good and 100 percent in your favor at all times. Then you have to find ways to get that trapdoor open so that you can update your energy pattern and send the message that those past life experiences you rejected have in fact been resolved—that you're okay and no longer need to live in emergency mode.

That's where I want to take you: to shifting the energy pattern that's creating your current life experience. This *must* be done through the body, by opening the central channel and establishing the circuitry for flow. It's not enough just to have a realization or enlightenment in your conscious mind; you need to *embody* your realization, because reality is created from the inside out—from the *energy* out. Only when we become embodied can we change the expression of our energy at the subconscious level, and therefore shift what we have been creating and attracting in the physical world.

In the Clearing Code, I will provide you with ways to access your subconscious reasons for being stuck—the things that, if you knew they were contributing to difficulty or dis-ease in your life, you would be willing to forgive and let go. This will happen underneath the level of the conscious stories that you tell yourself and others about the reasons you are unable to progress. It will happen beneath your mind! Once you can access your internal trapdoor, you can use the exercises in this Code, and the Codes that follow, to clear those subconscious interferences and reset your energy system.

We are rarely stuck for the reasons we think we are. There is almost always something deeper that is really the cause. When we use the practices in this Code to set those energies beneath the trapdoor free and allow them to become reintegrated into our system, we naturally move back into our core—into the Soulful Self, the only place from which we have tremendous power to create by conscious choice.

Before you learn the steps to do this, however, I'd like to share the story of one of my patients who received life-changing results from the physician-administered version of the B.E.S.T. practice. Rachel is a vivid example of how trauma can become trapped in the subconscious mind and affect us long after the event has seemingly been resolved.

RACHEL FINALLY RELEASES HER TRAUMA

Rachel was in the hospital delivery room, about to deliver her third child, when tragedy struck. The delivery room staff had her lying on her side to give her an epidural but, because they couldn't get the needle to go in, they sat her up on the end of the table and bent her over. They gave her the epidural, and it worked. Then both of the nurses attending to her happened to turn their backs at the same time. She started to fall off the table, and because the epidural had cut off all her control over her legs, she couldn't catch herself. She fell onto the floor in a horrifying heap, causing her to have a spontaneous delivery.

Three days later, she woke up in a hospital bed. The baby was okay, but she wasn't. She couldn't raise her head off the pillow without becoming violently ill. This vertigo did not improve. She spent the next three years in bed or on the couch because she couldn't sit upright without becoming terribly dizzy and vomiting for hours.

That's when I met her. She "walked" into my office with her husband on one side and her father-in-law on the other. Each step was extremely wobbly and uncertain, as if she were trying to stand up in a canoe. We talked only briefly that day because she was feeling so poorly that I wanted to get her right into treatment.

I immediately started working to identify what subconscious interference might be preventing her from getting well. I wanted to find out why, three years later, her body was in the same state it had been in three days after the accident occurred—why it seemed that her body hadn't even *tried* to heal.

In that first session, I treated Rachel using B.E.S.T., the BioEnergetic treatment protocol, and she got sick instantly, right there in my office. She felt a little better then, so we talked about what had happened and what was currently going on. She said she was involved in a lawsuit against the hospital and was finding it impossible to get the medical care she needed, as no other doctor wanted to get involved in what was obviously going to become a court case. By the time she came to me, she felt completely rejected and dejected and believed that this was just how life was going to be in her future. Clearly, the moment of the injury had been horribly emotional, and three years later she was still emotionally locked up.

Her next treatment with me revealed more of the picture. While outwardly, consciously, she was no longer really angry at the hospital and even said she was willing to forgive them, some part of her was still holding on to what had occurred. I told her that, in order for her body to heal, it was very likely that she needed to drop her lawsuit, because on a subconscious level her system might be trying to maintain her illness in the belief that it would be impossible for her to win her court case if she got well. (Of course, this was not her conscious intention at all, but that's what can happen at the subconscious level.)

So she dropped the court case. But even then, her system remained locked up in the defense physiology. The trapdoor was slammed shut. As I worked with her, reestablishing her neurocircuitry with bioenergetics and the Energy Codes practices, I could tell we had opened her system and she immediately began to heal. Three months later, she played third base on the softball team our health center was sponsoring. It was what many would call a miracle— and it happened because we opened the trapdoor to a trauma that had affected her physically, mentally, and emotionally. All that angst and anxiety and unresolvedness was being stored in her body, and her body was so locked into emergency mode—into survivorship—that it wasn't even trying to heal.

In the Clearing Code practices, you'll be doing the self-help versions of the practices that helped Rachel, and thousands of others, to finally heal.

The Clearing Code Practices

PRACTICE 1: THE MORTER MARCH

The Morter March is a daily practice that activates and unifies various high-brain centers and systems of the body. These include the sensory cortex, the motor cortex, and the integrative capacity of the brain; the right side of the body and the left side of the body, the right brain and the left brain, the upper body and the lower body; the visual centers and the respiratory centers; and, for balance, the cerebellum, which also houses subconscious memory. It causes all of these systems to become active at the same time, creating a kind of master reset button that allows us to integrate whatever we're trying to embody more easily, rapidly, and efficiently. This parallels the work of George Goodheart, DC (a colleague and friend of my father's) in the 1960s, known as Applied Kinesiology. Dr. Goodheart's work defined contralateral exercise, aka the cross-crawl, and its many self-healing benefits. The result is that we clear unresolved subconscious patterns and the tension they generate, and cultivate the presence of the Soulful Self.

Here's how you do the Morter March:

1. Stand with your feet hip-width apart and your spine straight and tall.

2. Take a step forward with your right leg and bend your right knee in a lunge so you can feel your right thigh muscles activate. Let your conscious awareness drop down into your body.

3. Raise your left arm in front of you, pointed at a forty-five-degree angle toward where the ceiling and wall meet. Turn your palm so that your thumb is pointing upward.

4. Extend your right arm back and down behind you at a forty-five-degree angle, toward where the wall meets the floor. The thumb will be pointing down. Extend your fingers to enliven them.

5. Tilt and slightly turn your head to the left and look directly up your left arm to your left thumb. Close your right eye.

6. Now, standing in this position, take in a deep belly breath and hold it. Focus on a deep sense of well-being, or the feeling of forgiveness, acceptance, and love.

7. Retain the breath until you can no longer hold it, or about the time it takes to slowly count to ten.

8. Then exhale and step back to center with your feet parallel and hip-width apart.

9. Repeat on the left side, then once more on each side, for a total of four repetitions. The more you do this Clearing Code exercise, the more shifts you will start to see.

Note: If you are unable to stand, this exercise can be done lying in bed.

How does this work? It's actually pretty fascinating. The body's survival system works on a priority basis, using its energy and resources to handle the most serious threats to life first. When a traumatic experience is not resolved, it is held at the subconscious level. There it makes the body continue to respond to it, as if it is still an emergency rather than a past event. In other words, in the event of being overwhelmed, the trapdoor slams shut. This stops the communication between the conscious and the subconscious mind, and the subconscious mind is never informed when the crisis is resolved and keeps replaying unnecessary patterns in the body.

In order for the body to feel and release the trapped energy from the old trauma, we first have to get the nervous system to think it's got something more important and lifesaving to attend to. That's why we hold the breath in the Morter March. When you hold your breath, the nervous system starts to question whether you'll be able to take another breath anytime soon. Assuming the possibility that you can't, it starts to relax the muscles it contracts for protection and needs less oxygen. This allows you to have more oxygen and energy for assessing how to respond *accurately* to your current situation. The feeling of being overwhelmed is reduced, the system can begin again to process efficiently, and the body and mind feel safe. The newly redistributed energy is available for healing rather than being wasted on a false unresolved sense of danger. When the areas in the brain are activated along with the body position of the Morter March, old circuits can reconnect and new ones can be built.

In that moment of release and realignment, we can focus on updating the nervous system to a *new* message for the subconscious. Perhaps we're forgiving someone or something, or we're willing to accept something we were unable to before, or we can be present for someone or in love although we couldn't before. When we visualize and feel ourselves forgiving or accepting at the very moment the reset is happening with the body positioning of the Morter March, this synchronization allows an integration to occur. The nervous system reevaluates how it's allocating its attention and energy; it redistributes that energy, and our energy field shifts accordingly. Energy flows through the body again as the nervous system accommodates to the fact that we have actually forgiven or accepted the matter that our subconscious was holding on to. The result is that we begin to operate closer and closer to the Front Side of the Model as true creators rather than being trapped as victims of things we aren't even aware of. We then have more kinetic energy to experience throughout the day; we feel free and enlivened, optimistic and inspired. We literally begin to feel ourselves more deeply rooted in the body as the Soulful Self.

I've loved sharing the Morter March with so many who find it to be a valuable integrative tool. A few years ago, I was in Heathrow Airport in London and someone far across the concourse caught my eye. A man was standing in the March position doing his homework! Of course, I had to cut across the rushing traffic of people to give him a hug!

To take your integration further, here is an advanced version of the Morter March, called the mPower Step. I recommend practicing the

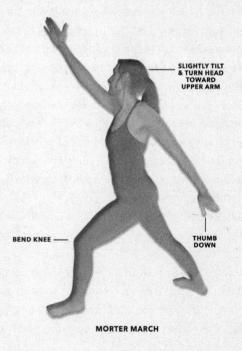

MORTER MARCH

Morter March first and becoming good at it. Once it becomes second nature, you will be able to add the mPower Step.

PRACTICE 2: MPOWER STEP

This advanced technique adds steps to the Morter March and enhances your subtle body energy field (including your chakra system) in combination with your nervous system. This synchronization enables new ways of being and perceiving so that you can engage as a creator in all of your life circumstances.

The mPower Step accentuates the central channel in order to create even more photon density in our core. By creating greater awareness there, we generate a physically tangible Soulful Self—one that your sensory nervous system can pick up on more readily. This greatly facilitates making the Quantum Flip, shifting out of the Protective Personality into the Soulful Self. By focusing on the core in the mPower Step, you open many areas of your brain and your body simultaneously, activating them in sequence with one another, which allows your nervous system—specifically your mind—to perceive more information more readily. The result is that old patterns release more quickly—which is precisely what we want.

How to do the mPower Step:

1. Set up your body in the same position as for the Morter March: right leg forward, left hand raised at forty-five degrees, right arm extended down behind you at forty-five degrees, head slightly turned and laterally tilted to the left, right eye closed.

2. "Open" the bottoms of your feet and the palms of your hands to awaken the minor chakras there. (Imagine that there are flowers blooming on your palms and soles.) Lift your toes and lay them back down.

3. Turn the palms of both hands so that the thumbs point up. Make sure you rotate your bottom hand outward to do so, so it doesn't feel like your arm is twisted behind your back. As an easy way

of making sure to do this correctly, place both palms together above your head and open your arms, with both hands palm-out to the right as you then lower the back hand down to the forty-five-degree point. Squeeze your shoulder blades together. Now lift your heart.

4. Then ground in your anchor points: squeeze *mūla bandha*, your root lock. Squeeze your heart center, as if you're hugging it within your chest. Constrict your throat so that you can feel and hear the breath moving up and down through it. As you look at the raised thumb, pull your attention back behind your eyes. In addition, pull your thighs toward each other to lift *mūla bandha* and pull the energy through the body even more.

5. Focus on breathing up and down the central channel as you did in the Anchoring Code. Breathe from above the head and into the core of the body—the belly. Squeeze the upper thighs together as you breathe in, and keep your anchor points engaged. Feel the energy pour into your body. Let it feel good; more of the real you is arriving! Hold the breath inside. Then exhale through your feet into the earth.

6. Take another breath up through your feet and legs, from two feet beneath where you're standing, into the belly. Then hold the breath in as long as you can; again, let it feel good.

7. Exhale out of the nose in a quick, forceful manner up through the central channel, and feel the energy of the breath shooting out of the top of your head as if you were a whale shooting water out of its blowhole. Try to clear out every last bit of air from your lungs.

8. When you run out of breath, take a deep inhale and step back to the center, planting your feet under your hips and straightening your spine.

9. Repeat on the left side, then once more on each side for a total of four repetitions.

Note that you may feel occasional "recalibration" happening in your system while standing in these positions, which is perfectly fine. If dizziness or disorientation occurs, stand near the back of a couch or against the wall for stability. You are generating the change you desire, moving toward living as your true, empowered Soulful Self.

In addition to clearing old patterns with this exercise, we're introducing a new model, a pattern "update," to the nervous system. We're starting to build a new energetic identity at the core of our physical being. We're also sending signals to the subconscious that this more-released state is our preference, our new foundation or set point. When you practice these positions with an added feeling of gratitude or joy, it reprograms your subconscious even more quickly, giving you more momentum for continuing the shift from the Protective Personality to the Soulful Self.

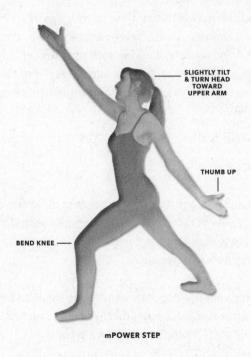

SLIGHTLY TILT
& TURN HEAD
TOWARD
UPPER ARM

THUMB UP

BEND KNEE

mPOWER STEP

Now that you know the Morter March and mPower Step, you're ready to approach the specific subconscious interferences that have been keeping you stuck or unfulfilled in life and release them through B.E.S.T. Release. Remember, we're never stuck for the reasons we think we are. This practice reveals the truth for us.

PRACTICE 3: B.E.S.T. RELEASE

With this Clearing Code practice, we're going to really go in and release an old pattern that just isn't serving us anymore. We're going to get very specific about where our greatest subconscious interferences lie—these are preventing us from being able to experience life the way we truly want to—and where we most need to build circuitry.

We'll start by identifying those blockages through a method called muscle testing. With muscle testing, we can tell what is hiding in the subconscious, because the subconscious communicates directly with the body via the central nervous system.

You can perform muscle testing alone or with a partner. When working with B.E.S.T. Release, use whichever method is more comfortable for you; however, I do recommend working with a partner initially if you are unfamiliar with muscle testing, as the results are easier to observe when using the larger arm muscles and working with another person.

Start with Muscle Testing: Test for the "Yes"

With a Partner:

1. Stand facing your partner and have her raise either arm directly out to her side, parallel to the floor. Her hand should be open, wrist relaxed, with her palm down toward the earth. She should be looking forward, eyes open.

2. Still facing your partner, place one of your hands on top of her extended forearm. Place your other hand on her opposite shoulder to help stabilize any movement when testing.

3. Ask your partner to "hold" there while you press down on her forearm with smooth pressure toward the floor. Look for a strong-arm test, indicating the partner can resist your pressure using reasonable upward force. Find the amount of force to use to be able to observe strength while she is attempting to hold the arm, being careful not to overpower her.

4. Have your partner tell a "truth"; for example, if her name is Mary, have her say, "My name is Mary." Test the arm strength. It will remain strong.

5. Next, have the partner tell a "lie"; for example, if her name is Mary, have her say, "My name is Betty." Test for strength and show that the arm is weak. Then have your partner *think* a "lie," and demonstrate that the arm goes weak just by her thinking a thought that the subconscious can't relate to.

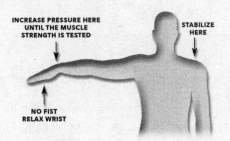

INCREASE PRESSURE HERE
UNTIL THE MUSCLE
STRENGTH IS TESTED

STABILIZE
HERE

NO FIST
RELAX WRIST

MUSCLE TEST FOR B.E.S.T. RELEASE

Self-Test Using the O-Ring:

1. Begin by making a ring with the thumb and index or middle finger of either hand (Ring 1). You will hold tight with this ring.

2. Make another ring with the thumb and index or middle finger of your other hand (Ring 2). You will use this ring to pry apart/test the muscle resistance of Ring 1.

3. Squeeze Ring 2 flat and insert it inside Ring 1.

4. State a "truth"; for example, if your name is Mary, say, "My name is Mary." Test for strength by prying apart with Ring 2 while holding tight with Ring 1. Ring 1 should remain strong.

5. Next, state a "lie"; for example, if your name is Mary, say, "My name is Betty." Test for strength by prying apart with Ring 2 while holding tight with Ring 1. Ring 1 should fail.

Take note of the difference in feeling between a "truth" and a "lie," and how each affects your muscle resistance.

SELF MUSCLE TEST

Identify the Reactive Subconscious Belief and Emotion

1. Using one of the testing methods above, think about (or ask your partner to think about) an ideal belief or goal—something that has heart and meaning. State it in the present time and in a positive sense. Don't express it as something you are going to do eventually; rather, state it as if it is already happening, such as "I am in perfect health," "I am happy and fulfilled," or "I am enough." Rather than frame it as something that you want to get away from—"I want to lose ten pounds"—claim instead the weight you choose to be as if you are there already: "I weigh 130 pounds." Test the arm strength if working with a partner (or ring strength if self-testing) using positive statements until a weakness (meaning the inability to hold strong) indicates a particular subconscious block.

2. Once you identify a belief pattern that demonstrates weakness, continue testing the arm strength (or ring) and identify the re-active emotion that causes the weakness by using the six words listed in the Clearing Chart (below). One or more of them will cause the arm (or ring) to test weak. If two or three weaken the arm (or ring), toggle back and forth between them until you get one that the body prioritizes with continued testing. Ultimately there will be one that stands out. This emotion is the stored pattern in your subconscious mind/energy field, which will be updated and released during the B.E.S.T. Release procedure to come.

If the muscle tests weak, it tells us that something overwhelming is stored in the subconscious. When that something is brought up and mag-nified by the conscious mind, it has a short-circuiting effect to the degree that the person can't maintain the thought and the muscle resistance at the same time. Something has to give, so the muscle goes weak. This use of the body's own communication system is what makes muscle testing an excellent tool for helping us sleuth out emotional experiences that are still unresolved in our system.

The Clearing Chart

Fear

Anger

Love

Sadness

Enjoyment

JUDGMENT

Easy to Remember:
F A L S E   JUDGMENT

This chart contains the four basic emotions identified in the study of psychology, from which all other, "secondary" emotions spring. *Anger*, for example, is a basic emotion, from which comes a spectrum of emotions from irritation to hate. *Fear*, another basic emotion, breeds anxiety, nervousness, and compulsiveness. By using these foundational emotions in this practice, we can identify the energy at the root of all other emotions, no matter how complicated they initially seem.

My colleagues and I have found in our clinical work that judgment and lack of enjoyment interfere with a person's ability to stay present, keep the trapdoor open, and maintain flow. In fact, judgment is the gateway to the separate self and the Protective Personality. We have found that patients initially generate a *judgment* about something that happened, such as, "That was bad and it shouldn't have happened." They then reject the event; they are no longer present with it. As a result, they do not participate in a whole and joyful life; hence, less *enjoyment*.

How does an emotion like love cause a problem of interference? It isn't actually love that is the problem, but how we think about and relate to love. For example, if we had a past experience that was hurtful or disappointing, the subconscious will hold love as potentially dangerous, and will actually guard against it. When you begin to love, the subconscious will sabotage the situation in order to keep you "safe" (in a very backward sort of way!) from ever experiencing that hurt again.

Update the Stored Belief Pattern

1. Assume the Morter March or mPower Step integrating position (depending on which one you are comfortable with at this point—remembering that ultimately using the finer details of the mPower Step is more powerful, so keep practicing!).

2. Holding the position, focus on the following thought: *I forgive any interference regarding [insert your reactive word—Fear, Anger, etc.] as it relates to my goal, known or unknown* (i.e., conscious or subconscious).

3. Continue to hold the integrating position, inhale, and then hold your breath. You may feel a literal shift in your body's energy pattern immediately. Then switch to the opposite side.

4. Complete this process two times on each side (alternating sides).

5. Using muscle testing, retest the reactive word. The arm (or ring) should test strong. (If it doesn't, retest for the correct word, as you likely missed the original priority. And clear it again.) Then retest the original goal/belief. Again, the arm (or ring) should test strong! (If it does not, it is due to the above reason; retest for correct original priority word. And clear it again.)

For video demonstration of B.E.S.T. Release, go to drsuemorter .com/energycodesbook.

If these exercises feel like a lot to do, try working just with the muscle testing or the mPower Step until they become more familiar. Then putting them all together will feel much easier. The technology in these Clearing Code practices has made my clinic a worldwide destination for healing and wellness, so please trust me when I say that you want to learn them. You may not always understand, at the story level, the changes they will bring about, but they will always improve your life. As you clear out old subconscious patterns and get stuck energy flowing through your body, your life will become more graceful, easy, and magical. Life itself begins to flow. Both small and large problems will resolve, often without you really understanding how or why.

Even at that very first session where my father, my brother, and I demonstrated B.E.S.T. Release with a group of clients, we saw tremendous results. I demonstrated the work onstage with a gentleman who didn't tell me his specific goal for the release. I didn't have him say it out loud; he just thought it while I walked him through the process. When we initially muscle-tested him, he tested weak. After we went through the clearing steps, he tested strong—completely able to hold the reactive thought without it short-circuiting his system. The next day he approached me and said, "I didn't know this was related to the stressful situation I was thinking of yesterday, but last night I slept through the night for the first time in five years!" The moment we enabled greater communication between the subconscious and conscious areas of the brain, his whole system shifted, relaxed, and began to heal.

At another workshop, a woman in the audience was in a wheelchair, having been unable to walk without assistance for many months due to excessive pain and weakness in her legs and back. We did the work with her, including B.E.S.T., and by the end of the event, she was not only out of her wheelchair but, to the delight of hundreds of onlookers, she was dancing onstage with us!

The Clearing Code Chakra Correlation: Third Chakra

The Clearing Code is related to the third chakra, the power center of our energy field, located three inches above the navel at the base of the sternum. Its Sanskrit name, *manipūra*, translates to "power of a thousand suns," and it regulates both the conscious and the subconscious. It sits at the core of the Self, where our identity is cultivated. Our ability to be open and to embrace circumstances, rather than resist or reject them, is greatly enhanced when this area is clear and flowing. When we clear the mental issues of previous rejections, we open the flow to our true selves.

People with a blocked solar plexus often have trouble distinguishing where they end and other people begin. They get caught up in "objects" rather than staying on "subject"—the Self. They often feel a weak sense of self-worth and purpose and may have trouble "standing on their own two feet" or taking action because they don't trust themselves and their own capabilities. Conversely, they may suffer from excessive ambition, or always be running on overdrive because of a need to prove themselves and establish a place for themselves in the world.

In general, people with a weak third chakra are the "overthinkers" of the world, with minds that are always seeking but rarely finding. They easily fall prey to beliefs like "I'm not good enough" or "I'm not worthy," and often have a deep well of subconscious shame, embarrassment, or guilt. Negative beliefs such as these limit our lives—but the truth is, *all beliefs are limiting beliefs,* because they come from the mind. When we connect with our core self, we learn to become more open. We free the raw energy underneath our stories and beliefs and work with it. By clearing all beliefs with the practices taught above, story falls away and a true sense of Self rises up naturally.

The third chakra also houses energies related to digestion and assimilation—physical, mental, and emotional. It governs the stomach, liver, gallbladder, spleen, and pancreas. Our ability to physically metabolize the foods we eat is a reflection of our ability to consciously metabolize or digest life on the energetic level. When energy gets "stuck" during the metabolic process, it affects our ability to transcend the thinking mind and experience ourselves as the Soulful Self.

The following chart offers a summary of some of the key characteristics of the third chakra. Again, notice how the energetic properties of the chakra mirror the physical body areas.

The Clearing Code Chakra Correlation: Solar Plexus Chakra

NAME(S)	Third chakra, *manipūra chakra*
LOCATION	About three inches above the navel, at the base of the sternum
COLOR	Yellow
MUSICAL NOTE	E
BODY AREAS AFFECTED	Digestive system, muscles, stomach, liver, diaphragm, gall bladder, lower back, trapdoor of the autonomic nervous system, spleen, *pancreas*
"BACK SIDE" SYMPTOMS	Oversensitivity to criticism, need to control, low self-esteem, stomach ulcers, digestive issues, chronic fatigue, allergies, diabetes
"FRONT SIDE" CHARACTERISTICS	Respect for self and others, personal power, flexibility, high self-esteem, spontaneity, uninhibited. "I allow my own way, and allow you yours." "I open my mind to possibility."
PRACTICES	• Morter March • mPower Step • B.E.S.T. Release
BREATHWORK (as explained in Chapter 8)	Solar Plexus Breath
YOGA POSES FOR GREATER INTEGRATION	• Camel Pose *(ustrāsana)* • Bow Pose *(dhanurāsana)* • Reverse Table Top *(purvottanāsana)* • Crescent Warrior *(anjanayāsana)* • Breath of Fire *(kapalabhati prānāyāma)*

By integrating the third chakra, the Clearing Code helps to balance oversensitivity to criticism, the need to control, and other issues of low self-esteem. It may also empower the body to heal digestive issues, including chronic conditions such as Crohn's disease, ulcerative colitis, diabetes, and food allergies.

The following yoga postures will further help to integrate the third chakra.

Yoga for the Clearing Code

Access to the solar plexus chakra can often be made easier through the practice of particular yoga asanas. One of the primary postures to create alignment and flow in this energy center is Camel Pose, or *ustrāsana*.

CAMEL POSE (*USTRĀSANA*)

Here's how to practice Camel Pose:

1. Kneel on a mat with your knees directly under your hips and your calves parallel to one another. Your feet should be aligned with your knees, not angling in toward each other. Toes are tucked for the easier version, untucked for the more advanced.

2. Lift your heart and, with a long spine, begin to bend backward, placing your hands in imaginary back pockets and supporting your spine. If you are more advanced, reach your hands toward your heels or shins. (If your feet feel too far away, place yoga blocks next to the outer edges of your feet, and rest your hands on the blocks.)

3. Lower your upper body toward the floor, lengthening your tailbone toward your knees. Lift up through the front of your body, engaging the hip flexors and muscles of the pelvic floor.

Drop your shoulder blades down your back as you lift your heart toward the ceiling.

4. If it feels safe and comfortable to do so, let your head drop back and open your throat, and stretch open your solar plexus area.

5. Hold for about five breaths. To come out of the pose, engage your abdominal muscles to "unroll" yourself back to a kneeling stance. Then sit back on your heels to rest.

6. Repeat two to five times.

Now let's integrate the Clearing Code and BodyAwake practices while in Camel Pose.

1. Holding the pose, find the energy base two feet underneath where you are kneeling. Imagine it as a large, disc-shaped energy base two feet beneath the earth. This is your connection to nature and its support.

2. Locate the energy center of your solar plexus chakra, beneath the center of your chest but above your navel. Lift this area toward the sky.

3. Engage *mūla bandha*, and squeeze the area in back of the heart by tightening the shoulder blades briefly toward one another.

4. Take a breath up the front side of your body and exhale out the top of your head. Roll your eyes up to feel the tension, and chart your course of breath through the central channel.

5. On your next inhalation, draw the breath down from above your head, into your central channel, and down into your core, then exhale down into the earth. Squeeze and release the core muscles in the front body, opening the mental aspect of the

chakra system. (Your legs should be engaged as well; this will happen automatically due to the stretch in that area, but to activate them more deeply, squeeze the muscles in the front of your thighs upward.)

6. Repeat the entire breath cycle several more times. Then come out of the pose gently with care for your neck and back, and sit back to rest on your heels.

Thoughts and emotions may release in this position in the form of tears or sweat. Welcome this as a release of stored energy from beneath the trapdoor of your subconscious. You are clearing a pathway for the expression of your Soulful Self. Repeat up and down the channel while in Camel Pose.

ADDITIONAL YOGA POSES TO INTEGRATE
THE SOLAR PLEXUS CHAKRA

You can use these asanas along with Camel Pose to enhance your work with the Clearing Code.

Squeezing areas of sensation helps to center you in these poses as you build circuitry, while relaxing in them helps you to feel the energy flow. However, even while you relax your musculature, *imagine* the energy flowing up the central channel pathway and into any areas of fragmentation or friction.

- Bow Pose (*dhanurāsana*)
- Reverse Table Top (*purvottanāsana*)
- Crescent Warrior (*anjanayāsana*)
- Breath of Fire (*kapalabhati prānāyāma*)

––––––

The anchoring, integration, and clearing of energy up to this point have introduced and established major changes in your system, including a strengthened connection between the central channel and the mind and a new path of access to the trapdoor of the subconscious. This has allowed you to lay the groundwork for the Quantum Flip—the moment when you truly begin to embody the Soulful Self and transform the Protective Personality into an engaging personality that is based in wholeness and love.

The Clearing Code sets the stage for living beyond the story and flowing in the energy of life. This is the work of true liberation. Clearing the unresolved blockages that have held us back, and integrating the lower three chakras, frees up an abundance of new energy to be used for carving our true path. We can now begin to embody the most powerful healing energy on the planet—the energy of *love*, which is concentrated in the heart chakra, and which is the very vibration of the Soulful Self. Love not only resides within us, it *is* us. You, the Soul, are made of love. Training your mind to find and magnify the real you—the you that is love—unleashes the greatest power of transformation on Earth. When we focus the mind on love from the inside out, we amplify its remarkable, unifying presence for all.

Are you ready to experience pure, world-changing love? That's what's coming up next.

Chapter 7

THE HEART CODE:
THE UNIVERSAL SOLVENT

For three weeks after my mother, Marjorie, passed, I just . . . sat. I had patients to tend to, classes to teach, and responsibilities that needed my attention, but I simply couldn't show up. Instead, I sat in my backyard looking up at the trees, wondering how my mom—my best friend—could really be gone.

On the day I finally felt it was time to get back into the world and start contributing again, I went to my backyard to "thank" it for holding space for my grief. As I allowed my gaze to sweep over the yard, I noticed rays of morning light beaming down through the trees. I walked across the patio and across the creek to where one particular ray was shining brightly onto the ground. Right where it touched the earth, there was a patch of clover . . . with a four-leafed one right in the middle.

Tears fell from my eyes. My mother found four-leaf clovers all the time, but I had only found one or two in my life. She'd even given me one that she found when she had been pregnant with me. It was our thing. I felt her presence; this was my sign that she was still here with me, and that I would be okay. I picked it and went to work, feeling a sense of connection to her, and to life, again.

That night when I returned home, filled with tears again, I went with my broken heart to that particular spot in the backyard. And there, as if I had not picked the first one, was another four-leaf clover shining in the evening light! Tears flew from my face. I picked it, too, and went to bed.

The next morning while getting ready for work, I found myself thinking about the clovers and the feeling I got from finding them. I noticed my anticipation that I would find another, and how I believed finding it would confirm for me that everything was going to be fine. As I was walking to the backyard for my third find, I stopped, and said internally, "Sue, you can't keep looking for this confirmation on the outside. You have to learn to find it on the inside. That's what you teach." My eyes fell to the ground as the thought landed, and a warm flowing feeling of acceptance dropped down through my body.

As I accepted the internal instruction of not looking for the answer outside of myself, right in front of my left foot was a third four-leaf clover! Yes, I picked it, and went to work!

The pain in my heart over the loss of my beloved mother actually allowed me to see beyond the layer of my regular senses. It was as if I had been connected to some deeper version of myself, and of life in general. My intuition was heightened, and as each feeling panned out, my mind grew more accepting of the unexplainable insights and knowings I was receiving.

Over the next several months, I found *sixty-nine* four-leaf clovers, in my own backyard and in everyone else's. I would see them at stop signs and jump out of the car to pick them. Walking in the park with friends, I would lag behind, busily picking four-leaf clovers to give to everyone around me. Friends helped me count them, and the neighborhood kids started showing up at the door, asking if I was the Clover Lady—and, if so, could I teach them how to find their own? We would then go to the backyard, where I'd say, "You have to look with your heart, not your eyes." Guided by that intuitive sixth sense that I'd begun developing in my own inner laboratory, I would stop and drop my hand to the ground . . . and, inevitably, there would be a four-leaf clover right where my hand touched the grass. The kids would shriek with delight—and so would I! It was truly a magical time.

Then, one day, it stopped. No matter how hard I looked, there were no more clovers. Two weeks went by, and still nothing. I did what we all do—I began to question myself: "What did I do to lose the connection? What will I do without my mom's delightful signs shining in my world?" No matter how hard I tried to force it, I couldn't find the clovers with my mind.

I didn't know that the secret ingredient was right in front of me.

Several days later was my mom's birthday; she would have been seventy. The moment I realized this, my heart lit up. I immediately ran to the backyard to find clover number seventy . . . and seventy-one . . . and seventy-two! I could hear her giggling in the ethers as I picked them. It was as if she had been there all along, waiting for me to figure it out. The secret of the clovers was my gratitude-filled, joyful heart.

That was how I could see beyond the veil of three-dimensional reality to the threshold of a larger world: I was seeing with my heart! I was so vulnerable and openhearted after my mom's passing that it allowed me to see things that I typically wouldn't have—and this openness was allowing a flow to happen in my life.

The magic continued until the snow fell—and even then, in a small patch of grass in between, a tiny four-leaf clover would be there, shining through.

This is what being open in our heart can do for us. Even in times of great pain—in fact, *especially* in times of great pain—we are held in a sacred space of connection. Many people have awakenings at times of anguish. This connection is what we all truly seek. Using the Energy Codes, we can connect gracefully, without the pain.

As the one-year anniversary of my mother's passing approached, people kept asking me what I was going to do to celebrate or commemorate her, and if I would do the "clover thing." I replied, "No, I'll just leave that intact as it was in my life and do something else." So that morning, I did some other things that led to another beautiful experience of her—but by four o'clock in the afternoon, I found myself drawn to the backyard to look for clovers after all.

I stepped onto the grass, and saw four-leaf clovers hovering everywhere! I picked them nonstop for forty-five minutes. Then I went upstairs to get something to put them in and came back down to pick them again for forty-five minutes more! I was picking two and three four-leaf clovers at a time! Projectile tears shot from my face as I gathered these amazing treasures; 124 of them in an hour and a half. I stopped only because I was overwhelmed with the bliss of experiencing my own heart.

When this had happened the year prior, I simply flowed with it, unsure what was really happening. This time, I was intentional about the experience. My heart was opening up for me, just as it had before—only this time, it was even bigger. I had known theoretically that we all have this ability, but I had gone beyond theory now, into experience. Now I knew that I could use my open heart to literally connect with—even exchange with—my mother, because she was, in fact, not "gone"; she had simply gotten back on the Cosmic Bus and dialed into another vibrational stop.

That day, overcome by my profound bliss, I committed to study and research with my clients how to activate such a heart blossoming within them so that they too could experience this level of love and oneness. This openhearted vulnerability and its flow of grace became my new baseline for living. It changed my awareness of how to connect intentionally with our deepest, most essential Self. We can't drive this pursuit with our mind; rather, we have to step into life with an open, vulnerable heart if we want to experience our true power and live the magnificent life that actually is meant for us. That's because the vibrational frequency known as love is the character quality of the Soulful Self. To truly establish and express the Soulful Self within ourselves, we must anchor in, emanate, and live in the vibration of love.

This Code will show you how to connect with a grounded version of your deepest "heart-self" and then remain there. You will learn to use your body to shift from *thinking* about love (with the mind) to *being* (embodying) the vibrational frequency of love. Once you do that, not only can you create clover-sprinkled miracles of joy and connection, you can, finally, fully love yourself and love others from a pure, healthy place.

What Is the Heart Code?

All ancient spiritual traditions refer to the power of love as divine. When we feel loved, we feel better. When we're able to love someone without reservation, we feel freer and more able to drop into a beautiful experience.

A key benefit of making the Quantum Flip from the Protective Personality to the Soulful Self is the way we experience love. While we can indeed give and receive love as the Protective Personality, it's different from what's possible as the Soulful Self. In the Protective Personality, we think we're separate from love, that love is something we need to acquire from someone or somewhere outside of ourselves. We spend a lot of time and energy trying to figure out ways to "get" love. We subconsciously try to control or manipulate people to get love by pleasing, dominating, and seducing them.

Because the Protective Personality tries to shield us from getting hurt, it automatically puts conditions on when and whom we can love safely. This conditional love says, "I can love you as long as you are behaving this way," or "I can feel safe to love as long as these conditions are present." These requirements greatly limit our experience of love, happiness, and joy because the world can hardly meet our conditions and expectations at every turn. So we withhold love. We bargain for love. We decide whether or not to love. We experience a lot of angst and unhappiness around the conditions we have about loving—and when we don't "get" love the way we think we should, we go deep into story about what this lack of love says about us.

These trials and tribulations are common to living in the splat—the condition of not embodying the Soulful Self and being self-referencing. They do more damage than simply stirring up story or drama, however; they actually keep our vibrational frequency stuck at a level that is too low for us to fully identify as the Soulful Self.

The Heart Code guides you to an entirely different practice of love, which eliminates conditionality, attachment, and bargaining. When we come from the vibrational frequency of love, we feel loved because we are actually *living* in love. We are generating the feeling of love *within* us, all the time. We give and love from a place without parameters. We love unconditionally because we don't need to "get" love from anyone else. Our sense of well-being is not dependent on others' behavior. We are no longer disappointed by the way others respond or interact. We can simply be present, and love—again, and again, and again.

If you do even some of the exercises in this chapter, you will gain a powerful, tangible sense of the love you hold within yourself. Before you begin, however, I want to assuage some common fears about living in this state of love.

I'm often asked, "Does loving without conditions mean I no longer care about anyone else?" Of course not! It simply means loving without *attachment*.

Loving from the Protective Personality is an experience of attachment. We cling to thoughts and beliefs that make us feel safe. Our love is conditional; we think it only exists within certain parameters. However, when we attach our identity to a felt sense of Self, rather than an externally directed thought, image, or goal, we are free to care about others out of delight, rather than out of fear for their safety or of what their loss might mean to our own security. We're no longer hung up on how things might turn out.

Becoming unattached to the outer world for our own well-being leads to unconditional happiness, joy, and availability to love. It results in better health and a better life experience in every aspect of our lives. A common theme in spiritual texts, this unattachment is considered the ideal way to engage with life and love. In the Buddhist tradition, for example, attachment is the root of *all* suffering.

Note that *unattached* is very different from *detached*. Unattachment is simply a sincere absence of worry about the outcome; the focus is on the *action* of loving, not its result. Detachment, on the other hand, is a sort of aloofness, a distance maintained not only between the Self and the outcome, but between the Self and the action of loving. It's an out-of-the-body experience that keeps us thinking we're safe, when really it just keeps stirring the untethered or unanchored experience of rapidly vibrating energy, which, ironically, feels unsafe. It causes us to be uninterested in life, uninspired, and even apathetic.

Detachment usually results from a trauma or a stressful environment that we believed we needed to escape. If we couldn't physically escape, we did so mentally and/or emotionally: we detached. Detachment feels protective in the short term, but in the long term it increases loneliness, feelings of isolation, and depression; reduces inspiration and optimism; and contributes to many health conditions such as dangerously low blood pressure, slowed healing, adrenal fatigue and thyroid problems, digestive problems, kidney issues, respiratory challenges, and other symptom patterns.

To heal the body, we have to be *in* the body. To heal most powerfully and quickly, we have to be in the body *in love*. The vibrational frequency associated with love is the ultimate healing energy—a universal salve that repairs all it touches. Love is the great neutralizer; it brings the mind, body, and breath into coherence. The energy creates an all-consuming bonfire in the heart space. Any issue, any problem, any dispersal, any interference that we can feed into that fire of love gets transformed by love's vibrational frequency. Confusion turns to clarity. Hate turns to forgiveness. Prejudice turns to understanding and caring. Separation and isolation turn to connection and togetherness. Grief turns to immeasurable joy.

Love is the universal solvent. The more we live from love, the more consistently we apply it to every situation and circumstance, the more we become unified as the Soulful Self. In fact, the Soulful Self can *only* inhabit our physical life through the doorway of the love vibration; love is the gateway to the Soulful Self.

Why is this so? Because the vibrational frequency of love is as expansive as we can get in human form. That very first compression of energy when we, as spirit, move toward physical matter—as we get off the Cosmic Bus at our earthly stop—is the vibrational frequency we call love. Wow! When we land in the core of our being, love is easy to experience because it's what we're made of.

Love is your true nature, not just a place to visit. The Heart Code practices teach you how to fall into the love vibration at will—at any time, and in any situation—and then to live from that place all the time. These practices are the pathway to the love within us. We don't need to remain in the "want" vibration of seeking love outside of ourselves, when we can develop the skills to remember—on a physical, feeling level—that *we are love,* and that we can drop into that vibration in an instant and ultimately learn to stay. When we can do this, we then share this love with others constantly and unconditionally, which amplifies the experience that we came here to have.

The Soulful Self is always anchored in love. This is why the Soulful Self is also called the bliss body—*anāndamaya kosha* in Sanskrit. When we are in the Soulful Self, we are blissful in a loving state. Through daily practice of the Heart Code, you will quickly learn to manifest that bliss, every day, for the rest of your life.

The Heart Code Practices

PRACTICE 1: GENERATING LOVING
PRESENCE: CHOOSING TO BE LOVED

This practice gives you a direct route to the vibration of love that is waiting to be ignited inside you. It provides the tangible experience of love we all seek and makes superfluous the need to seek love outside of ourselves. It also gives you tremendous freedom to be the truest version of yourself, without agenda. This clarity of Self is essential for living from the vibration of love and for healing and creating in your life.

1. Think of someone or something you dearly love. It could be a friend, a family member, a pet, your childhood sweetheart, your current sweetheart, or the soul mate you haven't yet met! It could be the love of spring, a favorite place, a cherished memory, or even an object that has great meaning for you. Choose anything that generates the sensation of love within you.

2. As you call up this person or thing that you love, understand that this object of love is actually *revealing* the vibration of love to you. It doesn't bring love to you; it *brings up* love *from within* you so that your mind can perceive the love you already have inside you—the love that you *are*. It causes *you* to "come out."

3. Now fill your heart with the presence of this person, object, or memory. Fill your senses with this image, and then take your attention to your body. Sense how you feel inside when you think of this image.

4. Next, turn up the volume on this experience. Double it. Then double it again. Fill your body with the love that you have for this person or thing and then let it overflow into the room. Then make it even bigger than the room by dropping into the experi-

ence completely with every part of your concentration. Again, notice how you feel in your body as all of this love is happening. Memorize how it *feels*.

5. Now place your hand on your heart and say to yourself, "This is for me." Receive it all. Drop the love that is bigger than the room into the center of your own being, and receive it fully. Call it home to you—come back onto "subject" (as we did in the Anchoring Code)—and feel it in every crevice of your body.

6. As you place your hand on your heart, squeeze *mūla bandha* to deeply feel this vibration on a physical level. Then take a breath up and down through the central channel and the anchor points in your core, as you have learned in previous Codes. You will start to sense the anchoring of love's specific vibration in your body.

7. Nurture this feeling and vibration of unconditional love for several breaths.

8. Next, repeat steps 1 to 5, only this time think of a moment that you felt completely, unconditionally, unwaveringly *loved*. Maybe it was being loved by your grandmother, maybe your mother, maybe a partner or a best friend; it could even be a pet. (If you've never had an experience of this at all, that's okay too. In that case, the invitation in this exercise is for you to *just make it up*—to imagine what it would be like to be loved completely and simply for who you are. You get to have it any way you choose.)

9. Notice if there is any area that has more of a charge, and squeeze it and breathe down through the central channel into the earth, opening the bottoms of your feet as you do. Open them by lifting your toes off the ground and then laying them back down,

envisioning *yourself*—not just the energy—reaching and rooting down through them into the earth.

10. Connect one line of circuitry all the way from the heart space in the center of your chest, down the torso, through the pelvis and the legs, and out through the feet into the earth.

The sensation you now feel in your heart is, indeed, unconditional love. In doing this simple exercise, you see that the love you once thought was brought to you by people or objects outside of you is in fact available within you all the time—you need only to connect with it. Building circuits through the Energy Codes allows you to have this experience often, even without an impetus from the outside world. You generated love just now because you decided to, and then received it fully because you could.

You created it, and you received it. No strings attached. This is vitally important! To allow the mind to perceive more of the love vibration within the body—to build the circuitry for that love to flow—you can't simply love everybody else; you also have to love yourself. Doing so specifically creates the photon patterning associated with truly knowing "I am loved." The truth, of course, is that we're made of love, so we cannot *not* be loved—but we need to give the Protective Personality the experience of *being loved*. We need to embody being loved to create the feeling of being loved *in the body*, where it will then reflect out into the world as being loved by others.

When you do this practice, your conscious mind recognizes that you are generating love, and your subconscious recognizes that you are receiving love—all at the same time. This is a signature pattern for you to practice multiple times every day. Cellular familiarity with this expansive vibration is a necessary requirement for moving completely to the Front Side of the Model. We cannot remain there without it, for love is the true identification, feeling, and sensation of the Soulful Self.

To illustrate the importance of this practice, I want to share a story about how my mom was always the one to serve others and didn't allow herself to receive the love she was giving to everyone else . . . until she did.

MARJORIE SAYS, "ME TOO!"

My mother was a lover of everyone. She was always giving to and caring about others—to the extent that it compromised her own life balance and health.

One day, while washing her hands in a hotel lobby restroom, she turned to grab a towel. With that simple movement, her leg snapped and fractured. Our first thought was that her bones were osteoporotic, which is more common in women over sixty than in younger women. But tests found that her bone density was that of a twenty-four-year-old!

But if calcium deficiency wasn't the cause of this spontaneous fracture, what was?

According to the science of bioenergetics, the study of the body's energy field, a "fracture" occurs first in the energy field, and *then* manifests in the physical world when we step off the curb and break our ankle. We step into what already exists in our subtle energy body. Something else was going on with my mom, since clearly not everyone who turns to dry her hands breaks a leg! It is possible that the fractured bone was caused by an *energetic* fracture—a dispersed energy that shot down her leg in order to be grounded. She had a blockage in her field, and it played out in that moment as she turned her leg. (If I'd known how we can anchor and integrate our own energy field using the Energy Codes at that point, I might have helped her avoid the fracture altogether by doing the practices I've been teaching you!)

Interestingly, at that time in her life, my mother was just starting to include herself in her efforts to help others. She was learning to identify her own needs and speak about them—which women of her generation did not readily do—as she searched for balance. But she had not yet put her finger on how to identify and articulate what she really felt or "take a stand for herself," and so the energy that was trying to anchor and awaken lacked a pathway to make itself known with grace. To allow her to learn to say, "Me too!" the energy gave her an external situation—a friction— that enabled this transformation. All along, life had been supporting her in a loving way, but the message needed to become a bit louder for her to hear it!

Well, it worked. My mom began to let her love flow for herself as well as for others from that moment on. When she would speak to me about her challenges with various circumstances, her words reflected a new perspective, and her experience of receiving love more abundantly grew each day. For people who are overgivers, these practices will help you find an energetic balance before the messages have to be so big!

Through the Energy Codes, we begin to rewrite how we look at love, and how possible it is to experience love in any situation. We soften any confining beliefs around love and what's required to experience it. People tell me all the time that they "fall in love" with this work as they do it—that is because the feeling of love is a by-product of landing the mind on the central core of the body and allowing it to perceive and magnify the presence of our true nature. Love is extraordinarily abundant. It is completely unlimited, so there is plenty for everyone. In fact, the more you receive love, the more you generate it, and vice versa!

PRACTICE 2: LOVING TRIAGE

Love is a catalyst to transformation—anything we love changes in the presence of that vibration. In this exercise, we're going to build on the work of the Energy Codes by adding the vibrational choice of love as the *nature* or *quality* of how we're working. This will ensure that our work won't be mechanical, that it will be performed in the spirit of love, and will therefore be made all the more powerful. Specifically, we'll be using the *breath of loving presence*—bringing together three life-changing components to create the transformation: the breath, for moving spirit energy through the body; loving, for bringing in the transmuting quality of love; and presence, for focusing the mind in specific internal locations.

Here's how it works: Ideally, when we're in an upsetting situation, we "take it to the body" instead of reacting into story. We find the charge as a sensation in the body, and we squeeze that spot to acknowledge that the conscious mind is making contact. We then breathe up and down through the central channel, bringing the charged area into the flow of energy through our core as we continue to squeeze it and breathe. However, we now know that we can increase our capacity for healing and transformation if we turn on the vibration of love as we breathe. Flipping on that "love switch" will tremendously increase our power to integrate the energy dispersal that is causing the charge.

This can be really challenging at first. It might be hard to access love in the same moment that you're trying to identify and integrate the area of dispersal, especially when you're first learning to access love on command. So I want to give you an alternative way to work with this, a technique I call Loving Triage.

These are the steps:

1. When you're in a challenging or stressful moment, take it to the body. Notice where in the body the charge is, squeeze that area, and memorize its location so you can come back to it later. This will not only minimize the energetic dispersal, it will keep you from doing anything in that moment to contribute to the story drama (for example, it will keep you from getting into an argument, stepping into fear, or doing something else that you're going to regret).

2. Later, at a time when you're under less stress (such as when you're lying in bed), approach the scenario again. Do the Generating Loving Presence exercise you just learned, imagining something or someone you truly love. Bring in sensory input like smells, sounds, or anything else that would add detail to your vision of love. Now turn up the volume on the feeling of love again and again, until the love is so big that it's causing the image you're holding to pale in the face of all of this love.

3. Notice how this feels in your body, and set the intention to maintain that pattern of energy no matter what. The goal here is to lock in and memorize what love feels like in the body.

4. While you're in this loving state, slowly breathe up and down the central channel six to eight times, sensing for a shift.

5. While performing Central Channel Breathing, bring the idea of the challenging topic into the mix. Squeeze the area of your body where you originally felt the dispersal, and allow the loving presence to dissolve the challenging situation and build new circuitry in the affected area.

In this practice, we stoke the bonfire of love and then bring the challenge to it. It's not unlike the common ritual of writing a challenge on a piece of paper and burning it; in this case, you're building the fire in your own heart space and performing the work internally, so you don't have to do the ceremony externally. Plus, by embodying this transmuting flame of love, you can more sustainably embody the changes you make when you set alight life's frictions.

The first-things-first approach of Loving Triage makes it much easier to dissolve our energetic interferences because we're not trying to ignite love in the midst of an upsetting moment. Whenever life is too much, whenever it feels overwhelming, tap into this practice as a way to work with what you need to let go of or heal. Working consistently with Generating Loving Presence will make igniting your internal love bonfire easier and easier. Ultimately, as we get the energy moving and melt all of our stuck and dispersed patterns into this flow, dropping into love and then living there will become "first nature"—as automatic as breathing. (For the health-care and bodywork practitioners reading this: blazing the bonfire of your heart when working with the energies of your clients, rather than placing a "bubble of protection" around yourself as we are so often instructed to do, is a more effective practice because the latter only affirms the duality of Protective Personality and Soulful Self.)

PRACTICE 3: SEEING EVERYTHING AS LOVE
(AKA "IT'S ALL IN MY FAVOR")

I've had the great privilege of sitting bedside with dozens of people over the last thirty years, many of them in their final days. Surprisingly, the conversations have all had a similar thread: "It's all been good. It all served.

Even the stuff I hated, I love now. It was all part of this amazing life I've lived." They talk about the huge gamut of experiences they got to have—the sadness and joy, victory and loss, birth and death, everything. This is what goes through people's minds as their lives here come to a close.

My question is: If we're going to eventually embrace all of our life experiences from that perspective, why not do it *now*?

When we decide right now that all of life happens for our benefit, and we operate intentionally from that place, we generate a different filter through which to experience life as it is happening. If we're willing to look at every scenario in our life as an act of love—as our true self lovingly giving our earthly self an experience so it can wake up to our own magnificence and expand in our capacity to love—we will naturally interpret those scenarios differently. Simultaneously, we stabilize the distortion that resistance, rejection, and judgment create in our energy field. The next thing we know, it becomes easier to see love. It becomes easier to experience love. It becomes easier to reveal and share love unconditionally.

Love is abundant. It's in everything. It's everywhere in the all-ness and wholeness of life. When we acknowledge this, we start to see that, from the Bus Stop Conversation perspective, even the hardest things in life are based in love. My mother's passing was the greatest pain in my life—but in the face of what looked like loss, in that moment, it also broke all of my previous records of what love could feel like as it reunited me with her in this deeply heart-based reality.

The truth is that *every* exchange in life is really the interplay of love with love; it's all just different versions of love coming to connect. Perceiving that all of life is a story of love finding love—of the Soulful Self awakening within us through our coming to the perspective of love in any given scenario—is a real action of the heart center and the love vibration we've been talking about. Until we lead with that intention, however, it's not likely that life will show up for us like that. As like attracts like, we need to embody love to invite love into our experience. This is what we are furthering with the Heart Code.

We can also understand this through quantum science, which tells us that everything in our reality is ultimately a reflection of our own consciousness—that, when something happens, it's because a part of our own consciousness is drawing that experience into our awareness. If my life is peaceful, it's because my inner world is integrated to a place where I can perceive peace. If there is turmoil, it is a reflection that there is circuitry that still needs to be hooked up in order for me to see without distortion. In essence, the three-dimensional world acts like a movie screen for me to see how I am integrated, and how I am not.

If we perceive that people, places, and things that are happening in the outer world are not a reflection of ourselves but instead are separate from us, we start wanting to change those circumstances because they're uncomfortable. But when we realize that there's nothing but love happening—that everything that happens is simply a guide to help us awaken the mind to the loving Soulful Self—we can experience the turmoil differently. When we encounter a really challenging situation, we can know instantly that it's a reflection of our own internal reality, a gift to help us find the ability to sustain love, peace, and harmony in the face of any set of circumstances. We can then take this gift of feedback to the body, where we can transmute it with love. And that's really our job here, to bring love to every aspect of our lives.

To practice Seeing Everything as Love, follow these steps:

1. Think about a situation that currently feels like a real challenge for you—for example, a relationship conflict, a health or financial crisis, a major loss or the threat of one.

2. Ask yourself, "If this circumstance were simply a gift or opportunity from myself to myself so that I can expand in my capacity to love, how might my view of it shift?"

3. Then, using the practices of Loving Triage and Generating Loving Presence, take the situation to the body and into your heart center, see where to build new circuits, and allow the bonfire of love to transmute the old and help forge the new.

4. If you like, follow up with action. Ask yourself, "In what ways can I now choose to more deeply love myself and others through

this experience?" Another way of framing this is: "If expanding in love is the reason for this experience, what is my heart telling me to do?" or "What is the universe asking of me now toward accepting my magnificent ability to live in love?" Then follow your heart!

Many people feel that they have to wait for external proof—a set of circumstances like my experience with the four-leaf clovers—to start seeing everything as love. But it's just something you have to decide to do. In the same way that you wouldn't expect to see in a dark room until you turn on the light, you need to flip the switch in your mind to start coming from that place. The more we start looking at everything and everyone as a loving presence in our lives (whether it looks that way at first glance or not), the more we can find the love vibration. And the more we do these practices for generating the love vibration, the easier it is to view the world this way. We melt the gunk in the central channel and remove the wobble that is thwarting our perceptive field. Love is reinforcing, leading us more and more deeply into embodying the Soulful Self.

This work will help you move through life without attachment, detachment, or distortion. When you embody love as the Soulful Self, your happiness level will soar, your relationships will transform, and your ability to heal, rejuvenate, and replenish will become automatic as you settle into a consistently peaceful state. In love, life begins to shift toward a state of collaboration instead of survival—a magical, blissful adventure created solely for your benefit.

The Heart Code Chakra Correlation: Heart Chakra

The Heart Code is correlated to the fourth, or heart, chakra, located in the center of the chest. This energy center—known as *anāhata chakra*, "the unstruck"—represents our very nature as love. It is the pathway to our mind's connection to that love and to the unified field, which connects everything in the universe. It governs all aspects of love's expression. While *manipūra*, the third chakra, represents our sense of self, *anāhata* represents the way we see ourselves in relation to the world and everyone in it. The love associated with the heart chakra is ever binding, the missing link ("the unstruck") in most spiritual inquiry.

Many people with heart chakra issues feel disconnected from others, from love, and from themselves. They feel "outside," as if the threads that bind other people simply don't stick to them. This can lead to anxiety, depression, and loneliness, as well as physical symptoms such as heart trouble, circulatory problems, and breathing issues—a literal manifestation of an inability to "take things in" or receive the energy of love.

The heart chakra is where the energies of the first, second, and third chakras—which represent our primitive, individualistic sense of self— meet and integrate with the energies of the upper chakras, which reflect the higher-frequency energies of our divine consciousness. The heart chakra is where our divinity and our humanity come together; it plays a key role in awakening our divinity *in* our humanity.

As we activate the energies of the heart chakra, we open to our most vulnerable selves and find strength and power in love. When we work with heart chakra energy, we become less prejudiced and more present—more divine, in that we are available to *what is* rather than pushing our individualist, lower-chakra beliefs onto every circumstance we encounter. We also become more patient, nonjudging, and forgiving of the judgments that others impart. We have greater ease and relaxation in the body because we're not triggering the fight-flight-or-fright response. And we appreciate life more fully, as we come to recognize that we are loving and lovable in new ways. Underneath it all, we are divine, and now we finally get to experience it.

A common misconception the world over is that we can't be in our power and be loving at the same time. We think, "If I'm in my power, I can't be loving. If I'm being loving, I can't be in my power." But that's not true. We can do both! Being vulnerable is not being weak, as our vulnerability brings us into the presence of our greatest power by giving us access to our heart and the gateway to infinite possibilities. To live both aspects of our nature, we simply need to integrate the energetic components of the third chakra—the mental, self-identifying self—with the fourth chakra—the Soulful, loving Self. This allows us to exist in an optimal state of being both powerfully loving and lovingly powerful—to be vulnerable, authentic, kind, *and* strong.

When our Protective Personality is trying to find love or to be loving, we might actually be trying too hard and not anchored and integrated in our personal power. This presents as the classic "doormat," where we're always doing for others to try to get love, appreciation, gratitude, and a sense of self. When we are in this space, we may find it hard to make choices that include love for ourselves. We create a vacuum, a vacancy, where all the love is going outward and none of it is being integrated in our own energy field.

The following chart offers a summary of some of the key characteristics of the heart chakra. Again, notice how the energetic properties of the chakra mirror the physical body areas.

The Heart Code Chakra Correlation: Heart Chakra

NAME(S)	Fourth chakra, anāhata chakra
LOCATION	In the center of the chest, beneath the breastbone
COLOR	Green, pink
MUSICAL NOTE	F
BODY AREAS AFFECTED	Heart, chest, circulation, arms, hands, lower lungs, rib cage, skin, upper back, ***thymus gland***
"BACK SIDE" SYMPTOMS	Fear of betrayal, codependency, melancholy, shallow breathing, high blood pressure, heart disease, cancer, inability to perceive or receive love
"FRONT SIDE" CHARACTERISTICS	Compassion, unconditional love, conscious lovemaking. "There is more than enough for all." "There is only one of us here – we are one." "Everything is a reflection of the Divine, and is in my favor."
PRACTICES	• Generating Loving Presence: Choosing to Be Loved • Loving Triage • Seeing Everything as Love (aka "It's All in My Favor")
BREATHWORK *(as explained in Chapter 8)*	Heart Coherence Breath
YOGA POSES FOR GREATER INTEGRATION	• Triangle Pose *(trikonāsana)* • Thread the Needle *(sucirandhrāsana)* • Fish Pose *(matsyāsana)* • Reclined Spinal Twist *(supta matsyendrāsana)*

In balancing the heart chakra, we heal codependency, fears about betrayal, detachment, and apathy. Compassion, love, and ease in relationships result. On a physical level, improvements in blood pressure, circulation, heart disease, and lung disease, as well as other benefits, may occur.

Yoga for the Heart Code

Along with the Heart Code practices, the following yoga posture will help you to activate and integrate the heart chakra, and get its energy flowing optimally again.

TRIANGLE POSE (*TRIKONĀSANA*)

Here's how to practice Triangle Pose:

1. Stand sideways on a mat with your feet three to four feet apart.

2. Turn your right foot outward so that it is facing the short end of your mat, pointing away from your body.

3. Turn your left foot slightly inward so that your heel is the farthest point of your foot from your body.

4. Swivel your hips slightly toward your right foot so that both of your knees feel safe and stable.

5. Draw energy up through your right leg, lifting the kneecap toward the hip and the femur into the hip socket. Enliven your left leg as well. Draw up through the pelvic floor to engage *mūla bandha*.

6. Now hinge the hips toward the back of your mat and extend the torso over the right leg as much as you can. Reach with the right hand far toward the top of your mat and then let it drop down to rest on the right foot, shin, or thigh (avoid putting weight directly on or hyperextending your knee). You can also place a block directly inside the right shin and rest your hand there.

7. Turn your torso toward the side without destabilizing your hips and extend your left arm straight out from your shoulder toward the ceiling. You should feel an elongation and stretch in your side waist and low back.

8. Slowly draw your arms back into your shoulder sockets to energetically activate the muscles around your heart.

9. Hold for several breaths. To come out of the posture, slightly bend your right knee, lift the torso back to center, then turn the feet back to neutral.

10. Repeat on the left side.

Now let's integrate our Heart Code and BodyAwake practices while in Triangle Pose.

1. While holding the pose, bring your attention to the space beneath your feet, two feet below the ground. Also bring your attention to two feet above your outstretched left hand. Imagine that you are tethered between these two points in space, above your hand and below your feet.

2. Pull the thighs together, extend your spine, and outstretch your arms fully while simultaneously plugging the arms into the shoulder joints and activating the muscles around the heart. Put life into your hands all the way to the fingertips. Collect yourself at your core.

3. Take a loving breath up through the legs and into *mūla bandha*, filling the pelvic bowl. Tightly pull the low belly back toward the spine and squeeze the back of your heart by pulling the shoulder blades together. This, in combination with the squeezing of the thighs, generates a "seat" for circuitry to transfer energy up from the earth and into the core of the body. (This is

tremendously helpful for allowing the mental body to release its constant effort to manage and/or control everything and to let love flow. It also allows for the building of the central channel on a deeper level, and for the Soulful Self to be more easily perceived.)

4. Press your lower hand (or your wrist, if your hand is on a block) against the inner shin of the front leg and rotate your heart to the sky. Squeeze everything in the core at the same time. Exhale this love through the entire core of the body and out the arms, hands, neck, and top of the head. On the next inhale, breathe love in from beyond the head and hands, through the neck and arms to the heart; then, squeeze the heart and *mūla bandha*, and exhale the love down through the body and out the legs and feet into the earth. Squeeze the thighs and lower legs as you exhale.

5. Release *mūla bandha*, and then repeat the whole cycle for three or four breaths, squeezing the core to build the sensory awareness with each breathing cycle. This allows you to begin to feel your loving self more within your core and build communication circuitry more quickly.

ADDITIONAL YOGA POSES TO INTEGRATE THE HEART CHAKRA

You can use these asanas along with Triangle Pose to enhance your work with the Heart Code. Remember to practice both while squeezing areas you desire to integrate and while relaxing the body and imagining and then feeling the energy (you) moving up and down the central channel. Again, having the feeling of love as you do each of them enhances their power tremendously.

- Thread the Needle (*sucirandhrāsana*)
- Fish Pose (*matsyāsana*)
- Reclined Spinal Twist (*supta matsyendrāsana*)

In the Heart Code, we embodied unconditional love, the most powerful healing ingredient that exists. The fire of love can transmute any limitation and challenge. We can apply the love vibration to "triage" stressful or hurtful situations to keep the energy of these challenges from becoming stuck in the body. Love is the key to every life solution, and you happen to be made of it!

In the next Code, we'll add more fuel to the fire that ignites the Soulful Self within by using the breath, which is the life-giving energy, *prāṇa*—Spirit itself. It's time to turn on your chakras and wake up your consciousness on every level.

Chapter 8

THE BREATH CODE:

THE POWER OF LIFE ITSELF

"Dr. Sue, is that you?"

I was walking down the hall toward the hospital waiting room, about to visit a dear friend after she underwent surgery for a stroke. The recovery area nurse on duty came briskly down the hall toward me. It was Nancy, whose children were former patients of mine.

"Do you remember me?" she asked. "You saved my son's life many years ago!"

"Of course I remember you! How are you, and how is Darren?"

"He's fabulous, in the armed forces now—he's strong as an ox!" Darren was one of Nancy's twins. Several years prior, when he was about four years old, I'd seen him for a "failure to thrive" diagnosis. His twin sister was bright and vibrant, while he was pale and weak, with multiple allergies and respiratory disorders. His vital force was declining and he wasn't expected to live for very long. The doctors didn't know what to do for him, so Nancy's sister—a patient of mine—had referred the family to me.

While observing Darren during our treatment sessions, I noticed that his breathing seemed "reversed." Most young children breathe into their belly first, and then their chest will move. Darren's shallow and rapid breath started high in his upper lungs, and his belly rarely engaged. I worked with him with the B.E.S.T. technique using pressure points around his head and body. I also worked with his breath. As soon as the blockages were cleared, his breath pattern shifted, and his health began to improve. Darren came to life. His skin color changed almost instantly after that first session—his lips turned pink and his cheeks became rosy within minutes! On his next visit, I observed that his new breathing pattern had continued. Over the coming weeks and months, he became playful as his vital force woke up. Soon he was teaching his sister what playtime was all about!

I shared Darren's story with other patients, giving them specific breathing homework to do. Their improvements were consistent with Darren's. I also shared these stories of improvement with my father so that we could incorporate the technique into the basic training of B.E.S.T. With that research and other reports of benefits, the doctors and health-care providers trained in B.E.S.T. began using specific breathing patterns in their practices as well, resulting in dramatic outcomes around the world.

Years later, as I began to understand that activating the energy in my core was fundamental for embodying high-frequency energy experiences, I was aware that conscious breathing would likely enhance them. As I breathed with intention into the areas of my own body that were not as enlivened, or that didn't emit the sensation of me "being in there," my hunch proved true. So I began to teach my patients and students various breathing patterns to awaken the areas of the body that correlated to their symptoms and patterns.

In the following months and years, I realized that we could even prevent many symptoms and typical responses to injury by activating those areas in a sequential manner that included all of the levels of energy in the body. This practice awakened the consciousness of each chakra level, which had previously been dormant because no one was "living in there" to do the awakening. People began to think, breathe, and behave more pro-actively, assertively, and compassionately—all because they were realizing a greater version of themselves. As they worked with their breath around their physical symptoms and patterns, their Protective Personality settled down and their Soulful Self woke up!

The breathing patterns in this Code are the same that I've used for years with my patients and students and in my own daily regimen. Many aspects of these techniques are derived from traditional rehabilitation modalities for strengthening the spine and increasing dynamic healing in the neuromuscular system. However, my personal experience of embodiment and the positive clinical outcomes while working with my patients led me to compile them in these specific patterns. If you utilize them regularly, they'll awaken aspects of *your* Soulful Self that may still be sitting dormant, waiting for your attention.

What Is the Breath Code?

Breath is spirit. Breath is life. Breath is *you*! When the breath is gone, spirit, life, and you have left the body, and life experience as we know it on the physical plane is over. But this isn't a one-way street. We can actually infuse more life, more of us, *into this plane* now, while we're here; we can bring more of the spirit, the Soulful Self, into our body. For this, we must use the breath. The Breath Code is all about breathing, and thus bringing, more life in. We breathe more of our true self into our energy field and physical body and get energy flowing, so that we can fully embody the life we came here to live.

At this point, we've worked with the breath several times—to anchor our consciousness within the body; to begin moving energy through our system and learn the language of the soul; to acknowledge, lighten, and clear densities or interferences; and to infuse the love vibration of the Soulful Self into the energy field. Now we're going to deepen and intensify the work we've been mastering in the previous Codes by focusing *specifically* on the breath, deepening our understanding that this energy is who and what we truly *are*.

Focusing the mind on an area of the body and breathing into it at the same time allows us to awaken and "be" in that space, and to begin living from there. The chakras are integral to this energy flow and interface with the breath to create transformation in the body and life. This is how we most quickly "build" the presence of the Soulful Self and manifest meaningful change. Remember, when energy isn't flowing in the body, it's not flowing in your life.

In this Code, we will emphasize the chakras, which are not simply centers of energy but also anchor points that house levels of your consciousness. Collectively, they are *you* (in a slightly less physical, more energetic form)! Using the breath to enliven the chakras gives you the ability to change *intentionally*, with ease and grace, rather than through years of challenging story lines and lessons learned in suffering and pain. When the chakras aren't activated with our life-force energy, they don't function properly, and that dysfunction is reflected in our external world. When their circuitry is activated, we experience far greater harmony in body, thoughts, and emotions.

When we're activated in the root chakra, for instance, we feel as though we belong, and that life supports and is a reflection of our well-being and happiness. We have physical energy and vibrant health. We have visions and dreams, and we take action to manifest them. If we're not active in the root chakra—if it's dormant, imbalanced, or even overstimulated—our thoughts are not balanced or harmonious, and we view ourselves in terms of survivorship instead of creatorship and support.

In the Breath Code, we'll breathe energy directly into each of the chakras. We'll therefore be breathing energy into the abilities and qualities that those activated chakras convey. The most exciting benefit of the intentional use of the breath is that it creates change *before the mind understands what has occurred*. For example, if you breathe into your solar plexus—into *manipūra chakra*, the seat of your personal power—and get its energy moving through your body, you're going to begin feeling and acting more empowered, even if you don't consciously know (with your mind) how to see and assess a situation from a place of greater personal power or self-esteem. You will simply do it, because you've changed on the level of your energy.

Because conscious breathing acts as an integrator—meaning that it weaves together the thoughts, feelings, sensations, and chemistries on the physical level with the vibration and circuitry on the energy level—it is the single most powerful transformational tool available to us, far more valuable than meditation alone. When we choose to breathe into a chakra or area of our body, we choose to create change there and to bring it online as part of our Soulful Self. We choose to breathe spirit and subtle energy into our physical energy and form and allow them to reshape us in the image of our greatest potential.

Seventy-two-year-old Pat was able to take a deep breath into her essential core for the first time in her life simply by using these techniques. In that same moment, she was able to embrace and forgive a lifelong emotional pain pattern from childhood abuse. These techniques can work for you too.

The Breath Code is all about manifestation—breathing your way into your dreams, desires, and visions in this world. For this reason, I also refer to this Code as the Manifesting Code. This work reminds us that our outer life is a reflection of the integration, activation, awakening, and circuit-building of our inner world. When our inner world is not integrated, anything that we manifest in the outer world will likely be impermanent and unsustainable. Without internal integration, it takes a lot of energy to create things, and even more energy to sustain them.

We *can* manifest from the Protective Personality, but that manifestation will look and feel very different from what we create as the Soulful Self, because it will be driven by insecurity and fear. Someone will have to lose in order for us to win. We might compromise our health for a successful career, or compromise our relationships in order to feel validated. In these scenarios, we might be "successful," but we won't have intimacy or health.

To have achievement with fulfillment, we must come from a place of integration. If we learn to integrate and come from deep within our core as the Soulful Self, we will not only achieve as much or more in the same time or less, we will manifest our desires in such a way that everyone wins, there is enough for all, and we don't have to rob ourselves or others of something important to create our desires. When we manifest from an integrated place, what we create will be *sustainable*. We will find ourselves attracted to things that are in alignment with our highest good, and so our desires themselves will become more divine and manifest naturally.

The more we awaken our chakras by breathing energy flow into them and integrating them with each other, the more our mind will be able to sense and feel our truth. Our actions will reflect our true nature. Our true life purpose will emerge and flow. When we have the circuitry built to support a greater flow of life energy, we won't view challenges as problems. We won't take things personally and get caught up in story-writing; instead, we'll stay in the flow and dissolve potential obstacles before they

for intimacy, so much more able to be vulnerable, and so much more able to listen and to receive feedback without having to sidestep it or push back against it. My perfectionism has softened into loving the imperfections of life, knowing that they're all part of a beautiful unfoldment into something greater and more meaningful. My need to achieve is completely settled into the celebration of who we are as human beings, and my availability for others is tremendously enhanced because my energy and resources are so available.

My visions for my life have also blossomed. I went from seeing myself as merely an individual trying to "do my part" in my singular practice in a singular city, to understanding and accepting my role as a global visionary and spiritual teacher. I have opened enough to allow circumstances, and the flow of energy within me, to support my being able to teach people in a dozen countries around the world. People from across the ocean attend my seminars, learn this work, and receive care at Morter Institute, because I have allowed a greater sense of self to be revealed and to manifest.

Looking back, I find it amazing that I used to be afraid to speak at all because I didn't think I had anything to say that was important or that my ideas were significant enough to make a difference for other people. By allowing myself to drop into my own Soulful Self using the same practices and principles you're learning, I learned that the very things I share are exactly what people need to hear. The deepest part of me knows that this was meant to be all along; I just had to breathe life into that which was already meant to manifest.

Each one of us has the ability to gain that kind of purpose—that which we have always deeply known but haven't allowed our mind to consider or support long enough to bring it to life. Let that sink in for a moment: everything you desire to be, do, and create is already within you, just waiting for you to connect the necessary *circuitry* to bring it to light.

In fact, at this point in the Codes, I'd love for you to really begin recognizing that your whole life experience *is* the Soulful Self trying to steer the mind in a more effective, masterful way. You are constantly moving toward knowing how magnificent, strong, and capable you are—so squeeze that blockage that's letting you *know* that you know, breathe through it as you will learn to do in this Code, and love it for what it's revealing!

These Codes give us the tools to bring the mind's attention onto what the body is trying to reveal. When the mind and body start breathing in collaboration with each other, our true destiny comes up from within and becomes obvious to us—so obvious that we cannot *not* honor it. Our unfoldment happens naturally, without us having to push and try, and without the tremendous energy drain of manifesting from the Protective Personality. I haven't *tried* to create any kind of greater expression or engagement in the world; I just keep getting invited into a greater expression and engagement because I'm developing the circuitry to resonate at the vibrational frequency where those opportunities live. You can too.

You awaken to your greater self with ease by breathing into the parts of yourself that have been sitting dormant. In the course of your lifetime, you might discover most of these expressions anyway—but through this work, you can discover them *immediately*, and manifest and celebrate them. This type of dramatic transformation is the promise of the Breath Code. Specific ways of breathing will activate each of your chakras individually and bring their circuitry online in a targeted and proactive way.

The Breath Code Practices

PRACTICE 1: BREATHS FOR CHAKRAS ONE TO SEVEN

Everything in this world is made of energy and every form is composed of atoms, which can further be divided into subatomic particles, which are constantly moving within an infinite amount of space. This space, which exists in and between all particles, is as significant as the form itself. In fact, the unified field provides the backdrop upon which all of life is positioned. Did you know, for example, that current scientific studies show that plant roots grow in the energy space between the dirt molecules rather than in the dirt itself? Or that we humans walk on energy "pads" rather than actually touching the ground as we once thought? Everything is indeed energy! To improve health and vitality, we must activate and maintain the invisible energy in the space between the particles that compose the body's tissues and bring it to life. Why? Because we actually *are* that invisible space! We are the spirit in between the particles. When we are breathing with awareness, a vital energy flows through the body, intentionally activating every aspect of our wholeness.

When the space between particles is reduced, areas of the body become denser and we become more compressed. When we get upset and contract, energetic blockages can form, which lead to emotional and/or physical symptoms. In order to optimize the energy flow, we want to keep the space between the particles expansive. You might even say that we want to give them "room to breathe"!

Ancient Eastern traditions of breathwork produce specific results in the physical body. I've included some of them as I adapted them in my own experience of embodiment. In these exercises, you will open to the vibrational frequencies of healing and creativity within each chakra and integrate those frequencies into your body and mind at the cellular level.

Remember that you *are* the breath itself, and you *have* a body to live in. So why not learn to move into your entire house?

The Central Channel Breath—1st & 7th Chakras

The Central Channel Breathing of the Anchoring Code (page 110) connects all the points along the central channel, but specifically gets energy flowing through the root and crown chakras. Here is a brief recap of this exercise. Remember to breathe deep into the belly, extending it on the inhale and compressing it on the exhale.

1. Visualize a vertical channel running from above your head, through your body to the tip of your spine, and into the earth below your feet.

2. Squeeze your anchor points: *mūla bandha*, the heart, the throat, and behind the eyes.

3. Concentrating on the space over the top of your head, inhale down through the center part of your head, into your throat, and into your heart; let the breath arrive in the belly.

4. Then, from the belly, exhale down through *mūla bandha*, out the tip of the spine into the earth below.

5. On the next breath, inhale from deep within the earth, up through the tip of the spine, and into the belly.

6. Exhale up back through the central channel, through the heart, the throat, behind the eyes, and out the top of the head.

7. Now practice *being* the breath as you move up and down the channel. Be the essence inside the elevator going up and down the elevator shaft. A deepened experience begins to formulate from this last step.

The most important aspect of this exercise is that you follow the breath with conscious attention all the way up and down the central channel, without skipping any portion as you go. Do this as if you *are* the breath moving through the channel. Just imagine it. This exercise connects the subtle, higher-vibrational energies of the universe with the grounding, physical energies within the body and the earth itself, creating a pathway for deeper integration of these various energies that make up you. Since all major chakras reside along the central channel, this channel is like the "motherboard" of the body; this breath flips the power switches to "on." From this activated place, more subtle work with each chakra center can commence with greater ease and specificity.

The Vessel Breath (Buddha Belly Breath)—Second Chakra

This breath builds upon Central Channel Breathing, concentrating on the lower abdomen in the area of the second chakra, *svādhiṣṭhāna*. By contracting the muscles below the navel and deep in the pelvic bowl as you breathe, you conserve vital energetic life force within the body, rather than simply moving it through the system. The contractions create a "funnel," rather than just a channel, and allow energy to be held longer in the body (and activate the tissues more completely).

This practice can benefit everyone but is especially important for working with a sacral chakra imbalance or blockage. Breathing in this way improves vitality, awakens the second chakra's creative energy, and cultivates inner wisdom or our ability to "trust the gut." Billions of bits of information bombard the energy field every millisecond, and this is where they are cultivated, in the lower abdominal region at the second chakra. Trusting our gut is trusting our ability to make decisions and assessments based on more information than our thinking mind can manage.

Perform Central Channel Breathing, moving from over the head and through the body's central channel to just below the navel in the second chakra area.

1. As you do this, contract *mūla bandha*, lifting the sphincter muscles upward from within.

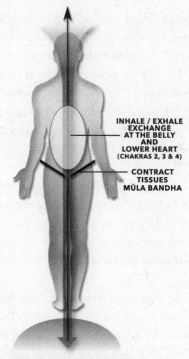

INHALE / EXHALE
EXCHANGE
AT THE BELLY
AND
LOWER HEART
(CHAKRAS 2, 3 & 4)

CONTRACT
TISSUES
MŪLA BANDHA

**VESSEL BREATH 2ND CHAKRA
(BUDDHA BELLY BREATH)**

2. Continuously hold *mūla bandha* during the inhale and the exhale. This may feel challenging because you are squeezing the belly and expanding the belly at the same time. Allow both to interact with each other, creating a sense of awareness in this chakra space. This is the intentional internal resistance or friction we have spoken of earlier.

3. Couple this breath with the entire central channel breath from above the head to below the tip of the spine and into the earth, and then back up again, while holding *mūla bandha* the entire time. This integrates the second chakra energies with the higher-frequency energies of the rest of the central channel.

Solar Plexus Breath—Third Chakra

The Solar Plexus Breath uses additional muscle contraction to activate *manipūra chakra*, the solar plexus chakra, and its related benefits. As this breath integrates the third chakra, it enhances decisiveness, strengthens self-esteem, and empowers us generally. If this area is not activated, it is tough to ever have a true sense of who you are—or have the power to honor it even when you do. This breath, when practiced along with the others, fuels the fire of your personal passion and can change your life.

Here's how to do Solar Plexus Breath:

1. While breathing through the central channel, and with *mūla bandha* contracted, contract the upper pectoralis (chest) muscles and draw the shoulder blades together and down. Squeeze the chest as if you are "holding" the heart center steady, or hugging yourself inside the chest.

2. Limit the area from which you draw your breath to only the space from above the belly button to below the ribs. (This is the space where, if you were hit there, it would knock the wind out of you.) I call breathing from this limited area the Baseball/Grapefruit breath.

3. As you inhale, push this high stomach area out, making it expand to the size of a grapefruit; as you exhale, return this area to the size of a baseball.

4. Practice breathing Baseball/Grapefruit and then simultaneously add the central channel breath. Inhale from overhead, making "baseball" enlarge to "grapefruit" at the solar plexus area; then exhale to the earth, making "grapefruit" decrease in size to "baseball." Then reverse and breathe from the earth up through the body to exhale overhead; "grapefruit" on the inhalation and "baseball" on the exhalation.

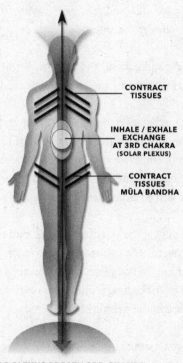

CONTRACT
TISSUES

INHALE / EXHALE
EXCHANGE
AT 3RD CHAKRA
(SOLAR PLEXUS)

CONTRACT
TISSUES
MŪLA BANDHA

SOLAR PLEXUS BREATH 3RD CHAKRA

Heart Coherence Breath—Fourth Chakra

Heart Coherence Breath focuses on the expansion of *anāhata chakra,* the fourth chakra or heart center, activating love energy and the connective dynamic of the heart while anchoring your consciousness in the Soulful Self. This breath also assists with conflict resolution and receiving love, and immediately invites greater joy and peace.

1. Begin with the Vessel Breath, filling the lower abdomen or belly on the inhalation.

2. Continue to inhale into the belly until the middle chest (heart space) also fills and the chest cavity lifts upward, filling the upper lobes of the lungs last.

3. Now expand beyond the body with the breath, imagining the breath overflowing the body and expanding out around it.

4. On the exhalation, deflate the chest and upper lung area first and then continue to empty the chest until the belly/abdomen begins to empty as well. Imagine exhaling your breath in every direction, out into the world, in a spherical fashion. The next inhale will be from every direction, into the belly.

5. Ultimately, at the end of the exhale, pull the belly button inward and upward, as if you are trying to touch it to the spine. Let your exhalation be complete, so that every last bit of breath is expelled from the lungs. This helps reset the fight-flight-or-fright response in the nervous system.

6. After practicing this sequence six to eight times, connect this breath with the central channel also, by inhaling to the belly from underneath where you sit or stand and exhaling overhead, then reversing the process, inhaling from overhead and exhaling to the earth.

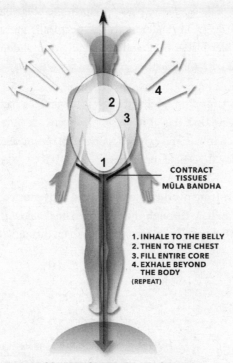

CONTRACT
TISSUES
MŪLA BANDHA

1. INHALE TO THE BELLY
2. THEN TO THE CHEST
3. FILL ENTIRE CORE
4. EXHALE BEYOND
   THE BODY
(REPEAT)

HEART COHERENCE BREATH 4TH CHAKRA

Manifesting Breath—Fifth Chakra

Manifesting Breath activates *vishuddha chakra,* the throat chakra and the seat of your truth. When this aspect of consciousness is enlivened, we can hear and speak openly and honestly. We are focused on manifesting the greatest truth, not just our personal or Protective perception or opinion. This allows life to unfold gracefully because we are open, free, and in true alignment with universal law.

Use this breath to assist you in proclaiming and manifesting yourself to the world, and to take action as the Soulful Self instead of the Protective Personality.

Here's how to perform Manifesting Breath:

1. With *mūla bandha* in place, perform the Solar Plexus Breath—
   squeezing your abdominals and pectoralis muscles with your
   shoulder blades back and down. Fill your abdomen and heart
   space with the breath.

2. Keep your chin level and draw it toward the back of the neck.
   Imagine "locking" it in place. Make this area the central focus
   of each inhale and exhale. Contract all the muscles in the rest of
   the core to isolate the throat.

3. Inhale from overhead to the throat with your conscious attention. Exhale through the entire channel below the throat, and
   into the earth. Inhale from the earth up through the body to the

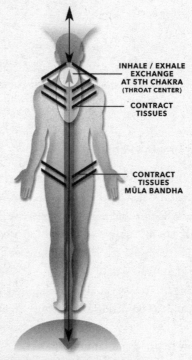

INHALE / EXHALE
EXCHANGE
AT 5TH CHAKRA
(THROAT CENTER)

CONTRACT
TISSUES

CONTRACT
TISSUES
MŪLA BANDHA

MANIFESTING BREATH 5TH CHAKRA

throat, and exhale out the top of the head. Let the throat be the pivot point of the breath exchange, but also make sure to *feel* the breath (yourself *as* the breath) moving all the way up and down the channel like warm, liquid light.

Visionary Breath (Inner Vision Breath)—Sixth Chakra

This breath activates the high-brain centers and *ājñā chakra*, the third eye. This will assist you in accurately perceiving what *is* and in seeing through the veils of the Protective Personality to the truth of the Soulful Self. This breath cultivates greater clarity and inner awareness, so that you can read the subtle energy messages of your own body. For best results, use it in conjunction with the other breathwork described in this Code in order to stabilize the channel below the third eye.

In this exercise, we initially deviate from the baseline of Central Channel Breathing and instead imagine inhaling from a focal point in front of the forehead through the center of the brain, then exhaling out the back of the head. As you do this exercise, keep the anchor points along the central channel engaged or contracted, especially *mūla bandha*.

With eyes closed, roll the eyes up so you can feel the tension in this anchor point. Keep your focus on this area as you relax the tension for the actual practice, re-creating the tension if you lose focus.

1. Perceive yourself inhaling from in front of your forehead to the center of your brain at the anchor point behind the eyes. Imagine feeling the breath fill the space between and within all the cells in your brain, activating and nourishing them.

2. Exhale the breath out through the back of the head an equal distance, opposite the entry point.

3. Now reverse the process, inhaling from the back of the head to the center of the brain.

4. Exhale the breath out the forehead to your focal point.

5. Repeat this action several times, and then connect it vertically with the central channel on each exchange. Inhale from overhead to the *center-brain anchor point*, and then exhale all the way down the channel to the earth.

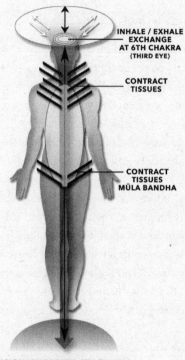

INHALE / EXHALE
EXCHANGE
AT 6TH CHAKRA
(THIRD EYE)

CONTRACT
TISSUES

CONTRACT
TISSUES
MŪLA BANDHA

**VISIONARY BREATH 6TH CHAKRA
(INNER VISION BREATH)**

PRACTICE 2: A THOUSAND TINY STRAWS BREATH

We literally are made of thousands of tiny tubes or channels of energy called *nadis*, and larger ones called meridians, in the subtle body anatomy. This breath practice allows us to begin bringing consciousness to those channels for greater enlivenment of our system. This practice is foundational to healing injuries and chronic pain, by breathing "space" into all muscular and connective tissues. It also enlivens the tissues of the outer layers of the torso, in addition to the central channel, including the arms and legs. It is highly beneficial for expressing your inherent gifts, talents, and purpose in this world, because it helps to remove blockages and awaken you to vibrations, realities, and capacities you once thought were beyond you. It is intricately integrative.

To do this breath exercise, you will visualize the body in three sections, as in the diagram on page 222:

- From the feet to the top of the hips.
- From the top of the hips to the shoulders, including the arms.
- From above the shoulders to the top of the head.

1. To begin, contract every muscle in the first section of the body (from the feet to the hips).

2. Now inhale up through the area, starting below the feet, as though your subtle energy body were made of a thousand tiny straws, and you were sucking a very thick milkshake up through them, inch by inch.

3. Keep constricting within the body, drawing the breath with great intensity. As you get to the next section of the body, exhale, but *do not release the area of contraction below*. Rather, add to it the contraction of every muscle in the next section (from the top of the hips to the arms and shoulders). On the next inhalation, pull the energy upward, inch by inch, through that part of the body, all the way to the tops of the shoulders.

4. Exhale into the neck and shoulder area but *do not release* the muscle contractions of the entire body beneath this level.

5. Next, add the third and final section (from above the shoulders to the top of the head, including the neck, face, mouth, and scalp). On the inhale, draw the energy through the straws in this section inch by inch until you pull it to the top of the head.

6. Hold the breath for a second, then exhale out the top of the head, without relaxing a single muscle.

7. Sense energy pouring out and down around the outside of the body—and then, relax everything! Think of the Torus Man and his three-dimensional energy, from chapter 3.

8. Take a deep breath in, exhale, and intone the relaxing sound of "ahhhh." Be aware of new energy pouring into your body from overhead, as if you're standing in a waterfall. *Let it feel good.* Your system is being energetically replenished.

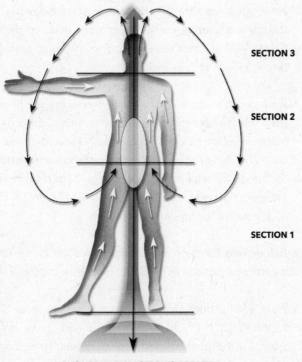

SECTION 3

SECTION 2

SECTION 1

A THOUSAND TINY STRAWS BREATH

9. Repeat the practice two or three times.

10. End with contracting all three sections simultaneously and breathing in from overhead and exhaling down through the entire body to the earth.

This breath is an advanced technique that is best learned with live instruction in the Energy Codes Coursework or via video demonstration (see drsuemorter.com/energycodesbook), but because of its tremendous healing benefits, I wanted to give it to you here. To be truly effective, it must be done regularly and with great attention to detail. But once you master it, you will have a powerful method for removing interference in the body's subtle energy flow—to really get your flow looking like that of the Torus Man. So give it a try. You'll find that it gets easier with practice.

You'll also be using the Thousand Tiny Straws Breath in conjunction with the final practice in this Code to target and heal injuries and chronic pain. You will love the effects!

PRACTICE 3: FERN FROND BREATH

The Fern Frond Breath is a technique to integrate fine details of energy flow in the spine, which helps sustain the changes we are trying to make. It builds circuits in detail, and while it may sound complicated at first, with practice it will begin to feel simple and natural.

Imagine a curled-up fiddlehead fern frond. See how it is coiled tightly upon itself. Now imagine that coil slowly unrolling, curves straightening, until the fern is stretched to its full length. This is sort of what we'll be doing: rolling into a curl, then unfolding to open the body again, drawing the breath through as we go.

As we do this, we'll be engaging a particular spot in the energy system—a place just behind the abdominal wall, above *mūla bandha* and in front of the sacrum at the tip of the spine. In some Eastern practices, it's referred to as the *dantian*. We want to take hold of this place and, with each inhalation, draw it upward through the body as we uncoil. We'll unfold the spine in a vertebra-by-vertebra fashion so that each segment becomes the apex of the curve as it unfolds.

Here's how to do it step by step:

1. Have a seat in a chair, or cross-legged on a yoga mat or the floor.

2. Contract *mūla bandha* and find the *dantian*, that space behind the abdomen above *mūla bandha* and in front of the sacrum. Think of it as a small ball of light, and draw it up through the central channel as you perform the next several steps and become that ball of light.

3. Exhale and tuck your chin down on your chest. Continuing to exhale, roll your chest down toward your abdomen and in toward your lap, coiling up like a fern frond closing. Go as far into the coil as you can without pain, exhaling until all air is released from your lungs. Imagine your spine curving in a perfect spiral like that fern, not just hinging at the base.

4. Now inhale, pressing your hands against your thighs. Pushing your spine backward away from your hands, roll your body up one segment of the spine at a time. Keep your chin tucked all the way up until you're sitting vertical again and it's time to unroll your neck segment; when you reach the cervical spine, envision yourself unrolling one vertebra at a time until you reach the base of the skull. (*Note:* You want to be inhaling the whole time you're uncoiling up to vertical, so this will take you two or three breaths initially; when you need to exhale, stop right where you are in the coil and exhale, then inhale again and pick up where you left off.)

5. Next, tip your nose up toward the ceiling, roll your eyes up and together, and exhale straight out the center of your forehead and top of your head.

6. Now inhale from that same position, and then exhale and start to coil again, emptying the breath as you close the fern frond

back down until you are back in your completely forward rolled-up position with the chin on the chest and the chest down toward the abdomen. Bring your forehead and crown toward the floor. As with the unrolling process, you may need to do this over several breaths; if you need to inhale, pause, take a breath, then continue to roll your spine down on the next exhale.

7. Repeat two or three times.

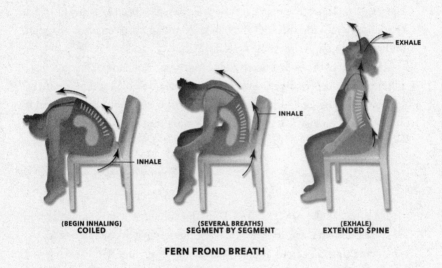

(BEGIN INHALING)
COILED

(SEVERAL BREATHS)
SEGMENT BY SEGMENT

(EXHALE)
EXTENDED SPINE

FERN FROND BREATH

Most important in this practice is to bring your conscious focus to one small segment of the spine at a time, so that integration happens all the way up the entire spine. Repeating the exercise in conjunction with the other breathwork—Chakras 1 to 7 and A Thousand Tiny Straws Breath—*greatly* increases the integration. As you work with these breath practices and become intimately familiar with their nuances, you will begin to truly feel and sense how the different energies can work together in your body. When you can feel your true self as the energy in the body, you begin to become masterful at moving energy. When you can move energy in your body, you can move it in your life; soon you will be able to shift your circumstances toward that magical life you dream of. You will move far beyond healing to living as a creator.

In the meantime, though, let's get some healing happening!

PRACTICE 4: BREATH PATTERNS FOR HEALING

Pain exists (or, more accurately, dysfunction or lack of healing persists) in the body because of a lack of energy flow through the affected area. A blockage causes an excess of energy to build up like a dam in a river, which causes pain. To restore optimal flow and therefore health, we want to get that energy moving through the blockage and get it circulating through and integrated into the whole system again.

If an area of the body is weak, it means there's not enough energy moving through the area, like the backside of the dam in the river. We want to increase the flow of energy there by putting our conscious attention on it and bringing energy to it with the breath, breaking through the dam. This breath pattern will begin moving the energy through the area to restore functionality.

Here's how you do it:

1. Squeeze the affected area. Don't just squeeze it mechanically; rather, squeeze it as if you were hugging it from the inside, making conscious contact with it and implying, "I'm listening. I'm not going to miss you this time. I'm embracing what you're trying to tell me. I now get that we're in this together."

2. Next, you're going to breathe from beyond the area, through the area, and into the heart center, and exhale out the other end of the channel. Breathing from beyond the area means going out beyond the nearest extremity and drawing in the energy from there. For example, if your knee is hurting, you're going to squeeze the knee as with A Thousand Tiny Straws, and then, in your imagination, go down beyond your foot to breathe the energy up from the earth, through the foot and lower leg, to

the knee—and then beyond it, to the hip, the abdomen, and all the way to the heart. Then you'll exhale out through the throat, brain, and crown. If the pain or lack of function is in the hip, you'd again go out beyond the foot as your starting point. If the problem is in a shoulder, you'd begin the breath beyond the hand, or from beyond the top of the head, whichever feels more involved in the issue. No matter where you start drawing the breath from, you will always inhale to the heart and exhale out the other end of the channel.

3. As you're drawing the breath through the problem area, squeeze the muscles all along the route. Squeeze them and stretch them at the same time that you breathe. This pulls the energy right through the tissues, awakening energetic circuits; so squeeze, stretch, and breathe!

4. Then reverse it all, taking your next inhalation from that new end of the channel, through the heart, and exhaling through the affected area and out the original starting point. Keep the muscles along the way fully contracted and stretched as you pass through them.

This breath pattern for healing can be used for any part of the body that hurts, feels tense, or is regularly problematic in some other way. I've given you a couple of common examples of issues and the specific breath patterns for healing them. For a video demonstration, go to drsuemorter .com/energycodesbook. See the Resources section on page 325 for additional options and support for this issue.

These breathing patterns for each chakra can also help heal mental and emotional traumas associated with physical, sexual, mental, and emotional abuse. Take It to the Body (page 130) was particularly helpful for me, as was practicing the specific breath pattern associated with the chakra indicated. Additionally, I recommend that you take special care to feel a deep and intimate connection in your heart as you do this exercise. (Reference the Heart Code practices starting on page 187 if this seems

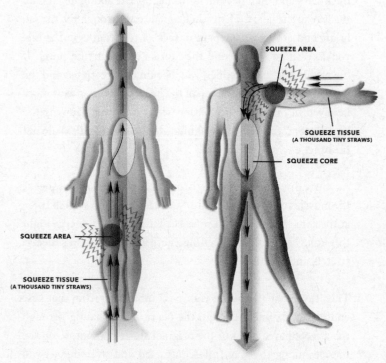

BREATH PATTERNS FOR HEALING

challenging.) Sharing this with my clients and patients has resulted in decreasing the emotional charge, shifting their entire perspective, and making the Quantum Flip. I know that it can help you too.

The Breath Code Chakra Correlation: Throat Chakra

The Breath Code is correlated to the fifth, or throat, chakra, located halfway between the heart and the throat at the base of the neck. This chakra is named *vishuddha chakra* in Sanskrit, meaning "especially pure." Beyond ruling the voice and the breath, it manifests our true path if we let it, because it is the spokesperson of the essential Soulful Self. It interacts with the outside world and expresses our true creative nature. It's also related to *using* the imagination. To operate as a creator, we often have to take action when there is no evidence that our action will be well received or safe. When enlivened with our conscious breath, this area allows that journey to feel guided and inspired.

The following chart offers a summary of some of the key characteristics of the throat chakra. Again, notice how the energetic properties of the chakra mirror the physical body areas.

The Breath Code Chakra Correlation: Throat Chakra

NAME(S)	Fifth chakra, *vishuddha chakra*
LOCATION	Halfway between the heart and the throat, centrally at the base of the neck
COLOR	Blue
MUSICAL NOTE	G
BODY AREAS AFFECTED	Mouth, throat, ears, neck, voice, lungs, chest, jaw, airways, nape of neck, arms, **thyroid and parathyroid glands**
"BACK SIDE" SYMPTOMS	Perfectionism, inability to express emotions, blocked creativity, sore throat, thyroid issues, neck ache, tinnitus, asthma
"FRONT SIDE" CHARACTERISTICS	Good communicator, ease with meditation, artistic inspiration, can listen. "I hear and speak the truth with love and compassion." "I manifest myself here fully." "My life is a reflection of my inner world."
PRACTICES	• Breaths for Chakras 1–7 *(Central Channel Breath 1 and 7, Vessel Breath [Buddha Belly Breath] 2, Solar Plexus Breath 3, Heart Coherence Breath 4, Manifesting Breath 5, Visionary Breath 6)* • Thousand Tiny Straws Breath • Fern Frond Breath • Breath Patterns for Healing
BREATHWORK *(as explained in Chapter 8)*	Manifesting Breath
YOGA POSES FOR GREATER INTEGRATION	• Cobra Pose *(bhujaṅgāsana)* • Plow Pose *(halāsana)* • Bridge Pose *(setu bandhāsana)* • Toning with Sound *(Oṁ, Ma, Ha)*

In integrating the throat chakra, we heal perfectionism, blocked creativity, and the inability to speak and share our deep truths. We begin to feel connected and free. Good communication, ease with meditation, and artistic expression are other common results. Thyroid issues, sore throat, tinnitus, and asthma, among other health concerns, also improve with throat chakra balance.

Along with the breathwork practices in this Code, the following yoga postures will help you to activate and integrate the throat chakra and encourage its optimal energy flow.

Yoga for the Breath Code

While Cobra Pose can be used for other chakras as well (most notably the heart chakra), and many poses can affect the throat center, I chose Cobra here because it is easy for just about everyone to do. Also, it allows a specific line of communication/awareness up and down the front side of the central channel.

COBRA POSE (*BHUJAṄGĀSANA*)

Here's how to practice Cobra Pose:

1. Lie on your belly on a yoga mat or blanket. If possible, draw your legs together so that your big toes touch; if that is uncomfortable, try to keep your legs no wider than hip-width apart.

2. With your forehead resting on the earth, bring your hands directly underneath your shoulders, fingers facing forward.

3. Press your palms into the earth. Press the tops of your feet into the earth, and activate your legs. Activate *mūla bandha* and draw your stomach and low belly up and in.

4. Now, keeping your chin slightly tucked, lift your head and heart off the floor as far as you comfortably can, keeping your legs and the tops of your feet pressing into the earth. Your back will arch into a C-shape. Draw your shoulder blades down your back; avoid scrunching your shoulders up toward your ears.

5. Lift your chin toward the place where the ceiling and the wall meet, exposing the throat. Don't simply hinge the head back; keep the neck long and engaged.

6. Breathe in and out here, feeling the breath running up and down the channel.

7. To come out of this pose, slowly drop the chin, then lower the chest and head to the floor. Extend the arms overhead or at the sides and turn your head to one side. Breathe deeply, relaxing the body. Then move on to the next part of your practice.

Now let's integrate our Breath Code with our BodyAwake practices while in Cobra Pose.

1. While lying on your belly with your hands placed under your shoulders and your legs touching, squeeze the inner thighs and knees together (or toward each other) as far as possible.

2. Press the tops of your feet into the floor and imagine a reservoir of energy two feet beneath where you lie.

3. Squeeze *mūla bandha*, and press the belly into the earth as you inhale energy up through the front of your central channel and into your core from beyond the bottom of your feet. *Feel* yourself inside the open belly space. Squeeze the shoulder blades together and down and pull your heart and chest through the front of your shoulders as you inhale, and open your throat.

4. Roll your eyes up to feel the tension, and exhale through that space and out the top of your head.

5. On your next inhalation, breathe from two feet above the top of your head and into the center of the brain to the throat and chest, down the front side of the body to the belly, pressing the open belly into the earth.

6. On your exhalation, squeeze *mūla bandha*, and exhale out through the tip of the spine, legs, and feet, keeping the legs fully

engaged, as with A Thousand Tiny Straws, and the tops of the feet pressing into the earth. Experience one full-body-long line of connection with this pose.

ADDITIONAL YOGA POSES TO INTEGRATE
THE THROAT CHAKRA

You can use these asanas along with Cobra Pose to enhance your work with the Breath Code. Remember that squeezing areas to which you want to draw attention is beneficial, but so is relaxing in the poses. Use your best judgment to work with the Breath Code practices in each of these poses.

- Plow Pose (*halāsana*)
- Bridge Pose (*setu bandhāsana*)
- Toning with Sound (*Oṁ, Ma, Ha*)

———

In this Code, conscious breathing activates and brings flow to each of our chakras to allow us to more fully embody the Soulful Self, manifest our desires and our true path, and create healing in all areas of our life. Next, the Chemistry Code will provide another crucial piece of the embodiment puzzle, both for understanding how embodiment works and for creating the conditions that are most conducive within the body for it to occur. Whole health and vitality await!

Chapter 9

THE CHEMISTRY CODE:

THE ALCHEMY OF EMBODIMENT

Twenty years ago, John walked into my office with a medical history chart so large he could barely carry it. One section, nine inches thick, was filled with test results, diagnosis reports, scans, treatment protocols, blood work results, orthopedic and neurologic opinions, and prognoses for a multitude of conditions: arthritis, gout, diabetes, ulcers and ulcerative colitis, chronic headaches, neck pain, back pain, knee pain, thyroid and adrenal fatigue, eczema, psoriasis, reflux, and a few others. "They're giving me less than a year to live," he said in a shaky voice. "I heard that your clinic is helping people in amazing ways with some of these types of issues."

He was the nicest man, and he was in trouble. I felt for him. "Have a seat," I said. "Let's see what we can find."

We spoke for a few minutes, looking at his reports, and I noticed that he would periodically reach into his pocket, grab a little something, and pop it into his mouth. My first impression was that he was managing his blood sugar with a handful of nuts or seeds, but it was too consistent, and far more frequent than sugar management would warrant.

I had to ask. "John, what is that you're eating? Is it a snack of some sort?"

"Oh, that? No. It's salt. I love salt . . . I just love it!"

"So that's *salt* you're putting in your mouth every minute and a half?" I asked.

"Yes. I get the driveway bag and dump some in my pocket every morning, and pop it in my mouth all day."

I immediately knew what was going on with him. It wasn't rocket science—it was an addiction to rock salt! The salt was toxic, dehydrating, and overstimulating to his system—causing high blood pressure and sending his pH off the charts on the acidic side. He was addicted to other stimulants as well: sugar, sodas, nicotine, and caffeine, to name a few!

For several weeks, we went to work on his body chemistry by natural means. We treated him with the bioenergetic procedures I used in my office, clearing the subconscious blockages connected to his need for constant stimulation. In the next month, John healed from the majority of his conditions. The remaining conditions were manageable and continued to improve as more months passed.

Seven years later, a much happier John ducked his head into my waiting room just as I passed by the front desk. I hadn't seen him in a few years; he'd moved to Florida, but was back in town to visit his kids. He wanted to thank me, and was celebrating his life as he showed me photos of his new grandchildren.

"Any snacks?" I teased.

"No way! I'm feeling way too good to mess with that!" he replied.

What Is the Chemistry Code?

Years ago, before he wrote *The Biology of Belief*, Dr. Bruce Lipton made presentations at the seminars that my father, brothers, and I gave about natural healing through bioenergetics. He would share the groundbreaking insights from his research in a new field of science called epigenetics. In a nutshell, epigenetics is the study of gene expression, or what triggers genes to act in certain ways, and how genes can be influenced by lifestyle, age, disease, and even thought patterns. This field has started to answer some age-old questions about our own capabilities to influence and heal the bodies we were born with.

For me, perhaps the most exciting discovery was that the surface of every cell in the body has antennae, or receptors, that tell our genes how to act based on the energetic and chemical messages they receive from their immediate environment. Regardless of our genetic makeup, the sequence of our DNA, or the predispositions we've inherited from our parents or grandparents, a cell will act in accordance with the "information" it receives about its environment from the receptor on its surface. The best news of all is that we have a great deal of control over what that "information" is, and what environment we create for our cells. We can therefore *consciously* and *deliberately* tell our genes how to act.

Like everything else, our cells rely on energy for information. That energy then becomes physical as our body produces chemicals (e.g., hormones, enzymes, etc.) according to the information from our energy field. Those chemicals, in turn, create the internal "environment" that directs cell function and creates our overall body chemistry. When our energy field shifts, so too does our body chemistry. For instance, the energy field determines how the thyroid gland and the adrenal glands ultimately produce hormones; the cells in these glands "sense" the energy in the body's field via the antenna-like receptors on the cells' surfaces.

Because they are equal partners in the feedback loop, the reverse is also true: our body chemistry affects our energy. This means that our body chemistry either facilitates or hinders our efforts to embody the Soulful Self.

In this Code, we learn how to create an environment that brings the body into its natural state of calmness, relaxation, balance, and efficiency. When the physical body is in an optimal state, the energy field is enlivened. We can bring closed-down circuitry back online, integrate fragmented energy, empower the body to do its innate work of self-healing and creativity, and allow the Soulful Self to come through. In other words, when our body is in an optimal state, we set the stage to manifest well-being in all areas of life.

Playing a major role in all of this is our body's pH balance.

The Importance of Body pH

Our story about John at the beginning of this chapter was, in essence, a story about body chemistry. I'm referring specifically to the pH balance of the fluids throughout the body—how acidic (low pH) or alkaline (high pH) the body is as an environment for our cells. This matters because cells stay healthy and vital and have the ability to self-repair in an alkaline environment, whereas (with the exception of stomach cells) they begin to break down or malfunction in a more acidic environment.

Ninety-five percent of all diseases occur when the body is in an acidic state. Cancers are the extreme result of a highly acidic state. Other common diseases—acid reflux, osteoporosis, high blood pressure, gout, arthritis, high cholesterol, hypothyroidism, diabetes, and excess fat retention, to name a few—are also symptoms of an acidic body environment. Unfortunately, most people's bodies are simply too acidic for cellular healing to occur; the result is today's epidemic of chronic illness and disease. And although most of us now know better than to chew on rock salt all day, there are many ways in which we unknowingly contribute to our inability to heal.

Our bodies always put energy into survival first. The pH level of our body's urine and saliva registers to our system as either a threat to survival (when too acidic) or a state of safety (when adequately alkaline). Our cells are designed to float in an alkaline environment and produce acid as a by-product of function. Being too acidic is actually a life-threatening condition! An extremely acidic state is called acidosis, and can lead to heart problems, stroke, and failure of the kidneys and the body's major systems. So even if the body has other—even very serious—problems or issues to heal, it's going to work to get the pH balanced before it allocates any healing energy and resources to other tasks.

This constant prioritization of maintaining alkalinity is a primary reason that injuries and illnesses become chronic—meaning, they never heal. For example, if someone complains of back pain and their pH is too acidic, as a doctor I could work on their physical symptom forever without seeing much improvement. Why? Because their body is using all of its healing energy to neutralize acidity and therefore prevent system failure. A person won't die from back pain, but could in fact die from a chemical imbalance due to excess acidity. Until chemical balance is restored, this system will choose to spend all of its extra energy on managing that more life-threatening problem, and healing of issues of less priority won't occur.

Thousands of cases in my practice over the last thirty years revealed that a chemical imbalance was keeping someone's back pain, knee injury, headache, depression, or anxiety from healing. As we remedied the chemical state by alkalizing the body, the system was able to change its focus and begin working on the lesser issues.

Even with all the evidence, pH balance is a topic of debate. The reason for the controversy is the many variables that can produce conflicting test results, including which body fluids are being tested and what the patient's dietary intake, emotional status, and concurrent health factors are during the testing period. (The saliva and urinary pH are used for testing, as the body will protect the blood pH as long as possible, even sacrificing alkalizing minerals from the bone and muscle to do so.) Additionally, pH findings and recommendations are often misunderstood. For example, a patient with Stage IV cancer may test with alkaline urine pH due to cellular breakdown rather than because of a proper chemical balance in the body. In the last forty years, I've seen many nutritional recommendations and fad diets come and go. What my father and I observed in the clinical setting was that eating an alkalizing diet in order to maintain alkaline "reserves" (found in the extracellular fluids and, ultimately, the muscle and bone tissue where even more of the body's minerals are stored) for the body to draw from as needed is what enables the body to heal.

Our body chemistry—not our mental willpower and not our emotional discipline, as some would purport—ultimately determines the ease or difficulty with which we heal and transform, because our body chemistry is an equal factor in our system-wide feedback loop with our energy field. In fact, the chemistry of our body is important to manifesting all of our desires in life, because it bolsters (or inhibits) our ability to connect with and draw forth the Soulful Self, feel inspired, be uplifted, take initiative, and self-heal on all levels.

Which leads us to the crucial question: *How do we balance body chemistry?*

Numerous things contribute to our body chemistry. I think of it as a complex homemade soup, with various ingredients going in to create the final mix. These ingredients include the obvious things—food and drink, the air we breathe, the substances and chemicals we take in or absorb, and so on. Other ingredients are less obvious, such as our thoughts, emotions, and beliefs—conscious and subconscious.

Interestingly, the "room" in the brain that houses the subconscious is also where the body chemistry soup gets made. Called the Cave of Brahma, the Cave of Creation, or the Cave of Collaboration by various Eastern traditions, this area in the center of the brain is believed to be where creative thought originates, and where generating a new reality begins. It is command central for numerous functions in the body, so what happens here has a major impact on body chemistry. While the interplay of hormones, neurotransmitters, and synapse reactions is quite complex, here's an easy way to think of it.

Imagine a small cave in the middle of your brain. The floor of the cave is made of an area of the brain called the hypothalamus, which receives information from inside the body—from the internal world—and responds chemically to that information. Chemical imbalances are ultimately regulated at this level. Now imagine that you're sitting in this little cave. If you were to stretch your foot out on the floor as far as it could reach, it would be in the neighborhood of the pituitary gland, the master gland that controls the hormonal system. The hypothalamus and the pituitary gland have a direct relationship with each other; the former is a "communication center" for the latter, exchanging information about which hormones are needed and in what quantity. The walls of the cave are made of the thalamus, which, among other things, receives nerve impulses from our five senses reporting from the *outer* world. And sitting in the back of the cave is the pineal gland—a gland whose cells contain rods and cones, similar to the rods and cones of your physical eyes. Both the pineal gland and the eyes perceive photons. Since there is no opening to the outer world in the center of the brain, this gland may perceive frequencies higher than visible light, such as those of our energy body and the Soulful Self. (I have personally experienced this to be so.) Finally, in the floor of the cave is a trapdoor, beneath which lies the subconscious, where the experiences we have denied, resisted, or cut off from our consciousness reside, along with all of the aspects of ourselves that have not yet been awakened. All of the reactions of these cells and glands continually affect our energy and physiology.

Several key ingredients are funneled into this cave through the information-gathering activities of the thalamus, hypothalamus, and pineal gland. The culmination of all of the dissemination and transmission within this cave is the body chemistry "soup" that is sent to our cells via the pituitary gland, the cerebral spinal fluid, and other neural messages. The cells of our brain and body bathe in this soup's messages and respond to them.

The chemistry of this soup not only determines how we heal, it determines how and when we eventually awaken to the great truth of who we are as a multidimensional, eternal energy being—as the Soulful Self. This chemistry contributes to our Quantum Flip.

Let's look at a couple of the ingredients that are making their way into our body chemistry "soup pot."

The Foods We Eat

You can think of your digestive system as a wood-burning stove. When you put wood in a stove, it is consumed as fuel, and the by-product is wood ash. The by-product created once a substance has been metabolized by the body is also called "ash." We call an alkaline by-product "alkaline ash" and an acidic by-product "acid ash."

The foods and drinks we consume affect body pH after they've been digested. Some items, like coffee, are acidic going in and acidic once metabolized. Some, like certain vegetables, are alkaline going in and alkaline once metabolized. And still other items, like oranges and lemons, are acidic going in and alkaline once metabolized, or, like a steak, are more alkaline going in but have a potent acid ash afterward.

To create and maintain a healthy cellular environment, we must eat far more alkaline-ash foods than acid-ash ones. If we don't, the body is forced to pull from its alkaline reserves to neutralize the acid ash so it doesn't pass the rest of the way through the digestive system and burn the tissues of the kidneys and colon, causing cellular breakdown, illness, and disease as it travels. When we eat a lot of acid-ash foods, we borrow more alkalinity than we end up putting back. This isn't a problem if it only happens occasionally, but in the long term, constant input of acid-ash foods depletes our alkaline reserves, until the body can no longer create a buffer. When this happens, the system just continues to get more and more acidic. Under these conditions, cells that are designed to float in an alkaline environment begin to break down and disease occurs.

Fat retention is a response to an acidic body chemistry. Because fat is alkaline, the body will retain fats and fluids in an attempt to dilute or neutralize the acidic condition that's building up in the body. Losing weight is easier in an alkaline environment.

This is where epigenetics comes in. For a long time, it was supposed that certain diseases (including diabetes, heart and circulatory conditions, and even cancer) were inheritable conditions. There may be some component of this present, but, as we learned earlier, what triggers gene behavior isn't simply our inherited DNA signature—it's the daily environment in which our cells exist. In many cases, this translates to long periods of acid-ash food consumption that generate an acid condition in the body and produce the conditions that encourage disease to develop.

This is incredibly exciting! The disease conditions you've come to believe are unavoidable and simply have to be contended with can, in fact, be avoided or even reversed by creating an alkaline body chemistry. Long-standing evidence from patient cases throughout the B.E.S.T. clinical community shows that when a person decreases his intake of acidifying foods and increases his intake of alkalizing foods, he becomes more self-healing. The body automatically starts to return to its natural state of wellness when we give it this kind of help.

The Chemistry Code will provide you with the tools to create a new "soup recipe" for your body chemistry and give your cells what they need to operate in an optimal, alkaline state. That alkaline state is necessary not only for proper individual cell function, but also for accurate relaying of information from the energy field to the surface of the cell and then to the inside of the cell, so that the cell can produce its chemistry that then translates information to the brain. In this way the sensory system produces accurate motor responses in life.

Alkalizing foods are primarily fruits and vegetables; other foods produce some percentage of acid ash to varying degrees. Animal protein is the most acidifying, followed by dairy and grains. Caffeine is highly acidifying, as are sugar, soda, alcohol, and highly processed foods that contain artificial colors and flavors. And, of course, nicotine and other addictive chemical substances create acidity in addition to other well-documented damaging effects. We can't necessarily offset the acidity of one type of food by eating more of the alkalizing foods. Too much animal protein in a day (more than thirty grams), for instance, generates more acid than we can alkalize in twenty-four hours, no matter how many vegetables we eat.

My father used to say, "Eat foods that are as close as possible to how nature prepared them." However, with the advent of genetic modification, even that solution is endangered. Some studies show that genetically modified foods affect the kidneys, liver, heart, adrenal glands, and spleen of mammals. I attribute this to their not being recognized by the body as "real food." Many believe, as I do, that the alteration of natural chemical bonds results in less complete or more challenging metabolism by the body, and therefore a greater accumulation of acid ash, which requires greater effort for the body to process. Therefore we should eat organic when we can, without GMO alterations.

Diet plays a large role in the health of our body chemistry, but there's another factor that is even more influential: our thoughts.

The Thoughts We Think

Thoughts create chemicals. Low-frequency thoughts create acidifying chemicals. High-frequency thoughts create alkalizing chemicals. The experience of love generates the most alkalizing effects on our system.

When we're under stress, for example, our body produces chemicals (such as cortisol, the "stress hormone") in response, in order to try to protect itself from the stress. Prolonged elevated cortisol levels create an acidic condition in the body because the fight-or-flight mode deals first with threats to our survival before the body's needs for filtering, cleansing, and healing. When we're joyful, the body produces different chemicals (such as dopamine, the "feel-good hormone") and we have a different result in the body's chemistry.

Arthur Guyton's *Textbook of Medical Physiology* states that the reticular activating system (RAS), a gatekeeper for prioritizing incoming stimuli to be processed, is eclipsed by our own thinking. This results in our inner thoughts having a direct impact on our fight-flight-or-fright response and subsequent body chemistry without any regulation. We know that thoughts can, and do, eclipse the beneficial effects of good nutrition on our body's chemical balance. This means that we can eat a perfectly alkalizing diet and end up still creating an acid condition in the body if our thoughts (conscious or subconscious) generate low-frequency emotions like anger, hate, resentment, remorse—or, the number-one cause of acid buildup in the body, excess worry. Yes, prolonged or habitual worry will produce more acid in the body than we can alkalize or neutralize, no matter how much alkalizing food we eat.

We can change our acidic pH within a few weeks if the imbalance is nutritionally caused. However, countless times I've tested clients' saliva and urine pH and found that they were running very acidic, only to discover when I asked them to log their dietary intake that they had a nearly perfect diet, and had eaten this way for some time—certainly for long enough that it should have made a difference in their body chemistry. (For more information about pH test kits and how to purchase them, see the Resources on page 325.) When this was the case, our next step would be to investigate the types of thoughts they were regularly having, and the emotions that resulted from those thoughts. Sometimes the patients were very aware of being in a challenging situation and experiencing stress, fear, worry, and anger. Often, however, we would find that they were not thinking or feeling negatively on a conscious level, but were in fact focused on healing, loving, and forgiving, yet their systems were still running in an acidic condition. In these instances, underlying subconscious patterns were causing the acidity; to solve them, we employed the Clearing Code practices, B.E.S.T., and B.E.S.T. Release to clear out the subconscious emergencies below each patient's trapdoor and reset the "command center" of the thalamus/hypothalamus relationship.

The subconscious's role in body chemistry cannot be downplayed. The body must get the message that the emergency is over and it is now safe. Then we can actually relax when our intention is to relax. When we go on vacation, we can actually rejuvenate. The body can reside once again in restorative chemistry and we can actually self-heal.

The conscious mind can't always do this by understanding and forgiving past experiences, so we have to build new neurocircuitry with the Clearing Code energetic practices in order to begin to resolve those subconscious interferences, even if we don't know exactly what they are. The Chemistry Code adds another powerful resource, because when we optimize our body chemistry, the actions we take to increase our energy flow and open to our Soulful Self will be greatly enhanced and empowered.

If we can create the types of supportive, welcoming chemicals that are present in the body, our chemistry becomes a stabilizing factor. It becomes a consistently positive part of the feedback loop between our energy field and our body chemistry, and makes it easier for us to remain seated in the Soulful Self under a variety of external circumstances. In other words, we handle stresses better. This is true, by the way, whether we're in the Protective Personality or in the Soulful Self!

Our goal in the Chemistry Code is to produce a body chemistry "soup" that is equated with peace, harmony, joy, well-being, and self-healing. The more our internal chemicals are correlative to living in a state of wholeness, the greater the chance of our staying in a state of wholeness when our external circumstances change. Changing the state of our physical body makes the state of wholeness more tangible and allows us to anchor more of our energy in well-being, the true state in which we are meant to live.

The story of my client Barbara nicely illustrates this.

Knee pain, back pain, wrist pain, moodiness, lethargy, and abdominal bloating were only some of Barbara's symptoms. She also experienced depression, anxiety, and insomnia, and was unable to concentrate at work. She found herself overly sensitive about many things, to the point she just didn't want to participate in activities or relationships. At times she was close to giving up on life completely.

After just ten days of alkalizing her chemistry, Barbara's joint pain noticeably improved. Within three weeks, her anxiety was greatly settled, and she was sleeping through the night. Her mood swings and concentration issues also improved daily. "It's like I'm birthing a new person inside my body!" she said. A few weeks later, Barbara was fired from her job. She had not been particularly happy with her work conditions: her boss was inconsistent and inconsiderate of her many contributions to the business, often planning meetings and canceling them at the last minute, and she failed to respond to Barbara's recommendations for improving the company. Still, Barbara had not expected to be let go—via e-mail, no less. She was upset, since her job was both her livelihood and her expression in the world. "Thank God I've been on this alkalizing program, and thank God I know this work. I've never taken anything like this quite so well. In the past, something like this would have laid me out for weeks, or months," she said. Thanks to her stronger, more alkaline body chemistry, Barbara had a stronger sense of who she was in the world than ever before. Deep down, she had always known that that job wasn't her destiny, and now she knew that everything was unfolding in her favor. Her stability no longer came from outside of herself, but from within—which was a magnificent place to be!

In the Chemistry Code practices, we will work with body chemistry through food and thought/emotion to create the alkaline environment that is required for healing, wholeness, and true illumination of the Soulful Self. Here I will outline for you my Alkaline Ash Nutrition Program for optimum body pH and provide exercises to help you master the kinds of thoughts you think. You will quickly start to generate a balance in your body chemistry, especially when you continue to practice the rest of the Energy Codes.

Let's start with my nutrition program.

The Chemistry Code Practices

PRACTICE 1: ALKALINE ASH NUTRITION PROGRAM

The Alkaline Ash Nutrition Program specifies the foods that contribute to the body's ideal pH and hormonal balance for healing and cellular rejuvenation and revitalization. The longer we alkalize, the younger we get.

75 to 80 Percent Fresh Fruits and Vegetables

Ideally, we would eat many of our fruits and vegetables raw. If this is a challenge initially, begin slowly. The body may be too acidic at first, and not produce the proper amount of enzymes to digest a lot of raw foods. This is often the case in older people's digestive systems and in those who have abused with junk, fast, and fried foods for prolonged periods. But by beginning slowly, you establish a greater tolerance, even if you are older. I have seen the digestion of people in their nineties become younger within a few weeks or months by alkalizing their diets.

If there are fruits or vegetables that you cannot eat due to reactions or "allergies" (such as sores in the mouth, skin rashes or breakouts, or sinus reactions), eat the ones you can, since your reactions reveal that you are too acidic, and you therefore need the alkalizing effect of whichever raw foods you can tolerate. As you raise your pH, you will be able to tolerate more varieties. The body produces many of its enzymes on a supply-and-demand basis, so if these are new foods in your diet, eat them cooked first and they will be easier to tolerate. Still, remain open to your own transformation and the possibility of being able to eat more types and more alive foods soon. If you want your body to be more alive, you have to eat "alive" foods!

The foods you eat together also play a role in the body's ability to metabolize them, since different foods require different enzymes for digestion. And enzymes that digest certain foods can be impeded by other enzymes that work on other foods. For instance, the enzyme protease, which digests protein, calls for a different environment than the enzymes amylase, maltase, sucrase, and lactase, which digest carbohydrates. When protein and carbohydrates are eaten together, the enzymes render each other less effective than if each had been consumed alone or with other foods that are more easily digested together. Because of their high water content, melons are best eaten aside from heavier meals, as they dilute the enzymatic environment of digestion. They slow the digestive process, which is why you often feel uncomfortably full when you eat a piece of watermelon with your lunch. For the same reason, it is best to not consume large amounts of water or other fluids with your meals.

The following guidelines will help when you're experiencing joint inflammation, chronic sinus congestions, allergies, muscle pain, and many types of chronic headaches, or when your saliva pH tests low. They will aid your digestion and increase your alkaline reserves.

- Eat protein with vegetables, and not with starches.
- Eat starches with vegetables, and not with protein.
- Eat fruit by itself.
- Avoid dairy.

Whenever your pH tests low, significantly decrease animal protein until your pH rises and symptoms improve.

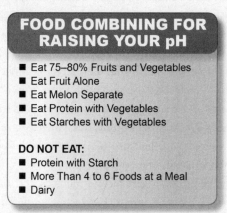

FOOD COMBINING FOR RAISING YOUR pH

- Eat 75–80% Fruits and Vegetables
- Eat Fruit Alone
- Eat Melon Separate
- Eat Protein with Vegetables
- Eat Starches with Vegetables

DO NOT EAT:
- Protein with Starch
- More Than 4 to 6 Foods at a Meal
- Dairy

Use this plan if your pH is too acidic and until it rises.

There are also times of the day that your system will respond best to digesting certain types of foods. From the early morning hours until about noon, your system digests fruits and vegetables most easily. When trying to alkalize, shift to eating less heavy protein at this time of the day. Your biggest meal is most easily digested in the middle of the day, from noon until about six or seven o'clock in the evening, when the body is in a *digestive* mode. The body then moves into an *assimilation* cycle, during which it benefits from all of the good nutrients you put into it that day and absorbs them into the cellular structure. This lasts until around three o'clock in the morning. During this time, your system begins working on *eliminating* all the toxins that were consumed that day and is still off-loading the by-products of digestion that are simply not serving you—the stuff you don't need to store—when you wake up in the morning and continues this cycle until about noon. Ideally, we would not eat after 7 or 8 p.m.

There are two reasons you might wake up in the early morning hours: One is that you may be consuming too many toxic or acidifying foods and thereby stressing the system during its elimination cycle by putting it into overload. The second is that, according to Eastern tradition regarding the development of consciousness, while in the elimination cycle you may be more available to higher-frequency energy and thus raising your level of consciousness at a subconscious and cellular level while the conscious mind is asleep. Because of this, oftentimes fasting was even recommended to further one's progress. I have guided many individuals through detoxification and cleansing programs that have helped them lose weight, raise their energetic vibration, and heal asthma, allergies, chronic headaches, back pain, colitis, ulcers, food sensitivities, hives, sleeplessness, irritability, food addictions, and other conditions. With these improved chemistries, your system may "want" you to wake up so that the conscious mind can be dialed into this new "vibrational radio station" and new circuits can be built.

So, never be upset when you wake up in the middle of the night, and don't fear that you will not be rested in the morning. Rather, gently begin Central Channel Breathing and scanning for densities to take advantage of this opportunity to raise your vibrational frequency. Then, during your waking hours, track your pH. If it is in the ideal range, you are raising your frequency. If not, make the changes necessary to bring your body chemistry into the ideal range so you can tune into this new vibratory frequency and bring more of your Soulful Self online. (For a demonstration of saliva pH testing, go to drsuemorter.com/energycodesbook, and see Resources on page 325 for information on obtaining pH test kits.)

pH Saliva Test - Interpreting the Results

pH	Color	Indications	Alkalinity	Dietary Suggestions
7.2 to 8.0	Blue to Blue	Worry, Anxiety, Headed for Body Exhaustion	Reserve is Available	Can Add Rice or Cereals if you are a Vegetarian
8.0 to 6.4	Blue to Green/Yellow	Trouble Ahead, Chronic Stress	Some Reserve is Still Available	More Vegetables, Brown Rice
6.4 to 5.5	Green to Yellow	Trouble Ahead, Chronic Stress	Some Reserve is Still Available	More Vegetables, Brown Rice
6.8 to 8.0+	Green to Blue	Preferred Response, Handling Stress Well	Reserve Levels are Adequate	75% Fruits & Vegetables, 25% Meats & Grains
5.5 to 5.5	Yellow to Yellow	Must Make Immediate Changes	Reserve is gone or Not Being Utilized	Gradually Add Only Cooked Vegetables
5.5 to 6.4 - 8.0	Yellow to Green/Blue	Not the Best, Not the Worst	Reserve is Okay. Body is Stressed	Less Meat & Dairy, Add Fruits & Vegetables
6.2 to 6.8	Green to Green	Less Desirable	Reserve is Available	Add Cooked Vegetables, Less Meat, Some Fruit

(IDEAL — marked alongside the "6.8 to 8.0+" row)

See video link for more instructions and recommendations on pH Testing.

Instructions

- Do not eat or drink anything, other than water, for _2 hours_ prior to testing saliva pH.

- Tear off a 1" strip and pool saliva under your tongue. Dip pH paper in it without touching your tongue. Do not touch the end you will put in your mouth.

- Compare the color of the strip to the chart on the paper dispenser _immediately_. The color will change even after a few seconds. Write the number down.

- Place in your mouth the juice of 1/2 a lemon and taste it throughout your entire mouth.

- Swallow four times to remove the lemon juice, then repeat the pH test with saliva under your tongue. Recheck the color of the strip _immediately_. Write the number down.

- Ideal Numbers: **6.8 1st number**
                     8.0 2nd number

Energy Codes Allowances

If, as you start to do this work, you get cravings for foods that we now know are acidifying, do not assume that you are undisciplined, because there is actually a deeper reason for your cravings. It has to do with that universal expanding-and-anchoring, expanding-and-anchoring cycle I've talked about that happens as we evolve. When we begin to integrate and change our body chemistry soup, an expansion may occur in our energy field—meaning that some part of our field jumps to a higher vibrational frequency with a corresponding expansion in consciousness. Suddenly we don't really recognize ourselves because we're thinking higher-frequency thoughts than usual. Our minds are opening up, and we feel unfamiliar to ourselves on a deep cellular and vibrational level.

When this happens, our subconscious starts looking for a way to feel more grounded and connected to familiar energy. The result is that we crave "comfort foods" that lower our vibration so our body and mind feel more at home. These "anchoring foods" tend to be heavy foods like meats and dairy, fatty foods like ice cream and fried foods, and stimulatory foods like sugars and starchy carbs. Not only are they energetically denser, these foods also have an acidifying effect on the body, and that acidity drops the vibrational frequency of our energy. (Even though sugar revs us up, which may seem expansive, that expansion only lasts for a short time. The long-term by-product of eating sugar is increased cellular activity, which produces acidity, so we end up with an acid-ash condition, which drops our vibration.)

Mechanics aside, what I really want you to know is that these cravings are *normal*. And if you allow yourself to have a craved food at a particular time, it will not only stop the craving but can even facilitate the anchoring and integration of what you've just expanded into on an energetic level. So consciously indulging in your cravings can actually keep you moving forward in your integration process. However, you'll note that I did say *consciously*! When we indulge in comfort foods unconsciously, two things often happen to throw us off track or make us backslide. When we indulge without awareness, we feel like we've "fallen off the wagon," and start to beat ourselves up. We tell ourselves that we're weak, and that we have no willpower, discipline, or self-love. This kind of self-criticism throws us right back into the Protective Personality, which wastes a ton of time and energy and really slows our momentum. If we have a different, more conscious way of interpreting what's happening, we won't blame or abuse ourselves; this is key to our forward progress.

Unconsciously indulging in cravings for too long also sets us back. We run the risk of surrendering emotionally to the idea that we are never going to be able to eat right and take good care of ourselves. For this reason, you want to be vigilant about how long the allowance period goes on. The body works in three-, seven-, and twenty-one-day cycles. If a craving or eating pattern continues for more than three days, then you need to have your eye on the seven-day mark as the stopping point. Keep working with the Codes you've learned to help you stay grounded and anchored throughout that seven-day period. You don't want to take a twenty-one-day cycle to get the anchoring done. This is important because many studies show that a habit takes root at the twenty-one-day mark; if you stay in a craving/acid-ash eating pattern for that long, it's going to be harder to get out of the cycle.

Ideally, when you feel that you want these comfort foods, you indulge—but only a little, and in a managed way. The rest of your grounding happens when you dig deeper into the breathwork, prescribed yoga asanas, and other practices of the Energy Codes. This balance has the further benefit of creating a habit around seeking comfort from the only place from which it truly and sustainably comes: being in the Soulful Self. In the long run, comfort from any external source—food or otherwise—might work in the moment, but it never lasts.

PRACTICE 2: CONSCIOUS EXERCISE

Another way to build positive body chemistry and create an ideal environment for the Soulful Self to move into is to engage in intentional, conscious physical exercise.

Often when people exercise, they're not fully present within their body. Many people distract themselves by listening to music or watching TV as they pound it out on the treadmill or weight machine; they take their mind elsewhere so their body can work more intensely for longer periods of time. They say, "It helps me get my workout done."

If you do Central Channel Breathing while you exercise, you will actually pare down the time needed to get the same—or better—results. I've trained professional athletes, triathletes, and adventure racing champions to break their own records simply by breathing through the central channel as they worked out. By breathing up and down the central channel with conscious intention as you exercise or train, you can go farther, faster, without fatiguing. This is because when you bring awareness to the Soulful Self, you actually start to draw from a greater source of energy. I call exercising in this intentional way Conscious Exercise.

If you move the body and intentionally use the breath at the same time, you start to build circuitry that connects the conscious concentration (mind), movement (body), and breath (spirit). This is the same unification of mind, body, and breath that our great ancient Eastern teachers spoke of thousands of years ago, and it creates real shifts in body chemistry in a relatively short period of time.

When done with this awareness, yoga is truly the perfect example of Conscious Exercise. BodyAwake Yoga brings this conscious element of Central Channel Breathing and mental focus together with traditional postures. If you aren't drawn to yoga, however, there are plenty of other ways to do Conscious Exercise and build circuits for the Soulful Self. Other regular types of exercise, such as calisthenics, jogging, and lifting weights, can be made conscious by adding Central Channel Breathing in specific ways, which I teach in detail in my coursework. For a video demonstration of Conscious Exercise, go to drsuemorter.com/energycodesbook. (See the Resources on page 325 for additional sources of Conscious Exercise instruction.)

On the following page is a diagram of a common exercise, weight lifting, showing the flow of energy moving through the central channel as you inhale or exhale.

1. When lifting the weight, breathe up from the earth, through *mūla bandha* and into the core.

2. As you release the weight, exhale through the central channel and out the top of your head.

3. Now reverse this, starting with an inhale through the top of your head.

4. Repeat, breathing through the channel with each repetition of your exercise.

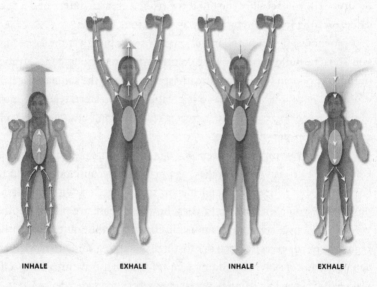

INHALE   EXHALE   INHALE   EXHALE

CONSCIOUS EXERCISE

I've taught hundreds of patients and clients to move energy through the body while exercising this way. The results are astounding. Not only does your daily workout become more enjoyable because you can actually feel, in the body, an immediate uplifting and strengthening effect, but you also have greater, sustained energy *all the time.* And, of course, by adding this to your Energy Codes regimen, you exponentially accelerate the transformation across your entire life.

PRACTICE 3: CHEMISTRY THROUGH THOUGHT

This exercise uses your thinking to intentionally cultivate an alkaline body chemistry. You focus on positive, high-frequency thoughts, and recognize and reframe any recurring low-frequency thoughts that contribute to an acidic state. This compounds your efforts in other areas to create healthy body chemistry and promotes both a physically beneficial environment for your cells and an energetically sound "home" for your Soulful Self.

1. Begin with Central Channel Breathing, tethering your anchor points.

2. Now focus on a victorious moment in your life—a moment where you triumphed over something challenging and that felt like a really big win. Recall it in detail, and notice how the energy moves in your body in response. Maybe you lit up above your head or around your shoulders, or your heart expanded. Gently squeeze that area to draw the mind's attention to it in a focused manner.

3. Now sit in that pattern and gently breathe up and down through the channel until that same vibrational sensation can be felt throughout your whole system—in other words, until what you were feeling in your heart, head, or throat (or wherever the sensation was) can now also be felt in your belly, hips, legs, and so on. You want to get your whole body to open and fill with that same sensation.

This is a reflective, meditative breathing practice. You are generating an open state so the whole system can resonate at the same vibrational frequency, because that vibration contributes to the body chemistry. You want the whole body to be involved in a victorious vibration. You want to *embody* it.

You can do the same practice with other even higher-vibration frequencies, such as inspiration, love, and joy. Tuning into different positive "radio stations" this way and embodying their individual frequencies is how we start to work with influencing body chemistry through thought.

Note that this isn't the same as "positive thinking," which by itself does not heal you. Thinking positively—even if the trapdoor between the conscious and subconscious is *open*—merely keeps you from thinking *negatively*, which would interfere with your body's natural healing process. (If the trapdoor is closed, our conscious thoughts have very little impact on our health and well-being.) Although you *are* focusing the mind positively in this practice, you're doing more than just thinking positive thoughts, saying affirmations, and dreaming dreams with the mind alone. You're bringing the *vibrations* of those things into the whole body in a big way—a way that raises the vibrational frequency of the tissues and "wakes you up" in there, and anchors it where it can much more strongly influence who you are and who you become.

You can also use this exercise to meld a *how* with a *yes*—to meld the possibility of a dream with the *feeling* that you can actually have that dream. Often our goals or dreams feel bigger than we are. We want them, but almost instantaneously think, "Who am I to think I can have that?" and "How can I possibly achieve it?" But if we don't believe something—if we don't "own" it—it means we're not tapped into the energy of it or that its energy is not really *alive* inside us. And, as we now know, if it's not there, in our core and in our energy field, either it won't happen at all or it won't last. Our manifestations become sustainable when we more than believe them, when we feel them and *are* them in our subtle energy and physical bodies. To get there, we need to embody the vibration of our dream and shift our energy flow into the pattern of what will create our desired outcome. This exercise will help.

To meld a *how* with a *yes*:

1. Sit and imagine "Yes!" Just that single word, as if the whole universe is saying "Yes!" to you, as if there's nothing but a big "Yes!" going on. It will be as if you are in the biggest state of acceptance and fulfillment possible—a hugely expanded state where you feel complete and whole.

2. Sitting in your best "Yes," notice how the energy feels in your body, how it flows. Is there some area that pulls your energy in one direction or another? Perhaps there's a big, round expansion, or a lighter feeling that happens everywhere.

3. Now think of a goal you have. Since it's still a goal and not something already manifested, I'm going to assume that when you think of it, your energy is going to shift. This could mean that there is some subconscious interference associated with the goal that's preventing you from having it. Perhaps it has to do with believing it's going to be hard, or that something so wonderful could never happen to you. Whatever the belief, the sensation you're getting is somehow different from a flat-out "Yes!"

4. Note the body's energy pattern of this desire for a goal. Anchor it in your awareness by taking note of what has a charge and where the energy is accentuated.

5. Go back to the "Yes!" pattern. Then slowly switch back and forth between them, allowing the two patterns to begin to connect with each other in your awareness. Soon they will find each other completely and carve a pathway of photon flow that includes the goal and the "Yes!" in the same energetic pattern. The body will then begin to adapt to the combined patterns and recognize this as a familiar way of being.

This exercise helps you master the tendency to hesitate when you have a dream but don't know how it is ever going to manifest, by carving an energetic pathway toward the manifestation of your greatest "Yes!"

Know that your dreams belong to you; they are a part of you. If they weren't, you would be dreaming of something different. They are "meant to be" when they serve your highest good. And whatever your intentions, wishes, and dreams are, always remember that everything happens in the body first!

PRACTICE 4: ENERGY CODES BRAIN YOGA

Yoga is about moving particular areas of the body at the same time that we're focused on that area of the body, with conscious breath. Amazingly, the same can be done to enliven the tissues of the brain, using what I call Brain Yoga.

Because the messaging that comes from the high-brain centers, and from the Cave of Brahma, is so key to the chemical balance of the body (among other things), we want to activate and enliven the tissues in this area and get them communicating with each other more effectively. We do this by "exercising" them—moving them and taking breaths while we're doing it. This wakes up areas of the brain and contributes to our ability to realize who we are as the Soulful Self.

The one general guideline for this exercise is that, when you move your eyes, you want to do so *without* moving your head. Here are the steps for doing the Energy Codes Brain Yoga:

1. With your nose pointing straight forward and your chin parallel to the floor, roll your eyes up as high as you are physically comfortable doing, as if trying to look at the ceiling. You'll immediately feel some tension behind the eyes.

2. Next, squeeze your other anchor points—*mūla bandha*, your heart, your throat—all while keeping your eyes rolled up. (You'll want to keep your anchor points contracted through the entire exercise.)

3. Take a deep breath in from the earth and bring that breath up through the central channel into your core. Do it in a relaxed way and just let it feel good. Then, from your core, exhale straight up through the central channel into that tension behind the eyes and out the top of the head.

4. Now imagine there's a giant clock on the wall. As your eyes are looking straight up, think of that as being at twelve o'clock. Now

roll your eyes to the one o'clock position. Looking at one o'clock, take a deep breath in from overhead down through where you now feel the tension behind the eyes, down through the central channel into the core. From the core, exhale through *mūla bandha* and down into the earth.

5. Now move your eyes to two o'clock. Draw the breath from the earth end of the channel up into the core. As you exhale from there up through the channel, feel the new tension behind the eyes and complete the exhalation, imagining it going out the top of your head.

6. Move your eyes to three o'clock and repeat the steps above, taking a breath from overhead down into the body, squeezing the anchor points, and exhaling down through the body in a belly breath.

7. Continue in the same fashion around the whole clock, one "hour" at a time.

8. Once you've completed the clock, end with an exercise known as *nadi shodhana* (*nadi* meaning "channel" or "flow" and *shodhana* meaning "purification" in Sanskrit). Place your index finger on your third eye, and use your thumb and second finger to alternate holding one nostril at a time closed. With the right nostril open, breathe in. Then close the right nostril, open the left, and breathe out. Then breathe in left, close, and breathe out right. End on an exhale out the right nostril. Repeat the full cycle six times.

Ideally, you'll want to do this Brain Yoga exercise a total of four times—once clockwise and once counterclockwise with eyes open, then again in each direction with eyes closed. And though you don't have to do all four options every time, I do recommend that once you begin the exercise, you go through all of the hours in one direction rather than stopping after just a few. And do one rotation in the opposite direction for balance.

Once you finish this exercise and you look neutrally straight ahead, you'll immediately feel something different happening in the center of your head. You'll have a greater sense of Self or subject—of being the presence inside yourself that is looking out at the world. Brain Yoga also activates the key areas of the brain we want to enliven—the areas in and around this third ventricle area called the Cave of Brahma, which increases circulation and the flow of electromagnetic energy, fostering an optimal environment for the creation of healthy body-chemistry "soup." In the same way that practicing the piano brings progressively greater sensory and motor dexterity to the fingers, this exercise builds sensory and motor communication in that key area of the brain.

The Chemistry Code Chakra Correlation: The Third Eye

The Chemistry Code is correlated to the sixth chakra, located in the center of the forehead, above and between the eyebrows. Known for its qualities of intuition, higher wisdom, clairvoyance, and inspiration, this energy center is also referred to as the third eye. In Sanskrit, it is known as *ājñā chakra*—literally, "command." It's no coincidence that this chakra is associated with the pineal and pituitary glands, which, as we learned in this chapter, are housed in the centers of the brain (the Cave of Brahma) and manage the chemistry of the body and the awakening of consciousness. The nutritional recommendations and mental and physical exercises prescribed in this Code are instrumental in activating these glands, and in stabilizing the third eye chakra and raising the body's energetic vibration for health, vitality, and empowerment. Here we merge the worlds of heaven (pineal) and earth (pituitary) by blending their energies. Integration is how we are able to develop our sixth sense, as we are intended to do over the course of our lives.

People who have third eye–chakra issues literally cannot "see" clearly what is happening inside and around them. They may ignore signals from their body about where energy or body chemistry needs to be corrected or might be blinded to low-vibration thought or relationship patterns that are creating stress in the body. They might have trouble trusting their inner knowing—the messages that are coming from the hypothalamus about what is happening in the body and energy field. They may have headaches, eye issues, or dizziness. They might struggle with depression or addictive behaviors because of compromised body chemistry and less ability to self-regulate.

The following chart summarizes some of the key characteristics of the sixth chakra. Again, notice how the energetic properties of the chakra mirror the physical body areas.

The Chemistry Code Chakra Correlation: Third Eye Chakra

NAME(S)	Sixth chakra, *ajñā chakra*
LOCATION	Inward from the center of forehead toward the middle of the brain, above and between the eyebrows
COLOR	Indigo
MUSICAL NOTE	A
BODY AREAS AFFECTED	Eyes, base of skull, ears, nose, left eye, left brain, sinuses, ***pituitary gland***, and ***pineal gland***
"BACK SIDE" SYMPTOMS	Nightmares, hallucinations, headaches, learning difficulties, poor vision, neurological issues, glaucoma
"FRONT SIDE" CHARACTERISTICS	Charisma, high intuition, healthy perspective, freedom from attachment, generating insightful creations, perceiving beyond the five senses, seeing the meaning "behind the scenes." "I am the one behind the eyes."
PRACTICES	• Alkaline Ash Nutrition Program • Conscious Exercise • Chemistry Through Thought • Energy Codes Brain Yoga
BREATHWORK (as explained in Chapter 8)	Visionary Breath
YOGA POSES FOR GREATER INTEGRATION	• Downward Dog (*adho mukha śvānāsana*) • Shoulderstand (*salamba sarvāṅgāsana*) • Child's Pose (*bālāsana*) • Exalted Warrior (*viparīta vīrabhadrāsana*), also called Warrior 4 • Balancing Poses

Along with the practices in this Code, the following yoga postures help to integrate and balance this energy center.

Yoga for the Chemistry Code

Downward Dog Pose is possibly the quintessential yoga pose. It's one of the first that new students learn, and one of the most common in any practice or lineage. Children do it naturally while playing. It inherently integrates the soul toward life on Earth. It's also highly beneficial for the third eye because it directs energy, attention, and blood flow to the brain.

DOWNWARD DOG POSE (*ADHO MUKHA ŚVĀNĀSANA*)

Here's how to practice Downward Dog Pose:

1. Start on hands and knees on your mat. Place your hands shoulder-width apart, with index and middle fingers pointing forward. Ground your whole hand into the mat so you can feel all five fingers and your palm in full contact with the earth.

2. With legs hip-width apart, tuck your toes under, and slowly lift your hips up and back. Straighten your legs as much as possible so that your body becomes an inverted V. Feel the ball mounds of your feet and all your toes grounded on the mat. (If your heels reach the floor, ground them as well, along with the whole outer edge of each foot.) Make sure the toes are facing the front of your mat or turned slightly inward.

3. Straighten your arms and allow your shoulder blades to slide away from your ears, broadening the tops of the shoulders. Rotate the inner elbows gently toward the ceiling so that both hands stay fully connected to the mat.

4. Tuck your chin slightly, without rounding your upper back, to align your cervical spine (neck) with the rest of your spine. Look toward your navel.

5. Hold for at least sixty seconds (or for as long as possible).

6. To come out, shift your gaze to your hands. Bend your knees, and gently lower yourself back to the floor.

Now let's integrate BodyAwake Yoga practices while in Downward Dog Pose.

1. While holding Downward Dog, imagine your feet anchoring into a reservoir of energy within the earth, two feet below your mat. Plug into that energy by grounding all four corners of each foot. (If it helps, you can lift your toes to connect the ball mounds of your feet more firmly to the mat, then lay them back down.)

2. Activate your legs. If your legs are straight, lift your kneecaps and thigh muscles, and plug the heads of your femurs into your hip sockets. If your knees are bent, simply hug all the muscles of your legs around the bones. Feel everything activated.

3. Squeeze *mūla bandha*. Breathe energy up through your legs and into your core from beyond the bottoms of your feet, like the Thousand Tiny Straws Breath from the Breath Code. Fill your core with energy as you inhale. Ground your hands into the mat, but don't let your shoulder blades shrink up toward your ears. Squeeze the area around your heart, wrapping the muscles around the sides of your ribs (latissimus dorsi) toward the center of your chest. Feel how this connects your hands even more firmly to the earth.

4. Roll your eyes firmly up to feel the tension behind them as you exhale out the top of the head—but also through the arms and into the earth beyond the hands.

5. On your next inhalation, keep your eyes rolled up, and breathe from two feet beyond the top of your head as well as from two feet below where your hands connect to the mat. Let the breath move through the head and the center of the brain, the throat, and the chest; simultaneously, let the breath move up the arms,

through the shoulders, and into the heart. Then let the commingled breath move all the way into the belly. Squeeze the heart and let it feel good!

6. On your exhalation, squeeze *mūla bandha* and exhale out through the tip of the spine and down through the legs and feet, keeping the legs fully engaged and all four corners of the feet pressing into the earth.

ADDITIONAL YOGA POSES TO INTEGRATE THE THIRD EYE CHAKRA

You can use these asanas along with Downward Dog Pose to enhance your work with the Chemistry Code. Remember that squeezing areas to which you want to draw attention is beneficial, but afterward so is relaxing in the poses. Use your best judgment to work with the Breath Code practices in each of these poses.

- Shoulderstand (*salamba sarvāṅgāsana*)
- Child's Pose (*bālāsana*)
- Exalted Warrior (*viparīta vīrabhadrāsana*), also called Warrior 4
- Balancing Poses

––––––––

You've learned a great deal about your authentic nature and how to release and/or integrate anything keeping you from experiencing yourself as who you really are. You've learned to process thoughts, emotions, and even food in a way that promotes the expression and expansion of your Soulful Self.

In the next, final Energy Code—the Spirit Code—you'll see what it's like to have connected with your core, essential self and then to live life with that connection intact.

Chapter 10

THE SPIRIT CODE:

WHERE THE MANY BECOME ONE

Many years ago, after I'd already been working with the Energy Codes practices for some time and was seeing incredible physical healing and mental and emotional shifts for myself and my students, I felt compelled to delve into a daily yoga practice. To my delight, I found that the yoga actually accelerated my ability to bring my circuitry online and to interpret and integrate information about my body chemistry, my energy field, and my Soulful Self.

Whenever I was in a yoga pose and felt tension in an area of my body, I would make contact with the tissues in that area by squeezing them. Then I would take a breath "through" them. Though in yoga class I'd been instructed to breathe "into" an area of tension, breathing "through" turned out to be very different, as it built connective circuitry of communication that nothing I had been doing previously addressed. When I did this, I found that the tension would release immediately and I could go farther into the pose with greater strength, stamina, and ease. My body felt lighter even as it was becoming stronger.

One day I got up early and drove half an hour to the yoga studio where I'd been practicing. My intention was to take a class from a particular teacher whose methods I especially enjoyed. When I arrived, I saw that that teacher wasn't there, and that a substitute teacher would be leading the class. I was disappointed! Even though I'd been practicing and teaching the Energy Codes principles, I got caught up in predetermination, anticipation, and expectation on the drive—and I felt let down when I realized things weren't going to go as planned.

I'd taken a class with this teacher before, and simply hadn't enjoyed it as much. It wasn't that his class wasn't good; it was just that his pace was considerably slower than I wanted at the time. In the first few minutes of the class, I found myself frustrated, thinking, *This is* not *what I need today!* Then, about ten minutes in, I thought, *Sue, this is ridiculous. It's 6 a.m. You've been up since five, and driven half an hour to be here. You're either going to spend the next hour being completely frustrated, or you're going to surrender into this and remember that everything that happens is in support of you.* With that thought, I released into the slower intentional pace of the class.

As I slowed my breath to the pace of the instruction and dropped into my core, I recognized that the movement we were being guided through held something new and beneficial for me. As we moved through a repetitive flow of three different positions, my mind was able to release into complete *presence*, both inside myself and in the room. I was listening to the instructor, but at the same time I was also extraordinarily attuned to the deep, core, internal version of myself.

Suddenly I could perceive a misty white substance suspended inside my body. If I closed my eyes, I could "see" this energy fashioning itself into a pattern that corresponded to the pose my body was holding. Then, as I slowly initiated movement into the next pose, the misty substance would begin to move with the intention—and if I settled myself enough, it would actually lead me into exhilarating details of the pose that I had never experienced or heard instructed. Then its powerful presence would lead my system into the next pose with a sense of wisdom. I felt at the cellular level that this was where the origins of yoga had started; something internally just "knew" it. The poses were being guided by our essence, and by placing ourselves in the poses intentionally, we could more easily find that state of being that would tap into this ancient wisdom.

I was witnessing a spiritual version of myself and wanted to just stop moving and be present with it—yet I knew that what had brought this energy into my awareness was the perfect combination of my focus, intention, *surrender*, breath, and the movement of my body, and I wanted to keep that happening! I found myself slowing down, not quite keeping up with the instructor's cues, because I didn't want to lose focus on what was happening inside me. Ironically, I found that the instructor who'd been teaching a class that was too slow for me now seemed to be teaching too fast.

The situation illustrates perfectly how we must embrace the pace of life and the speed with which things are delivered to us, trust what is happening, and collaborate in its perfection. By doing so we actively begin to use the chakras and the significant components of the Cave of Brahma and other high-brain centers, which contribute to our ability to operate as creators, truly living in the spiritual vibration of oneness. We are internally aware of what's arising at the same time that we're trusting and working with our external life as it unfolds. When we learn to breathe, stay present, and honor both the inner world and the outer world simultaneously, we begin to move with ease through life as the Soulful Self.

Thinking about that yoga class later, I realized that, through the collaboration of mind, body, breath, and movement, I had been able to experience a subtle and comprehensive version of myself that had formerly been accessible only through the complete stillness of meditation. Additional circuits were coming online for me that were allowing me to perceive more of my own subtle energy frequency—and this vibrational frequency *generated* the new circuit-building process automatically, without my conscious effort. Previously, any distraction (such as the yoga teacher's cues or the others in the room) would have dispersed my concentration slightly, and I would not have been able to pick up on such a subtle reality of dialing into a different "radio station." But most exciting was that, if I could find that level of integration, *I could teach others to do the same.*

After this event, I began teaching my students how to dial into the misty white spirit-like substance and to drop into that deep sense of self while in motion. Soon they were able to have deeper perceptions on and off the yoga mat. It was simply a matter of training the mind to perceive that we are tangible spirit beings, and that the reality of our true nature can be visible to us.

What Is the Spirit Code?

I often meet people who say, "I'm not very spiritual." This is impossible, because we are *made* of spirit. Spirit is energy. Spirit in the body is breath. True spirituality is more tangible than religious or mystical. It's our daily, minute-by-minute merging of our mind, body, and energy into one unified force—the Soulful Self.

When we engage with ourselves in this unifying way, and take action from that place of unity, "spirituality" becomes something that we experience, express, and live. It becomes inseparable from who we are. When we allow our gut feelings or intuition to guide the mind, we are living spiritual lives. When we realize that we are not being guided by spiritual energy, but rather that we *are* that spiritual energy—that spirit is the "real" us, not something we find or use—we take action as *spiritual beings.*

The Spirit Code anchors this truth for us by giving us tools to readily connect with the deep core wisdom that is rising in our body's system all the time. In this Code, we go beyond sensing and managing our energy, and we focus the mind in such a way that it stops perceiving that energy as separate from itself. Like two people who spend so much time together that they start finishing each other's sentences, no physical cue from one to the other is required to achieve harmony; they both reside in the same stream of consciousness.

This is our ultimate goal: to get to a place where the mind and the spirit collaborate so intimately and so consistently that they become one. This oneness *is* the Quantum Flip. It is a complete infusion of the Soulful Self into the Protective Personality, where the mind and body take their proper place as servants to the soul, which expresses itself in this world through them. The result of this merging is a soulful personality that lovingly, powerfully engages with life. Rather than trying to achieve, control, or please others, we now know that we're good as we are, and that life is not only safe but always unfolding to our benefit. In fact, we don't have to think much about it at all; life is simply ours for living. In this relaxed place, we're able to be present and available to whatever comes our way, regardless of the pace at which it is delivered. More, we are able to create rather than look for better ways to respond; we can generate life experiences without hesitation or second-guessing, and those experiences in turn reveal even more about our essential nature and our true purpose for being here.

While living in the Protective Personality, we focus our five senses externally, and occasionally have hunches or gut feelings. But as we retract our attention to the inner world, we perceive that a deeper truth is revealing itself *all the time*. Arising from the second chakra up through the central channel, this truth has been available to us all along, but our mind has been too distracted by thinking about how life is "supposed" to go to actually perceive it.

As the mind starts to hook into that soulful reality and trust it profoundly, it more quickly perceives and translates these constantly arising evolutionary impulses. Soon every thought, action, and response is underwritten by a deeper knowing. Our responses become collaborations, essentially cocreating and manifesting new possibilities. This is what we're cultivating with the Energy Codes—building more circuitry for sensing these impulses until perceiving them becomes natural and instinctual, and they become "louder" to the mind than all external cues. Then we solidify this dynamic even more by consciously choosing to act (or to *not* act) based on the soulful communication the mind receives. Living life in this way, according to our own inherent wisdom and truth, *is* living as the Soulful Self.

I've taught and traveled for thirty years, and spoken to tens of thousands of people, and I've never heard even one person say that he or she regretted going with a gut feeling. I *have* heard hundreds of times that someone had a gut feeling and overrode it, and later said: "Boy, do I regret it!" We should "do the math"!

We've all had moments when we didn't know what to do. If we had been able to direct our attention into our core, we likely would have felt an impulse rising that would have guided us along our highest path. But we weren't trained to direct our attention that way, and so we couldn't perceive that gut feeling. Instead, we probably made a decision based on the Protective Personality's limited mental, emotional, or sensory information. The results of such choices vary, but they are not usually the ones to which we would have been directed had we had access to our full inner knowing. With the Spirit Code, we move toward total integration of body, mind, and spirit, where our direction is clear and certain, and where instructions come to us effortlessly, as needed, from within—because that is where we live.

Even when you have fully integrated your mind, body, breath, and energy, however, you will still occasionally look for a gut feeling . . . and it's simply not there. You can't sense any impulse; it just feels blank and dark inside, like a void. There's a very good reason for this, so don't start telling yourself an old story that you are inept, inadequate, or lacking in any way, thereby thwarting your ability to follow your truth. The reason is that you're inside the Void of Creation.

STEPPING INTO THE VOID OF CREATION

Many people believe that the life experience progresses in a straight line. But, actually, it unfolds in more of a circle—in multiple circles, in fact, which, if stacked on top of each other, would look like an ascending spiral. With each trip around the circle, we complete a *cycle* that brings us to a higher vantage point, closer to our potential for wholeness. This is how we evolve. I call these systems the Cycle of Life and the larger Cycle of Evolution. As one cycle completes, it moves us upward to the next round of evolving experience.

The cycle has three phases or parts. First, we *create*. We get a new impulse, a new inspiration, and take initiative to make it real. In this phase, we bring something new into the world—a business, a relationship, a child, a work of art, or a piece of music. Next is the *sustain* phase, where the "project" is serving its purpose and we're gleaning the benefits from it. Here, we're contributing, feeling alive, and possibly even having abundance and success. Then, once the project has run its course and served its purpose, we have a sense of fulfillment or completion and a need to move on. If we're not attached to what we've experienced in the *sustain* cycle, we'll be more easily able to move through the final phase, *deconstruct,* where the project comes to a close and we must let go in order to begin a new cycle.

Not surprisingly, the *deconstruct* phase is the one we typically have

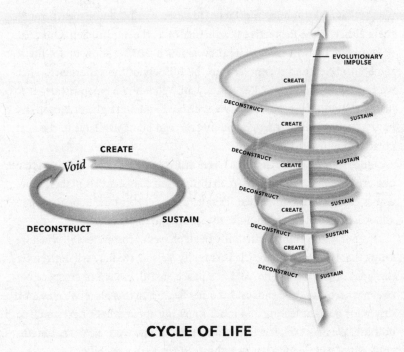

CYCLE OF LIFE

trouble with. If we're not aware that we're in a cycle and that our next new beginning is just around the bend—when we can't see beyond the place we're currently standing—it can be hard to let go. This is especially true if we haven't been fully present with our deep truth as we went through the cycle, and if we haven't recognized how it contributed to our evolution and expansion.

We can see this reluctance to let go most clearly in relationships. How many times have you stayed in a romantic partnership, friendship, or work relationship for too long? How many times have you been reluctant to part ways, even when you knew that doing so would be for your highest good? When we build something, we want it to last forever. But although love lasts forever, perceptions in the physical world last only until their cycles are complete.

Going around the cycle isn't optional. We can't choose to avoid the phases that make us uncomfortable. However, we *can* choose to go through them either as the Protective Personality or as the Soulful Self. Our goal, of course, is to awaken our circuitry so much that we show up for life as the Soulful Self and surrender into the fullness of the experience. Then we can say, "I showed up, I gave it my all. Whatever happens is meant to happen." If, on the other hand, we withhold and don't give it our all, we have a harder time letting go, moving on, and being available to the next creative impulse that arises.

Once we recognize that this Cycle of Evolution is happening and that our creative nature is always rebirthing itself here on this planet, it becomes easier to recognize that it's safe to just let this flow happen, and to allow each evolutionary impulse to rise up and to perceive it.

Even if we do embrace life fully in all phases of the cycle, and when we know that the end of one cycle isn't really *the* end, we may still encounter the Void of Creation. The Void is a pause, a stillness, an open space between where one cycle ends and another begins. In this place, we may look inside for our gut feeling and inner knowing about what's next and find nothing. We may even feel like we don't know who we are. We are untethered, out of a cycle for a few heartbeats, floating in possibility.

This is normal. When we reach the Void, it's because we have come to the edge of an old boundary, surpassed it, and stepped into an as-yet unexamined part of ourselves. We have no point of reference yet, even as the Soulful Self, so our intuition can't yet direct us. We need to get comfortable sitting in the Void, in the unknown, and learn to surrender to it as we ready ourselves for the next round of creation. Some ancient Eastern traditions state that *everything* is simultaneously present. The sound of AUM (*Oṁ*), the sound of *all* vibrations combined, and *nada*, the "inner sound," its corresponding silence, together represent the Void. When we are comfortable here in this "nothingness," we are available for the Quantum Flip into our fullest expression of Self.

This is vital to learn because, paradoxically, the Void is made of abundance! It is impossible to identify any particular thing within it because nothing is missing or absent. Our job, therefore, is to assign meaning and identity to what is in this vastness—in other words, to create what we desire from a smorgasbord of possibilities!

The practices and tools in this chapter will help you stop hanging on to attachments from the past and move gracefully through the Void and into the next creative phase of your life. The more easily you can do this, the more easily you will stay anchored in the nature of the Soulful Self and build energy circuits for expressing your true self. Fear, questioning, or uncertainty will not pull you back into the Protective Personality. Ultimately, the Spirit Code is about learning to live in a state of grace, to trust that your life is unfolding as it needs to, and to immediately see whatever is happening as beneficial and as a guide to your continued growth. Through embracing all of your experiences, rather than suffering, grieving, doubting, or otherwise fighting the natural cycle of life, you can grow and integrate more quickly, and manifest more of what you really want.

This Code's strategies will still the overactive mind and tune into the Soulful Self, become truly present with it, and identify as its constantly rising impulses. This Code takes us beyond where the general study of energy medicine has gone so far. We will identify with our energy, live from it, and create a very different reality. The more we know that there is no separation—that we're actually made of spiritual energy, that we *are* it—the more we can identify *as* it and the sooner we can take action without having a second thought about it—without questioning, doubting, or having to ask others for their consensus before we feel safe to move into something new. When we are consciously translating the information from the spirit self and rolling it into physical life, we invite Heaven to Earth. We become true Creators, living in HeavenEarth—where there is no separation of the two.

This is what the Spirit Code offers. Here are its practices.

The Spirit Code Practices

PRACTICE 1: DISCOVERING YOUR MEDITATION STYLE

To train the mind to acknowledge that its job is to steward the real you, it has to *start listening to* the real you. This "you" we are seeking is the you who exists as your deep, true, authentic Soulful Self—the one you know yourself, in your heart of hearts, to be. To live your truest and most fulfilling life, your mind needs to serve this version of yourself constantly and consistently, always referencing it. In order to do that, you have to teach the mind that its job is not just to think thoughts all the time; it needs to slow down for long enough to do its real job—perceiving what the real you is revealing.

You can do this by spending some time every day interrupting the mind in its current habit of obsessive thinking. Ultimately, remember that the mind—like a puppy—is trained through repetition, yet the energy field can change in an instant. Your objective is to instruct the two to work together for efficient lasting change. You don't have to do this training for long periods, but initially you do have to practice it regularly. The best way to begin to slow the rapid-moving ceiling fan of the thinking mind into collaboration is through meditation.

In meditation, we retract our focus from the external world and turn it inward to listen to the true us, the Soulful Self. It's similar to what we've already been practicing in the Energy Codes; only now, instead of perceiving the energy field (as though it's something separate from us), we are focused on training and taming the *mind* (which is just our tool) so that it learns to perceive and interpret the real us automatically, just as it happened for me in that yoga class.

Getting the thinking mind to be free from thought, or even slowing it down, is not easy. It's counterintuitive to what the mind as the Protective Personality wants to do. Some meditation practices will suit you better than others. Some people learn best through visual means; when they see something drawn or written, they remember it better. Some people learn best kinesthetically; when they act something out, going through it in their body, they learn it. And people who are more auditory learn best by hearing instructions or explanations.

Following are specific methods for meditating based on three primary learning styles. They utilize the circuitry you already have in place. A consistent, regular practice of, ideally, twenty minutes a day will help you train your mind to be still when you need to listen to the Soulful Self and build even more circuitry that will keep you attuned to your inner guidance.

If you're a visual learner:

1. Sit comfortably and place a lit candle in front of you. Set a timer for five minutes.

2. Take a few deep belly breaths, and then squeeze your anchor points: *mūla bandha*, the heart, the throat, and the eyes.

3. Begin slow, gentle Central Channel Breathing, and continue it for the duration of the exercise.

4. Now simply look at the candle flame. Your goal here is to stay fully present with the flame for the entire five minutes. This means that you will need to interrupt the thoughts that will inevitably enter your mind. When a thought starts to come in, say, "I'll think about that later. Right now—candle flame— nothing more." You may even get a few breaths in before the next thought pops up!

We meditate to train the mind to be thought-less so we can perceive the deep presence rising up from within, and also so we can consciously put our attention on what we choose in the outer world without being controlled by the mind's overactivity. Thoughts like, "I wonder if I'm doing this right," "I can't do this," or "This is crazy!" are common—and perfect, because they illustrate just how much the mind is running the show. So, again, when thoughts enter, simply say, "Nope. You don't get to do that right now. For now, just the candle flame." Giving your mind a visual focus will help it step more easily into its proper role: perceiving the real Soulful you!

If you're a kinesthetic learner:

1. Sit comfortably for a few moments and breathe slowly. Do not try to drive the breath up and down the central channel. Just follow the breath—paying attention to how it's naturally moving through the nose, high up into the sinus area, down into the throat and lower lungs.

2. Take a few breaths, and gently and slowly squeeze the heart, then the throat. Continue gently following the breath. Really focus on how the squeezed areas and the breath feel, as if you are in there with them—inside your body. For example, you might pay attention to the cooling or warming sensation in the nostrils or the noticeable flow of air as it enters the sinuses. As you exhale, you might feel what happens in the throat, or how exhaling happens in the lungs. Sometimes the breath will be more obvious coming upward, sometimes going down. Notice as much as you can about how each moment and movement *feels*.

3. Now begin to purposely extend the breath, taking a slow inhalation to a count of four, six, or eight. Then exhale to the same number of counts. Ultimately you'll work your way to slowing the breath down to ten, twelve, or fourteen counts, and even longer—but wherever you're starting, the main idea is to inhale and exhale for the same length of time and to feel the breath as it travels through the body. While at first the counting is helpful and even necessary, as you continue this practice with regularity you'll be able to just allow your system to feel and perceive that rhythmic breathing without counting.

By giving the mind the job of tracking the breath in this way, kinesthetic learners interrupt the mind's typical mode of "runaway train" and give it the opportunity to land on the flow of energy in the core that is the Soulful Self.

If you're an auditory learner:

1. Sit quietly in a place where you won't be disturbed.

2. Close your eyes and speak or sing a mantra of your choice—a simple word or phrase that carries a particular energetic resonance and is repeated (or sung) over and over. A few of the common mantras used for meditation practices are "Oṁ" (or "AUM"), which is the "universal sound"; "Sat Nam," which means

"truth, identity" or "I am truth"; and *"Oṁ Namah Shivaya,"* which is translated in Siddha Shaivism to "universal consciousness is one." You could also choose an English mantra, such as "halle-lujah" or "alleluia," "I am that I am," or simply, "I am."

3. Sing, speak, chant, or (preferably) silently repeat your mantra continually several dozen times, or for at least five minutes. With practice, you will start to feel your mind recede as the sound of the mantra takes precedence in your awareness. Even-tually you will increase your time until your practice lasts about twenty minutes. If your mind wanders, just gently squeeze *mūla bandha,* come back, and begin again.

For auditory learners, the repeating of a mantra is a very helpful tool for meditating with greater ease. The repetition of the word or phrase creates a trancelike effect that facilitates stillness in the mind. As the sound you make reverberates throughout your system, you feel yourself inside the body, which makes you more aware of being the "one behind the scenes." This gives you the perspective you need to no longer identify as the mind. Even silently "saying" or internally "intending" your mantra activates the circuitry that responds well to auditory learning, and the mind will become stilled.

Once you perfect your ability to gently reside within the core of your body during meditation, purposely relax all muscle tension to allow max-imum benefit from each of these three practices.

Additionally, any mantra that incorporates the deep vowel sounds—*ah, a, ee, o,* and *oo*—starts to bring our energy centers online, and therefore cultivates the awakening of aspects of our consciousness. As we've seen in the chakra charts in these Energy Code chapters in part 2, each chakra correlates to a particular musical note that vibrates on its same frequency. This is, in part, why we all love music, and why we're so often drawn to humming, whistling, or singing—because of the vibrational frequencies these expose us to. Classical music in particular brings us into a state of full "keyboard activation," where we feel delighted, rejuvenated, and in-spired. This is because so many different vibrational frequencies are hit together, simultaneously, in different rhythms, activating the chakras in a very gratifying and fulfilling way. Other sequences of tones and vibrations, such as chants from Eastern cultures, also activate the energy centers in a manner that cultivates stillness and presence while still allowing us to feel lucid and awake. For these different reasons, toning vibrations through the body through mantra and music brings an integrative quality to the different energy centers and their levels of consciousness.

————

The most frequent comment I hear from people who are learning to meditate is, "I try to meditate, but my mind just starts *thinking*." That is normal, and it's *the reason you want to meditate*! Embrace that experience instead of judging it, and build a better relationship between your Soulful Self and your thinking mind. Love into it.

When performed even three to four times per week, these meditation exercises will stop the constant flow of thoughts so that you can experience yourself *beyond* your thinking mind—so that you can experience the deep state of presence we are all seeking. We need to lovingly slow down the ceiling fan blades in order to get "between" our thoughts and see what exists beyond them.

The next practice combines several individually powerful elements that together create a moving meditation that facilitates the shift into the Soulful Self.

PRACTICE 2: WALKING IN NATURE USING
CENTRAL CHANNEL BREATHING

In nature, you are more relaxed. Stress disappears and you feel more comfortable in your own skin, more like your "true self," as though what is false about you has dropped away. You may feel buoyant and joyful; perhaps you gain clarity.

The energies in nature soothe and enliven us and support our most creative thinking. They shift us out of the survival physiology of the Protective Personality into the creative physiology of the Soulful Self. When we walk in nature, its energy calms, revitalizes, and grounds us in a beautiful expression of ourselves. A knowing emerges that isn't distorted by the lens of the false self. In the vibrational resonance of nature, the most potent ion-exchange environments on the planet physically and energetically support us in making the Quantum Flip.

Much of our work up to this point in this Code has been done sitting in meditation as we work with our energy field and Central Channel Breathing. This tool puts us *in motion*, helping to build circuitry in the subconscious, which supports the animation of this true, essential version of ourselves. It's not enough to just retreat into meditation and contact the beautiful stillness of the Soulful Self (although that is a good starting place); ultimately, we have to bring forth that Soulful Self into the world through action. We have to *live* as the Soulful Self and set ourselves in motion in our real-time daily lives, where we can change our entire experience in the physical world, and not simply allow our true self to exist only in a meditative vacuum.

Walking in nature is the perfect action for Energy Codes work. The vibrational frequency of nature *is* the vibrational frequency of the Soulful Self. We are not separate from nature; nature is what we *are*. When we spend time in nature, it is easier to find our true frequency and come into harmony inside ourselves. Central Channel Breathing heightens awareness of our energy field, creates new circuitry for awakening our essential self, and integrates dispersed pockets of stuck energy that are keeping us from recognizing and living as our wholeness. When we combine the two and add the natural and regular movement of walking, a powerful alchemy is created in the body, brain, and breath.

Here are the steps to Walking in Nature Using Central Channel Breathing:

1. Choose a place to walk in nature—in the woods, in a meadow, at the seashore, along a river or stream, in the mountains, or even in your own neighborhood . . . anywhere you're in contact with the natural world.

2. To bring your attention to an additional energy center known as the eighth chakra, or North Star, located about a foot and a half

to two feet above your head, reach your arms straight up over-head and snap your fingers. Memorize that space. This chakra is home to the high-frequency energies of our life's purpose.

3. Now engage your four foundational Energy Codes anchor points and perform Central Channel Breathing, and include the North Star as an additional anchor point for the breath as you move it through the channel. As always, let this feel good.

4. Practice matching, vibrationally, the sensations of the beautiful settings in the natural world around you with your inner world. Let the outer sanctuary model for you what the inner sanctuary seeks. Allow them to become coherent. It's a fabulous exercise! One of my teachers commanded, "One hour in nature every day." It deeply helped me embody.

Elements in nature correspond to aspects of our system and phases of the Cycle of Evolution. For example, water is the element of the emotional body and is associated with the *create* phase of the Cycle of Evolution. Among other things, moving water facilitates the movement of stuck emotions and the flow of creativity. Earth is the element of the root chakra and the *sustain* phase of the Cycle of Evolution; walking through the woods has a tremendous grounding and balancing effect. The element of fire is associated with the mental body in the solar plexus and the *deconstruct* phase of the Cycle of Evolution; it burns through old paradigms and illuminates shadowed places in the psyche. The element of air (in the form of wind) is associated with the Void of Creation; it allows expansion and helps break up dense energies to allow a new cycle to emerge.

These elements together help us to integrate our energy. When indigenous people dance around a fire, for example, they are grounding into the continuity of culture and shared memory while burning through dense energies and mental blocks to invite clear vision. When we stand in the wind atop a mountain, we might feel as though time has stopped—that we have stepped into the Void—yet we are anchored to the million-year-long cycles of the mountains.

When we're integrated, when more circuits are in place, we interpret the evolutionary impulses rising through us more accurately, more holistically. Our desires come from an inner-rising vision, and our choices come from a higher place within our Soul purpose. Our ideas seem innovative and creative because they're based in wholeness. We can then act to apply this wholeness and integration in our daily lives and live more fully as the Soulful Self.

Yes, all this can start with a simple walk along the beach or through the forest!

PRACTICE 3: MINDFUL AND THINKLESS PRESENCE

When the runaway mind is doing its thing, we're not really *here*. We're somewhere else—in the future or the past—or just mindlessly repeating our habitual way of processing information and putting ourselves in certain circumstances because it's what's predicted or what we're familiar with. We've bought into that prediction. We've predetermined or prematurely arrived at an outcome before life even has a chance to unfold. To change this, we must cultivate a new pattern of "thinklessness."

My life is a tremendous example of this.

From Prediction to Presence

Years ago, before I began to live as my Soulful Self, from the moment I opened my eyes my body would be carrying all the tension of the coming day—of running my clinic, managing the other doctors and staff, handling the patient load, teaching my father's practices, and keeping up with the breakneck pace required to complete everything. Before my feet even hit the floor, I was already in high-performance mode. Because I had created that energetic pattern of high-performance stress and busyness in my body, my day had no choice but to unfold accordingly.

This is what being on autopilot looks like. There is no room for growth. No room for creativity or spontaneous joy. No room for the Soulful Self—the real you—to emerge and be known. If you are on autopilot, *you* will never have the life you intended when you came here.

To shift out of this program, we have to drop deep into our core and come completely into the present moment, where we are *right now*. After all, when you're in the present moment, no problems exist. You can utilize this different energy to your advantage.

Today, my intention is to wake up and move into the day before I have a single thought about how it might go. If I find my mind starting to try to understand, interpret, predict, analyze, or categorize anything, I simply drop into Central Channel Breathing. As I focus my mind completely on the breath and the loving presence of my Soulful Self, I engage with the circuitry of just living.

When my students are anxious or fretting about something that's coming up, I ask them to drop in and ask themselves, "In this moment, right now, am I okay? I understand that tomorrow might be a horrible day, and that next week could likely be challenging—but right now, am I okay?" The conscious mind will have to admit that, indeed, "Right now, in this moment, I'm okay." So how about the next moment? And the next? The answer will be the same.

When you walk yourself through a few of those moments, you start to awaken the realization at the subconscious level that, if you come to *right now*, you'll be fine. It's only when you get out ahead of yourself, projecting ahead in time without being grounded in the present moment, that you feel anxious or afraid.

Here are the steps to cultivating Mindful and Thinkless Presence:

1. As you're waking up in the morning, before you get out of bed, do a central channel scan and notice where your body is activated or if there is any area that grabs your attention more than others.

2. Squeeze any area that is activated or where energy seems to not be flowing easily. Slowly and gently breathe that area through the central channel, integrating it.

3. Refer to your chakra chart to see what aspects of consciousness this area of the body and energy system relate to. Consciously

intend to give this area more of your attention throughout the rest of the day. Notice how it's revealing itself in your life and may be asking you to enhance it.

4. As you put your feet on the floor and walk into the world, see how long you can stay completely present while going through the motions of your day. As you walk from the bed, look in the mirror, brush your teeth, use the bathroom, etc., see how far into your routine you can remain totally present and refrain from thinking about the future or the past. Simply delight in what you are actually doing. The more present you are, the more you can live joyfully as the Soulful Self.

At first it may feel like you have to walk in slow motion in order to stay present. However, the more circuits you build, the more you can readily, rapidly go through life with the ability to "be here now." This is a tremendous habit to develop, and the perfect time to practice it is first thing in the morning, before the mind has fully kicked into autopilot. The conscious and the subconscious are most attuned to each other at this time and can more easily develop new patterns of function. The more mindful and thinkless presence you can bring into your day, the more circuits you can build for maintaining that deep inner stillness, even when you're in motion.

As you become anchored and integrated in the present moment and have the needed circuitry online, you'll be able to stay in the physiology of the present moment even while thinking about the future. You can approach the future with a complete sense of comfort, knowing that, when you get to each moment, you will know *exactly* what to do, because you will approach it in the same way you are, right now, approaching this moment—without conditions, attachments, judgments, rejections, or fear.

PRACTICE 4: BLENDING PATTERNS TO ENGAGE THE SOULFUL SELF

The fastest, most direct route to change—in your body and in your life—is on the energetic level. That's because energy moves faster than anything else—certainly faster than we can change our thinking patterns and be-liefs! The immense power of thought can direct photons and cause "real-ity" to manifest in this three-dimensional world. In this exercise, we will work with thought and energy together to move even closer to identifying as and embodying the Soulful Self.

How we define ourselves to ourselves has a tangible effect on what we create in our lives. Whenever we use the words "I am," we're creating a powerful directive pattern in our energy arrangement, which our phys-ical world will follow as its blueprint for manifestation. Therefore, it is extremely important to be conscious of the things we say "I am" about.

Right now, I would love for you to become aware of how it feels phys-iologically inside the body when you make an "I am" statement. There's a certain energy that rushes through the body when we stake a claim of "I am," regardless of the quality we are intending to affirm. "I am" statements that align us with the Protective Personality feel different energetically from "I am" statements that anchor us more deeply into the Soulful Self.

I would like you to get to know the pattern of energy flow that hap-pens through the body when you make a claim of identifying as the Soulful Self. (The Soulful Self is the absolute unwavering presence of the Divine in you, whereas the Protective Personality represents the rel-ative world of perception, judgment, and limiting beliefs. This practice allows the two patterns of energy associated with each to become one.) Notice where the energy patterns in the body are flourishing. Where are they rushing? Where are they integrating? What is accentuated? What seems to recede into the background, to pale in the presence of this new identity?

One noticeable pattern, for example, is that the exterior muscles of the body—the fight-or-flight muscles that would engage if a bear walked into the room—release as we move into our core. As we bring our mind's focus to the central channel of the body, work the muscles deeper in the core, and breathe there, those outer muscles automatically release. We become more centered, physically and emotionally, as we align along the body's central plumb line.

As my personal shift toward my Soulful Self and inner guidance began to integrate, I noticed a tremendous change in how the muscles behind my eyes worked together inside my skull. A release occurred regularly as I began to build the circuits for operating from the inside out, rather than responding from the outside in. As my third eye opened, my crown chakra area began to connect to this other world of seeing energy and living as an energy being.

You too might place your attention on your eyes as you comprehensively drop into your core. The muscles will relax more easily and you may feel like you are "sitting down" effortlessly behind your eyes. Noticing this myself, I started to work with my eye focus as a doorway for consciously shifting into the Soulful Self. The clockwork breathing of the Brain Yoga in the Chemistry Code helps to activate the energies of the essential Soulful Self. In the yogic tradition, this practice of directing the gaze is called *drishti*; it is used to enhance and direct the energy of a posture to awaken the high-brain centers associated with the particular eye positions. You don't have to be holding a yoga pose to get the benefit of this directed focus, however.

This exercise will help you start blending the Protective Personality and Soulful Self, which ultimately will help you emerge as the powerfully engaged and loving earthly version of who you really are—the absolute, divine you.

1. First, to trigger your Protective Personality perspective, think of something that you are not so good at but wish you were—for example, you might wish you made more money or were physically fit and strong. Or perhaps think about how you need to get a lot of things done today but don't have the time you think you need. Just pick something where you see yourself as less than comfortable, capable, and/or prepared. The pressure you feel in the body because of these thoughts is the presence of the Protective Personality.

2. Ponder that idea for a few moments and notice what thoughts and emotions come up for you. Sense what is happening *in your body* as you focus on these scenarios. Do you get locked up in

your neck, feel a surge of energy through your heart, or feel no power in your legs? Take a minute to explore what's happening inside you energetically and make a mental note of it.

3. Now, to develop a greater sense of Self, drop deep into the core of the body, bringing focused presence to the area around the spine, belly, and heart space. Breathe from there with deep relaxation in the outer musculature. State to yourself "I am" as you do so. When you focus like this, energy shifts into a dramatically different flow.

4. Notice for a moment what different thoughts and emotions come up for you; then, *feel* into what is happening energetically within your body. Do you feel a sudden sense of groundedness or a huge expansion in your heart center? Spend some time with this, allowing the mind to perceive all the subtle shifts coming from your core, and take a mental inventory.

5. Now you're going to blend the two patterns. Breathe the deep-flowing energy from the Soulful Self's core through the central channel and into the bound-up pattern of the Protective Personality. Breathe them "together." The two will become one, and you will generate a new, positive energy pattern while dissolving an old pattern associated with a limiting thought. The electromagnetic energy will flow in a more integrated, grounded, and unwavering way. You will be able to observe yourself having limiting thoughts throughout your day, while still feeling deeply seated in a place of absolute well-being. It will feel good! A new baseline will set itself regarding your tendency to compare yourself to the outer world, and a new set of circuits will come online for your inner "I am" guidance.

Connecting the two isolated energy patterns in this way gives physiological evidence to your subconscious that the coast is clear—that this issue no longer needs to be considered a threat. You're showing the subconscious physiologically that you're feeling more empowered because the body is more relaxed when you think about the old topic. This is very powerful! If the subconscious can have the experience of shifting energy, it starts to get the feedback of success. It starts to feel, "You know, I can shift this. I just took this locked-up, big energy in my throat and shoulders from the Protective Personality's version of this exercise and shifted it into my system's true version of empowerment."

This Spirit Code practice shifts the body's inherent communication system from a one-way exit ramp to a two-way superhighway, where we're constantly sensing how the energy flows and then immediately inviting it into another flow that we correlate with something more inspired, victorious, or expanded. We want to continually move the energy of the body in accordance with what we would prefer the body to experience; this is how we consciously change and create our lives. This, again, is true Creatorship. We have the total ability to create a life we love *through the body* as we become aware of how it works and utilize its genius.

Once you have identified how the Soulful Self feels in the body, the active mind can dramatically increase the speed at which you fully embody *as* it by affirming—using both words and your energetic disposition—that it is *who we are*. In other words, *we* can dissolve energy patterns previously associated with a limiting thought by affirming what you want through "I am" and other creative statements while embodying the energy pattern of the Soulful Self. This is how you stop trying to change yourself and your life in an outside-in, upside down, and backward sort of way and begin transforming in the only manner that really works—from the inside out.

The Spirit Code Chakra Correlation: Crown Chakra

The seventh, or crown, chakra is all about the higher aspect of our nature, sometimes referred to as our "superconsciousness." Known as *sahasrāra chakra* in Sanskrit ("the thousand-petaled lotus"), it is our access point to dimensions beyond the physical.

As the crown chakra becomes more integrated, we shift out of the fearful, constantly thinking mind and into the superconscious, thinkless mind—in other words, out of the Protective Personality and into the Soulful Self. Obsessive thinking stops. We become peaceful, focused, open, available, and nonjudgmental. As this happens and we begin to identify as the spirit self, the false self of the Protective Personality crumbles, dissolves, weakens, or wobbles—and all of a sudden, for the first time in our lives, we don't mind! We don't mind that we can't continue to hide. That it doesn't work to maintain our egotistic self-image. That it just doesn't seem important to be defensive or to have the last word in an argument. All of a sudden, we can remain present with someone when they're challenging us. Statements that would have led to an argument—such as "You don't get me" or "You're not enough this or that"—no longer bother us. Because we are anchored in our own energy and connected as our actual spiritual source, we won't spin out, fragment, or lose our desired focus or intention based on others' actions or reactions. We've built up the essential Soulful Self energy so that our personality in myriad circumstances no longer needs to be protective. We simply remain in our heart and lovingly present, because we know that everything is happening in a divine fashion in service of our greatest purpose.

As we become the Soulful Self, all of the insecurity, paralysis, and self-doubt that goes on with the Protective Personality goes out the window. We know who we are. We're clear about what's important to us. We know how to act. We don't have any shame, or reluctance, or embarrassment. We are comfortable being our true Soulful Self and taking loving action in the world as that Self.

When our crown chakra is not integrated, we feel stuck. We perceive ourselves as separate—from others, from spirit, and even from our own energy. This can lead to battles of will or ego, obsessive thinking, depression, anxiety, and other mind-associated disorders like epilepsy and Alzheimer's. Conversely, when the crown chakra is integrated, our energy system blooms like that thousand-petaled lotus. We are ever-expanding, ever-receptive, and ever-evolving into our most natural state: that of the lovingly present Soulful Self.

The following chart offers a summary of some of the key characteristics of the crown chakra.

The Spirit Code Chakra Correlation: Crown Chakra

NAME(S)	Seventh chakra, *sahasrāra chakra*
LOCATION	Top of head
COLOR	Violet / White
MUSICAL NOTE	B
BODY AREAS AFFECTED	Upper skull, skin, cerebral cortex, right eye, right brain, central nervous system, **pineal gland**
"BACK SIDE" SYMPTOMS	Depression, obsessive thinking, confusion, sensitivity to pollutants, chronic exhaustion, epilepsy, Alzheimer's
"FRONT SIDE" CHARACTERISTICS	Divine Personality, magnetism, miraculous achievement, transcendence, peace with self, collaboration with higher purpose, inner vision. "I am a divine being." "I am that." "Life is a reflection of all that I am."
PRACTICES	• Discovering Your Meditation Style • Walking in Nature Using Central Channel Breath • Mindful and Thinkless Presence • Blending Patterns to Engage the Soulful Self
BREATHWORK (as explained in Chapter 8)	Central Channel Breath
YOGA POSES FOR GREATER INTEGRATION	• Corpse Pose (*śavāsana*) • Headstand (*śirṣāsana*) • Rabbit Pose (*sasangāsana*) • Wide Angle Forward Fold (*prasārita pādottānāsana*)

Along with the practices in this Code, the following yoga postures help to integrate and balance the crown chakra.

Yoga for the Spirit Code

Śavāsana is the pose practiced at the end of most yoga classes—usually everyone's favorite! It translates as Corpse Pose, but simply means a posture of total stillness and surrender. It has tremendous benefits to the central nervous system and is associated with the crown chakra.

CORPSE POSE (ŚAVĀSANA)

Here's how to (traditionally) practice *śavāsana*:

1. Lie on your back on a mat or the floor with your feet hip-width apart and your arms by your sides. Let your feet flop open, and your hands relax with palms facing the ceiling. Let your neck settle into its natural curve, with the back of your skull resting on the floor.

2. Consciously relax your entire body, starting with your feet. Let a wave of total softness and surrender move up your legs, into your hips, your core, and your heart. Feel the relaxation spreading down your arms to your wrists and hands. Then relax your upper chest, throat, neck, face, and the skin of your scalp. Feel the energy moving more freely through your entire body.

3. Let your breath relax into its normal rhythm—not too deep and not too shallow. Turn your attention inward. If any place in your body is not fully relaxed, let your mind discover it, then consciously soften it. Then completely let go into the realm beyond all active thinking.

4. Remain in this relaxed state for at least five to ten minutes (or longer, time permitting).

5. When you are ready to come out of the pose, begin by gently wiggling your fingers and toes. Move your head from side to side, feeling the back of your head in contact with the mat. When you feel ready, gather your knees into your chest and roll onto one side. Take a breath or two in the fetal position, then slowly lever yourself into a seated position.

Now let's integrate our Spirit Code and BodyAwake practices while in *śavāsana*.

1. While performing the posture, supine on the floor, become aware of the huge pool of energy two feet into the earth beneath you.

2. As the wave of energy moves up through your body, consciously allow it to follow the central channel, rising up through the body as the torus field flow rises in the core.

3. Begin Central Channel Breathing. As each body part relaxes, drop more fully into your core and the center of the brain.

Allow the mind to release to the place beyond thought, and let that thought-less state be anchored deep within your system—the pelvic floor.

4. Begin to relax each aspect of the body in an order akin to *releasing* each muscle with A Thousand Tiny Straws, starting with the feet and working your way up through the whole body, but with the heart and *mūla bandha* being the very last to let go.

5. Spend several minutes in this space of deep stillness to allow the Soulful Self to rise to the surface of your awareness.

6. When you are ready to transition out of the posture, move from the core first, with a gentle squeeze at the four anchor points and a Central Channel Breath. Releasing a quiet whisper, a deeply internal sound of *"Ma,"* will accentuate the revealing expression of the Soulful Self in this significant moment.

7. Once the core has been activated, begin to move your small muscle groups (fingers, toes, etc.). Remember, you are here to cultivate new circuits from the *inside out* with the Energy Codes; this practice enhances those circuits.

ADDITIONAL YOGA POSES TO INTEGRATE
THE CROWN CHAKRA

You can use these asanas in addition to *śavāsana* to enhance your work with the Spirit Code. Remember that squeezing areas to which you want to draw attention is beneficial, but so is relaxing in the poses. Use your best judgment to work with the BodyAwake practices in each of these poses, first activating the core and then relaxing it.

- Headstand (*śirṣāsana*)
- Rabbit Pose (*sasangāsana*)
- Wide Angle Forward Fold (*prasārita pādottānāsana*)

———

Congratulations! This concludes the seventh and final set of practices that make up the Energy Codes program. You now have all the tools and know-how you need to make your own Quantum Flip to living as the Soulful Self. All of these Energy Codes have awakened you to your ability to expand your perception, embodiment, and expression of the Soulful Self, the divine creator of your experiences.

Next, in part 3, I'm going to show you how to make the Codes an easy-to-implement, daily, ongoing practice to best expedite your own Quantum Flip. We then look at what life is like from the Front Side of the Model, where you begin to operate in the state of true Creatorship.

Part III

A New Way of Living—
The Embodied Life

Chapter 11

MAKING THE QUANTUM FLIP,
ONE DAY AT A TIME

In part 1 of this book, we gained a new way of seeing ourselves, our life, and the rest of the world. We learned that we are actually brilliant souls—energy beings—on a path to awakening to our own magnificence and that our life and everything in it is a reflection of where we need to wake up. In part 2, with the Energy Codes program, we learned how to go about awakening. We learned a new way of being with ourselves and in response to our life. Here in part 3 we're going to look at a new way of living—how we can not only make the Quantum Flip once and for all, but also continually build circuits for the Front Side of the Model so we can embody more of our Soulful Self, every single day.

Now that you've experienced the sensation of "waking up" your Soulful Self, you likely want to bring all you've learned together in the easiest possible way that will also make the most difference in your life. That's what this chapter is about: to get you using the Energy Codes now and making them a new habit and way of life, I'm going to give you several clear, easy ways to start implementing the Codes, to begin actively and efficiently doing the work that will lead to you fulfilling your destiny here in physical form, embodying the Soulful Self.

These practices slip seamlessly into even the most hectic of days. You will have several different ways to incorporate them into your schedule. If you do better with structure, you may like the short, formal routines. If not, I'll share other ideas for an unstructured, adaptable (but equally powerful) daily practice. Simply choose the option that works best for you, and start. Because that's really the most important thing . . . that you begin *now* to consciously engage with the energy being that *is* the real you. That you begin today consciously living your true nature, as the spiritual being having a spiritual, physical experience. There is literally nothing in this world you could do that would make a bigger difference in your life.

As always, your goal with these practices is to build circuitry as constantly and consistently as you can—bringing in high-frequency energy to lighten your energetic gunk and densities, thereby infusing and activating those not-yet-awakened parts of your consciousness and body with the Soulful Self. Once you experience this infusion and integration, you will never look back! However, it's important to remember that this isn't a "one-and-done" kind of thing. The Quantum Flip and living on the Front Side of the Model don't happen just through cognitive understanding. They happen through *embodiment*.

To make this transformation happen in the spaces between the particles—where the real you resides—you'll need to *live* these practices, to do them continuously, as your new way of being in the world. This will entail repetition, which trains the mind. You want the mind's default role to be following the energy flowing through the body, rather than protecting, defending, and otherwise reacting to the story in your head. Continually doing the Codes practices will curb the mind's urge to push and drive life, which draws your attention away from your core and pulls you away from the intuitive realm.

Like any other practice, training the mind to perceive your true nature as an energy being requires dedication and conscientiousness. It will take some time (although not necessarily a *lot* of time) to thoroughly work your way through your entire system, building new circuitry everywhere it's needed to fully experience the Soulful Self within the body. If you do these practices mindfully, you will start to feel a difference almost immediately—but full integration won't happen in an instant (at least, probably not). Be patient. You will integrate at the pace that perfectly serves your personal evolution and the agreements you made at the Bus Stop before you came here.

Don't worry—it will actually feel good! And once you start doing the practices regularly, they will develop momentum. Cellular memory is similar to muscle memory: once you begin resonating at the new, higher vibration (of the Soulful Self), all of your integration practices will compound. In other words, you won't start over each day; rather, every single time you do the Energy Codes practices, you pick up where you left off. The practice becomes self-supporting and self-sustaining.

The vibration of your devotion to awakening to and embodying your divine nature will add to this compounding effect, because the vibration of true devotion, a form of love, *is* the vibration of the Soulful Self. Your devotion brings you to the very place you're trying to get to. Your sincere, heartfelt, precious intentionality generates an energy that is the same as your destination. Energetically, it's the vibrational match to the high-brain centers above the primitive brain. By approaching it this way, you arrive before the mind even knows it took the journey. By embodying this vibration through your sincere devotion . . . you are there!

Something I said at the start of this book bears repeating here: you could be a whole new version of yourself—healthier, happier, more empowered—in just a few months, or even a few weeks. But that will only happen if you *apply* what you've learned. Time will pass regardless of what you choose to do; it's up to you how you use it. Therefore I invite you to embrace this work with devotion, passion, and purpose with regard to your own expansion and embodiment. I promise, you'll be grateful you did.

So let's look at how you can best apply all of this to your daily life. The question I always get from students of my coursework is, "When do I do these practices?" What I tell them—and the first option I'm going to give you—is "Never not!"

Never Not!

After my exalted opening, I became obsessed with re-creating it. As a doctor, I approached the effort scientifically, and was able to systemize (and consistently reproduce) a state of being that was generally considered esoteric and out of reach. During my research, I discovered that these practices can be done just about anywhere, at any time—while doing anything! While I'm not suggesting you approach this work with the same fervor I did, I do believe that you should try to work with the Energy Codes practices every day.

We can do almost any activity as we simultaneously develop our sensory neurocircuitry. The more you practice integrating these simple neurocircuitry-building practices with your everyday activities, the more natural and effortless they become.

Challenge yourself to see just how often, and during how many different regular daily activities, you can "never not" practice these two foundational exercises—Central Channel Breathing and Subject-Object-Subject/Take It to the Body. Start a contest with yourself to see how much of your day you can spend building circuitry in one or both of these ways as you go about your regular schedule. Make it your "go-to" until it becomes your "come-from."

The following list of possible circuit-building scenarios will get you jump-started; it isn't exhaustive, by any means, so feel free to make your own additions.

You can build circuits when you are:

- lying in bed
- talking on the phone
- texting
- surfing the Web
- watching TV
- cooking
- eating
- washing dishes
- going to the bathroom
- bathing or showering
- walking, jogging, or doing other exercises (see Conscious Exercise in the Chemistry Code)
- standing in line
- practicing yoga (double points for this one!)
- shopping
- spending time in nature (double points here too!)
- petting an animal

- driving
- commuting to work
- reading
- working on your computer
- making love
- teaching or speaking to a group
- trying to make a decision
- doing laundry
- ruminating on something challenging
- brushing your teeth
- gardening
- vacationing
- _____ (Your choice!)

As I was developing the Codes, and working to build circuitry any-where and everywhere, I used an act as simple as reaching for my seat belt before driving as a reminder and opportunity for practicing. By twisting just a little bit extra when reaching over my shoulder for the seat belt, then squeezing the heart, and then inhaling and exhaling up and down the central channel, I built new circuits—without creating any disruption to my day. Then I took it one step further: As I turned to look out the rear window while backing out of the driveway, I would rotate my neck just a little more consciously, tuck my chin, and feel behind my eyes while I did so. Then I would draw my breath up into the center of my brain and out the top of my head—building circuits to the high-brain centers and opening a highway from my heart to my creative genius.

When you approach it like this, the great adventure of life then becomes: "How can I build circuits when I'm lifting groceries, or putting things away? When I'm picking up a suitcase, or moving boxes out of a storage room? Am I not only being mindful of proper lifting techniques, such as bending my knees and holding the object close to my body so that I don't injure my back, but also taking a breath up and down through the central channel?"

The invitation is to see how creative you can be with doing the prac-tices *while living your life*. What other ways can you think of? For many more ideas, and to join in the conversation yourself, please visit my Facebook page at Facebook.com/DrSueMorter. You'll find all kinds of support and discussion about how my coursework students and others are implementing this work.

To help make this a new way of living, you may want to give yourself some friendly reminders at first. Put sticky notes in the places where your eyes land often throughout the day—your bathroom mirror, your refrigerator, the dashboard of your car. Set a recurring alarm (for every fifteen, thirty, or sixty minutes, for instance) on your smartphone or other digital device. Or simply couple certain activities with an Energy Codes practice, so that whenever you do the activity, you simultaneously do the practice. One of my students has established the habit of doing Central Channel Breathing every time she goes to the bathroom. While she started this as a way to naturally heal a urinary tract infection (and it did heal, within twenty-four hours), she then kept it as part of her new Energy Codes regimen. She figured, "Why not? What else am I going to be doing in that moment? I can make great use of the time!"

Following are some additional, informal ways you can integrate the Energy Codes practices into your life without having to "find more time" in your regular day.

ON YOUR "BREAK" FROM SITTING

One of the big health warnings today is that sitting for very long is detrimental to our health, so we're being advised to take frequent breaks from sitting. Some experts say that, within every half hour we sit, we need to stand for eight of those minutes and move around for two. I invite you to use your breaks from sitting to do a few BodyAwake Yoga poses. Doing yoga is much more beneficial than just getting up and stretching; it has a whole different effect. Yoga puts the body into sacred geometrical shapes that allow higher-frequency energies to flow through it automatically, tuning into the radio station of the Soulful Self—our ultimate goal—with little effort. You could practice just one asana for one chakra on each break (and aim to cover all seven chakras every day), or do a quick scan on each break to see which chakra needs attention in that moment and choose a pose for that. (For a list of the yoga poses recommended for each chakra, see Thirty-Minute Routines on page 307.) As an alternative to yoga, you could do the Morter March or mPower Step on your break instead, which will have tremendous integrative effects on the central nervous system and the electromagnetic system.

Another powerful use of your "sitting break" would be to do breath-work practices. You can practice the Fern Frond Breath whenever you get up out of a chair: curl yourself forward as you get ready to stand, and then unroll your spine as you slowly rise up to a full stance. Equally powerful would be to do A Thousand Tiny Straws Breath.

If you are unable to stand for your break, you could reach back with your right hand and take hold of the back of the chair on the right; place your right foot forward and the left back behind you, perhaps under the chair. Contract the four anchor points. Reach toward your right knee with the left hand (cross over the body). Turn your chin over your left shoulder. Then take a big central channel breath up through your legs, up through your body, and exhale out the top of your head. Come to a neutral seated position again. Take a deep breath in from overhead, squeeze it in through the heart as it's coming into the body, then exhale it down through the legs into the earth. Repeat on the other side. Moving the energy with the breath alone is nearly the same as actually standing, as far as building circuits for enlivening these important pathways of embodiment.

You can choose any of the breathwork exercises that suits what you perceive you need that day: the Vessel Breath for creative wisdom, the Solar Plexus Breath for personal power, the Heart Coherence Breath for love and joy, the Manifesting Breath for speaking your truth, or the Visionary Breath for accentuating your inner vision for your ultimate life mastery. Each of these serves to bring more vital life force into the central core of the body to unify and conserve energy instead of dispersing it and losing it throughout the day. (A refresher on these exercises appears a bit later in the chapter.)

KEEPING ONE EYE ON THE INSIDE

Finally, while this chapter is really about *proactive* measures for developing circuitry, I want to remind you that you always want to have "one eye on the inside" and practice "taking it to the body" as your way of responding anytime (and every time) you get emotionally triggered and feel a charge in your energy field. This is *the* fastest, most direct route to the evolution of your consciousness (and the healing of your life) because, through the sensations in the body, you're getting direction straight from the Soulful Self about where you most need to put effort right now.

I'm always taking it to the body. I'm always paying attention to what's happening inside my body when I think a particular thought, or when I'm trying to work through a plan for my future or how to answer an invitation. I'm constantly referencing the internal flow within my core and noticing whether it's flowing when I'm thinking the way I'm thinking. If I find that it's not flowing—because of a block, backup, or gap—then I get busy building circuitry by squeezing the area where I feel the sensation or charge and breathing it through the central channel. So I really want to encourage you to see this not as something that's done as a formal practice, but rather as something you do all the time.

When we approach life with this "never not" level of intention and awareness, we see that every experience or moment is an opportunity for building the circuitry that will facilitate our healing, expansion, and evolution—in other words, our awakening as the Soulful Self. It simply comes down to how quickly we want that transformation to occur. If you're like me and many of my students, you'll be so eager to begin celebrating life on the Front Side of the Model that you'll be in a constant state of focus! That's okay; you absolutely cannot overdo this.

This inner referencing, breathing, and visualization will actually make you *more present*—both to the moment you're in and to your entire life. It wakes you up and keeps you alert, preventing you from sliding into autopilot or a rote way of living. Because you will be constantly turning your attention more deeply onto your core, you'll have access to more of your innate resources, which will give you a greater capacity for handling experiences with grace, ease, and consciousness. It also makes you more available to love.

———

Let's look at some more formal options for incorporating the Energy Codes into your daily schedule. You can pick and choose among the structures offered or do them all—whatever you have time for. The more, the better, and none excludes any of the others!

Morning and Bedtime Routines

Some of our greatest opportunities for building circuitry occur upon awakening in the morning and just before we're falling asleep at night. In the semi-asleep/semi-awake state, the trapdoor between the conscious and subconscious minds is widest, and the two can most easily communicate with each other. When the conscious and subconscious connect, our deep truth rises to the surface of our conscious mind, where it can guide us in accomplishing our heart's desires in the most authentic way. I invite you to make it a routine to begin and end the day with Energy Codes practices. In this routine, you start the day with a Central Channel Scan and end the day bathing in the transformational vibration of love.

MORNING SCAN

Before you begin your day, while you're still lying in bed, perform the Mindful and Thinkless Presence exercise in the Spirit Code: Scan the central channel and squeeze and integrate any areas that need your attention. Set your intentions for the day by utilizing these energies as a priority. Reference the chakras chart on page 76 to determine further recommendations to focus on throughout your day, and encourage your energy to flow in those areas by breathing through them regularly. For instance, let's say that during your scan you feel a pain in your neck. Squeeze your neck in response to this awareness and begin to breathe through the area, connecting it to the central channel. Reference the diagram and read what else is involved with the throat chakra (in this example). Include whatever catches your attention from the chart in your intentions that day (perhaps "perfectionism" and "inability to express emotions" jump off the page as you read). Set your intention to release and soften your perfectionism and allow yourself to express your emotions as best you can as you breathe through the throat area, connecting it with the central channel. Your body is revealing what you need to focus on next for your evolution.

BEDTIME GRATITUDES

When I crawl into bed at night, I always say, "Oh, I love bed!" Don't you just love bed too? It is the perfect cocoon in which to do this work, because we feel safe and protected there, and we can build circuitry there like nowhere else. The most effective effort is made in a state of *loving presence* and *breath*. Love is the vibration that opens the trapdoor between your subconscious and consciousness. Presence is complete focus and awareness with the mind. And breath moves the energy or spirit through the body. Cultivate your ability to go to love for no reason at all in the comfort of your own bed.

A perfect bedtime routine, which complements the Mindful and Thinkless Presence morning routine, is the Generating Loving Presence exercise from the Heart Code, on page 187. Like the morning routine, do this while lying in bed, just before you go to sleep. Fill your whole body with love and deep gratitude and breathe through the central channel to anchor that vibration in your energy field. Notice where there is any interruption in your continuous flow through the central channel, and do the circuit-building work in this area as you slip into your gracious slumber.

You can amplify this exercise by doing the mPower Step on both sides at least once before you get into bed.

———

Everyone talks about the importance of gratitude, but I'd like to talk about the importance of gratitude as it relates to living as the creator of your own life. When we do exercises like the one above, we purposely bring to mind things that generate the sensation of gratitude—not for any result in our outer world, but so that we can learn how to "do" the sensation of gratitude. We express gratitude in order to model the Soulful Self vibrational frequencies (joy, love, appreciation, and presence). Eventually, we want to generate those for ourselves all the time. Once we are able to call up the frequency of gratitude by thinking of something we appreciate, we can take the next step of calling up the sensation of gratitude for no particular reason at all—which in turn helps us arrive at the disposition of "It doesn't matter what happens in my life today; I'm doing gratitude. And there's nothing anyone can do about it!" It's truly empowering to know and feel ourselves as the masters of our internal experience, regardless of our external circumstances.

Ten-Minute Routines

If you can set aside ten minutes each day to devote to your Energy Codes practice, there are several highly integrative ways you can spend that time. Ideally, we become so versed in the Code practices that rather than choose with the thinking mind which to do, we let the energy that is the real us direct our mind to what is needed. The more familiar we are with all of the practices, the easier it will be to just reach for the one that is being called for from our toolbox and use it on that day. Nonetheless, a few different routines follow; they will take virtually no time out of your day and still provide you with structured support.

TEN MINUTES OF MINDFUL, THINKLESS
CENTRAL CHANNEL BREATHING

In the practice of Mindful and Thinkless Presence, we bring to a stop the runaway mind with all of its preoccupations with the past and the future, and we draw the mind's full, conscious concentration to the present moment, without any thoughts. It's the opposite of being on autopilot. We step into each day and each moment anew, without expectations and with an openness to possibility, where we simply observe what is actually unfolding in front of and within us.

I'm going to encourage you to work your way up to doing this for ten minutes straight. This will be especially effective on a break in the middle of the busy workday, when your mind is racing, but it is beneficial at any time. Engage the four anchor points while you do it, and add Central Channel Breathing. *Be the energy on the inside* that is moving through the central channel, rather than merely visualizing the energy going up and down inside the body. To begin identifying as the Soulful Self, you want to come into the channel with all of your conscious concentration and *be that* without thinking about anything else—to put your total focus on *being that* energy, on the inside.

So challenge yourself here: "Can I relax my mind and use the four anchor points to find my central alignment and then release all my muscles, but *stay focused* in the aligned core presence and breathe in this central channel state? Can I work up to ten full minutes of that?"

TEN MINUTES OF CHAKRA BREATHWORK

The Breath Code practices are based on breathwork from ancient traditions (known as *prāṇāyāma* or "breath control"). Yogis and adepts studying consciousness use these practices as a way to unify the layers of being and to build momentum toward enlightenment. Breathing these individual breaths, one on top of the other, builds an awareness inside the body that ultimately allows you to truly awaken to your Soulful Self. So this is a lot more than just taking a deep breath.

For one ten-minute routine, you can simply go through the six foundational chakra breathwork practices. Give yourself just over ninety seconds (about five to ten breaths) for each practice. Following is a quick recap of the practices.

1. Central Channel Breath (Chakras 1 and 7): To begin, activate *mūla bandha*, squeeze your heart, constrict your throat, and gently roll your eyes up. Then do Central Channel Breathing up and down.

2. Vessel Breath (Chakra 2): Inhaling from your last Central Channel Breath, distend the belly as much as you can outward, in front of you. As you continue to inhale, press down against the muscles that are lifting up with *mūla bandha*. Then as you exhale, pull the belly way back toward the spine in this Buddha Belly, or Vessel, Breath for creative freedom.

3. Solar Plexus Breath (Chakra 3): Next, roll that up into a Solar Plexus Breath, where you're contracting everything in the upper body, and everything below the navel; then, right where the ribs splay apart, breathe "baseball, grapefruit, baseball, grapefruit"— isolating the third-chakra area for personal power.

4. Heart Coherence Breath (Chakra 4): From the Solar Plexus Breath, inhale into the big Buddha Belly again, and then keep inhaling up through the Solar Plexus area and raise the breath up into the upper lobes of the lungs and chest, so that you're breathing in the belly and in the upper lobes of the lungs simultaneously in a big inhale. Keep inhaling until the breath expands beyond the body, and then exhale out in every direction in a giant sphere. Now inhale from this giant sphere into the belly and keep inhaling until you fill the upper lobes of the lungs again. This activates your love and joy.

5. Manifesting Breath (Chakra 5): From the Heart Coherence Breath, exhale completely and then inhale. Contracting everything in the lower body beneath the throat area, accentuate breathing into the throat-chakra area with all of your attention, opening the throat as you would if you were yawning but wanting to keep your mouth closed during the yawn. (Inhaling in this fashion allows the throat to open.) Exhale out the top of the head. Now reverse, inhaling from overhead into the throat, accentuating in this same manner to open the throat, and then exhale down through the whole body into the earth. This exercise is similar to Central Channel Breathing, but with the point of changeover being at the throat instead of the core/heart/belly region.

6. Visionary Breath (Chakra 6): Locate the sixth chakra by rolling your eyes up and feeling the tension behind them; memorize that location. Pick an object on which to focus your attention (such as a candle flame, a talisman, a simple stone or flower, or

some other object in your space) and place it two to three feet in front of where you're sitting. Breathe as if you are drawing a line in the air from that focal point to the center of your brain, as if it is the inhalation that "moves" the point of attention toward you to the center of the sixth chakra or third eye. Then exhale out the back of the head the same distance. (Just imagine it.) Now reverse, inhaling from behind you to the center of the brain and exhaling out in front. Now connect the Visionary Breath with the familiar Central Channel Breath, only this time with the change point at the third eye, rather than lower in the channel.

You can easily do this routine at any time while you're going through your day: on a ten-minute work break, while waiting for someone at a lunch meeting, while waiting for your kids to get out of karate class, or on the commuter rail platform. In other words, it doesn't require that you sit alone, close your eyes, and focus so intently that you can't be presentable in public. (Just try not to make funny faces!) It is safe and integrative, so you remain highly functional. (Obviously, I don't recommend doing these practices at work if you're operating heavy machinery or performing surgery, but otherwise you should be just fine.) If on occasion you desire extra support to ground your new vibrational pattern following the exercise, you might choose to take a short walk before returning to your tasks in order to integrate the new circuitry.

TEN MINUTES OF BRAIN YOGA

For Brain Yoga practice (see page 256), which enlivens the important high-brain centers in the middle of the head, you keep your head still, move your eyes around the hours of the clock, and breathe through the central channel. For this ten-minute routine, I recommend doing Brain Yoga for the first six to seven minutes. This should get you around the clock both clockwise and counterclockwise at least once. Then spend the last three to four minutes doing several Central Channel Breaths with yoga poses from the Anchoring Code. This sequencing is important because Brain Yoga is an accelerated technique for activating high-brain centers; therefore we want to make sure to ground and integrate the transformation in the whole body. If you experience any light-headedness, do this one at home. With practice, it will be easier to do throughout the day at any time.

TEN MINUTES OF FERN FROND BREATH

Do Fern Frond for five to seven minutes, then Central Channel Breathing and a few different yoga asanas from the Anchoring Code. (For a reminder of the details for doing the Fern Frond Breath, see page 223.) This exercise engages the *dantian* (a major energy storehouse) and integrates the energy flow in the spine. This fine-tuning integration is key to sustaining the transformation you're undergoing with all of the Energy Codes.

Thirty-Minute Routines

Again, while it's most beneficial to be attuned to what your body is telling you it needs and to then choose from among all the Energy Codes practices to suit, having a set thirty-minute daily practice will also bring about transformation quickly and powerfully. So if you can devote a half hour, and want some formal structure to help you build circuitry efficiently and effectively, choose from the following half-hour routines.

A BREATHWORK–MEDITATION COMBO

This combination is far more integrative than meditation alone. In this routine, you're going to use the meditation style that comes most naturally to you based on your primary learning style (visual, auditory, or kinesthetic). First, you'll do the chakra breathwork practices. There's an important reason for this. Getting the *prāṇa* or energy moving through your system as a precursor to meditation greatly increases the effectiveness of the meditation for creating breakthroughs in circuit-building.

This "living meditation" has been the focus of my meditation classes for the past seventeen years. With it, we bring together our daily life and our felt sense of the Soulful Self—so that every day becomes a walking, expressive, *integrative* meditation experience. This has been profoundly helpful to my patients, clients, and students. To approach meditation otherwise, I feel, increases the distinctions between two *different* worlds—the inner and the outer. We're here to bring it all together—to experience HeavenEarth—not exclude one or the other.

This combined routine will help beginners and seasoned meditators alike get the most out of their meditation efforts, so that we benefit from all the amazing experiences we have in meditation and infuse them into our nervous system.

Here's how to do it:

1. Sit in a chair, or cross-legged on the floor or a yoga mat.

2. Do the Ten Minutes of Chakra Breathwork routine (see page 304).

3. Spend the next five minutes doing a version of *prāṇāyāma* called *kapalabhati*, which translates as "skull-shining breath" and is also known as Breath of Fire. It is essentially the same as other breath patterns but is done at a faster pace. It has a cleansing effect on the electromagnetic circuits in your system—a sort of energetic housecleaning that burns up the gunk.

   Begin with a complete exhalation through your nose, emptying all the breath out of your belly by pulling the belly/low abdomen back toward the spine. Then release it, and let the belly draw more breath in automatically. Exhale again, forcefully, through the nose. Repeat, and then pick up the pace. You will notice that you are actually only focusing on the forceful exhalation; the inhalation is reflexive and takes care of itself as you momentarily relax the abdominal muscles between exhalations. To complete this breath exercise, connect the breath to the central channel with a few deep, slow Central Channel Breaths. (These Central Channel Breaths can be performed as alternate nostril breathing [*nadi shodhana*] for brain balance. For video instruction, go to drsuemorter.com/energycodesbook.)

4. Now release the structured breath pattern and any muscle tension throughout your body, and, for the next fifteen to twenty minutes, sit in meditation using the method of your choice. (For short, guided meditations, go to drsuemorter.com/energy codesbook.)

5. When you come out of your meditation, do two spinal twists to each side (alternating sides), extensions, and flexions, as these allow the body to integrate and memorize what you've just experienced. Lie on your back on the floor. Take a breath up and down the central channel as you bend your knees and gently drop them to the left while rotating the spine, neck, and chin to the right. Release and repeat on the other side. (If you cannot lie on the floor for any reason, you can do this rotating while sitting in a chair. Use the back of the chair to support you as, with your knees facing forward, you rotate your spine, neck, and chin to the right, and then to the left.)

   For spinal flexion, while lying on the floor (or sitting in a chair), contract the front side of the body so that you curl into a ball, hugging your knees in toward your chest as tightly as you can. For spinal extension, use Camel Pose (see the Clearing Code, page 176, for instructions), or lie on your stomach on the floor and lift your chest upward with your arms extended along your sides. (You can also carefully extend over the back of a low-backed chair, lifting the chest upward all the while to protect your back.)

Yoga also gets the energy actively moving through our body. Too often, though, we have a nice yoga class that finishes with a few short minutes of *śavāsana* (Corpse Pose); then we sit up, the class ends, and we leave. Yet if we would do *śavāsana* and then just sit there in meditation for a while, we would integrate much more of the great work we just did on the yoga mat. Because this may not always be possible inside your yoga studio, I highly recommend moving to a quiet space outside the studio or sitting in your car and performing a short meditation before you leave the parking lot.

BODYAWAKE™ YOGA POSES

1ST CHAKRA:
- Chair Pose
- Warrior 1
- Pyramid Pose
- Tree Pose
- Standing Forward Fold

2ND CHAKRA:
- Boat Pose
- Pigeon Pose
- Yogic Bicycle
- Seated Spinal Twist
- Breath of Fire

3RD CHAKRA:
- Camel Pose
- Bow Pose
- Reverse Table Top
- Crescent Warrior
- Breath of Fire

4TH CHAKRA:
- Triangle Pose
- Thread the Needle
- Fish Pose
- Reclined Spinal Twist

5TH CHAKRA:
- Cobra Pose
- Plow Pose
- Bridge Pose
- Toning with Sound (Oṁ, Ma, Ha)

6TH CHAKRA:
- Downward Dog
- Shoulderstand
- Child's Pose
- Exalted Warrior (Warrior 4)
- Balancing Poses

7TH CHAKRA:
- Corpse Pose
- Headstand
- Rabbit Pose
- Wide Angle Forward Fold

Ten extra minutes of dropping into your deep inner self while in this wonderful state of presence will be highly beneficial for your body's circuit-building. Be sure you're fully lucid before you drive!

THIRTY MINUTES OF BODYAWAKE YOGA

Yoga is highly integrative in and of itself, and especially when done with the mindful breathing in the Energy Codes. Throughout the Codes, I've given basic yoga poses that help to open each chakra and increase its flow. You can perform these poses in the order they are given, or preferably integrate them into your flow practice to activate all chakras in sequence. For your convenience, I'm listing here all of the poses we've discussed, sorted by the chakra they most affect.

I've also brought those poses together for a short but highly effective BodyAwake Yoga routine to help you build the restorative circuitry needed to reprogram your Protective Personality and activate your Soulful Self. To see the practice flow, please go to drsuemorter.com/energycodesbook.

THIRTY MINUTES OF HEALING BREATHWORK

If you are injured, have a physical weakness or pain, or have a health issue—all of which indicate that an area in your body has an energy blockage or inadequate flow—you may want to spend your thirty minutes a day on a Healing Pattern Breath for the area affected. For example, if you have persistent or recurring urinary tract infections, you could spend your half an hour breathing deeply and intently through the first and second chakra areas in the manner shown in the video found at drsuemorter.com/energycodesbook, and take it to the body when you think about the symptoms you are having. You could also do B.E.S.T. Release to clear any subconscious interference and unresolved emotion that might be contributing to the problem's persistence. (Unresolved anger, for example, is a common factor behind urinary tract infections.) Let your body tell you which emotions to clear, as the solution will likely unfold in an organic fashion. If you have knee pain, make sure you are putting just enough pressure on the knee joint to accentuate the sensation in the knee while you do the breathwork, pulling the breath through the joint area as the video shows. Specific work on various body areas is a perfect way to spend even short periods of time one, two, or three times a day. Keep in mind that the process is similar no matter what the condition is. This way, you can translate this technique to address other conditions such as headaches, neck pain, shoulder pain, stomach upset and tightness, shortness of breath, tension anywhere in the body, and other ailments. For additional information on Healing Patterns, see the Resources on page 325.

Energy is always trying to move upward through the body as it attempts to integrate; therefore, the blockage will always be *above* the painful or nonresponsive area. Always work with your breath patterns *through* the area from below it to above it for best results. And always include the entire body in your final breaths of the practice and incorporate A Thousand Tiny Straws Breath to finish. (The video will help!)

All of the practices in this chapter magnify the Soulful Self. Integration feels good to the body—the body *wants* its flow to be restored. It's built to be self-healing, self-regulating, and self-illuminating—to move toward its true Soulful nature and original design. In other words, the body is *designed* to do what we're now asking it to do. It needs only a little help from the mind and our intention, and then its own momentum will take hold. Our job is to facilitate, and then go with that natural flow.

When we view the transformation we're seeking as being about flow

Chapter 12

LIFE ON THE FRONT SIDE:

LIVING AS THE SOULFUL SELF

Seven years after my dramatic initial opening to my own Soulful Self, I was invited by a friend of a friend to speak at a women's conference in Copper Mountain, Colorado. After my talk, someone in the audience approached me and asked if I'd be interested in presenting at a speakers' conference in the upcoming year. "Of course," I said, not really knowing the magnitude of what I was saying yes to.

Very soon after, an organizer contacted me and asked if I had a sample video so that they could see what my presentations were like. I didn't have one, but was in the process of creating one, because someone from the Tony Robbins organization was asking for the same thing so that I might speak to the coaching team there. So I hurriedly got the video completed and sent it off. A response came quickly. Not only did they want me to speak, they wanted me to be the opening keynote speaker on the first morning of the event!

Excited about the opportunity, I began to think. I thought about what I wanted to say and how I might say it . . . but to my surprise and dismay, *nothing* came to my mind! Try as I might, I was a big blank. I would be addressing an audience of two thousand or so professional speakers at the National Speakers Association's annual convention—their biggest event of the year. This "nothing coming to my mind" status was not going to cut it! My old circuits were convinced that I had to plan, and I continued to try.

With my mind so embroiled with how I thought it should be, another way of going about it never even occurred to me.

With the conference still months away, every few days I would sit down and give it some thought. But despite having pen in hand and paper to spare, still nothing would come. Weeks and then months passed this way. I fretted over the process every moment in between sittings, the tension building with each attempt. I even decided that the pen and paper were the problem, so I ditched them for my computer! And still . . . nothing.

Soon the conference was two weeks away, and then only one week. *Still* I could not make my mind come up with what I should say. I had one thing I was certain I wanted to talk about, but that would take only fifteen minutes and I had an *hour* and fifteen minutes to fill! I decided to fly out to the conference location early and "get away" so I could get clear. A day and a half in the hotel room, and still nothing was coming. On the night before my presentation, I was still working at it. I stayed up until after midnight, then got up early the next morning, hoping for a glimpse. "I'll take a shower! All kinds of genius happens in the shower!" I said optimistically, hoping to convince myself. There I made my last gallant effort, to a resounding zero results before it was time for me to go. Getting dressed, walking down the hallway to the elevator that morning, I felt as though my career had ended before it had even begun. It was the most painful walk of my life!

Backstage, being fitted with my microphone, I heard my name being called as they introduced me, and the nice stage manager said, "That's you, I believe!" as he gave me a nudge. As I walked the ramp that led to the stage, it felt like I was walking the plank. My end was near, I could feel it!

As I stepped out from behind the curtain, into the lights, something massive took over inside of me. It was as if Niagara Falls had opened up over my head and was pouring in! All I could do was be present and give every ounce of myself to forming the words that were flooding through me. I flew across the giant stage from one end to the other in a way that felt as though I weren't even touching the floor. Looking out into the audience, I could see that they were fully engaged; it was one of the most magical moments in my life. As I finished my last sentence, I looked over at the time clock. To my amazement, it zeroed out just as I looked. The audience was up in a roar with the exercise we had just completed. Before it was all over, they gave me three standing ovations. As I stepped backstage and started to breathe again, the president of the association came rushing over with tears in her eyes, to tell me that my speech had been "more than she'd ever expected!" and that I'd "raised the bar on what had to happen on that stage in the future!"

Following the conference, I received e-mails and letters about the profound impact of the talk. Some of them quoted experts in the field of speaking, asking if I had studied with them. (I hadn't even heard of any of these experts.) They insisted that I must have rehearsed countless times and studied the structure of the talk over and over for it to go so seamlessly. But no, what came through me that day was far greater than anything I could have studied, planned, or rehearsed. It was far more than my thinking mind could ever have come up with. What came through me that day was pure Presence. It was *flow*. It changed me and what I was able to do from the inside out.

It also changed others. Seven years later, when I returned to the NSA convention, people stopped me in the hallway and glowingly stated how they'd been affected by that first speech all those years before. The flow had changed them too—more, I am certain, than I ever would have on my own. Ever since then I have allowed my intuitive mind to be in charge and steward the flow that emerges from within in response to each audience's needs. This is how the Soulful Self operates. It has access to a wholeness and a greater knowing than intellect alone could possibly predict.

This wonderful experience (despite my fighting it until the last moment) is an illustration of where we're all heading in the evolution of our consciousness. With the Energy Codes, we all can become like a funnel where pure Presence flows unobstructed through and out of us to magically transform our own and others' lives. Once we establish and allow that flow, and realize that the Presence moving through us *is* the real us, we've begun to make the radical and comprehensive Quantum Flip.

Even with a spontaneous, miraculous glimpse into the truth of my essential nature, as I had through my initial exalted experience, we still have to build circuits in order to fully embody and live our daily life as the Soulful Self. That's okay! It's the way it works. Rather than a sudden arrival at the final destination of total and all-encompassing perfection, we actually unfold into becoming who we really are, piece by piece, like the many petals of an opening lotus. We begin to heal on every level, richly and fully, and expand into our deep beauty and greatness.

In this final chapter, I'd like to give you a glimpse of what life looks like when we begin to really *become* the funnel for the unimpeded flow of the Soulful Self. While life on the Front Side of the Model will be unique to each of us in its individual expressions, some common characteristics will color our perspective and interactions as a whole.

Life on the Front Side: The Big Picture

The most significant attribute of Front Side living is that we stop identifying with the mind and identify with the Soulful Self. We speak about "my mind" rather than "my soul" as the outside, third party. We no longer work to master the mind, as the mind settles naturally into its role as an observer and facilitator. Here, we are simply in a different state of being—a trusted relationship with the universe, a state of flow.

Once on the Front Side, we know with absolute certainty that our inner world is the real world, and the outer world is merely a reflection. Therefore we know that, no matter what happens, "we've got this." The analytical mind steps into the background, no longer overthinking but rather recognizing that we *are* the essence we perceive, and serving our unfolding instead of competing with it. There is nothing to "do"; we need only be what we truly are.

Our thoughts are in alignment with the greater good, and we can see the greater good in everything that is coming through. We know without a doubt that everything is serving our own expansion—as well as everyone else's—and that no matter what happens, "it's all in our favor." Because of this, love is automatic. There is no judgment or rejection, only total acceptance and complete compassion that is grounded and integrated.

We trust in our desire because we know it is filtered through love. No longer afraid to speak out or manifest, we carry through with our visions, taking bold and loving action. We know we are made of goodness and so we trust our desires and our actions without hesitation. There is no reservation; we're all in! We know that we wouldn't desire a particular vibration if it wasn't a part of us that is ready to birth onto the planet, even though it may look very different from what we thought it would. We unattach from how we think things will be, because we are grounded in HeavenEarth, where all things are ultimately serving our highest good.

As we own our desire, our visions, and our power, people begin to experience and perceive a strength and a presence about us that has them wanting to come closer. They start to listen when we speak. We find ourselves getting the promotion or getting the advance or accepting the role of being a visionary, though it was never something we set out to be. As my story at the beginning of this chapter illustrates, life flows to us and through us—as us—surpassing anything we could have dreamed.

Remember that the ultimate plan at the Bus Stop was to experience our divinity—Divine love. And so, we will ideally come to see the challenges that we experience as the greatest support available for precisely that outcome. Family relationships, finances, and work all engage our circuits, and so offer the bottom-line challenges that we requested at the Bus Stop and lead us to the discovery of our magnificence and capacity for love. When, for example, after I got the news that I had been largely left out of my father's will and took it to the body with loving presence whenever the hurt came up, it built the circuitry for love to flow around my family again. (And I was delighted to even one day receive a package containing some of my mother's teacups!) This is possible for all of us.

Sometimes it's hard to believe that we can make the choice to "just love" and have it truly work in our lives. I invite you, once again, to try it on. Most of us (myself included) were not raised in an environment that taught us that "just loving" was smart, or even possible. But as you accept your power of free will in this manner, you will begin to experience yourself as a powerful loving presence in the world. That love will truly be unconditional, since no conditions are required to experience it other than your own conscious choice. The *real you*, the one who resides as the true essence behind the scenes in the stories of your life, is the one ingredient in the larger recipe of life that has the power to integrate you back from the splat, dissolve the rocks in the river, transform your life and the lives of those around you, and manifest as the power of the universe.

The Path of Purpose: Making a
Front-Side Impact in the World

We are here to be the creators of our lives and masters of our reality. Everything in this life is energy, meaning *there is nothing that you are not.* Everything you experience and encounter in this life is a perfect reflection of your inner world, meaning that you are the one who determines and reveals Heaven-Earth within you. It is your task—your destiny—to realize the truth of your magnificence and allow it to unfold from within by building circuits to embody a greater capacity of brilliance flowing through you. Using the Energy Codes, you come home into your body and learn to feel your truth from within. You establish yourself in your core, learning to live from the Soulful Self as you expand into a greater capacity for love. You breathe more life into your cells, animating the space between as you awaken your true creative potential. And finally, you connect fully with Spirit, opening your system to embrace a greater version of yourself as you embody the truth that you are made of love, and that everything in this life is working in your favor.

Since the moment you landed here from the Bus Stop, and in every moment, situation, and experience since, life has provided you with exactly what you need to evolve into a greater awareness of love—and it will continue to do so for as long as you are here on Earth. The world was created in love, and the purpose of your life is to discover your Creatorship within; you are on a path of unfolding.

You are the breath of life itself, and if you want the Soulful Self to be alive and well, you have to breathe more of that breath of life into it than you do into the outer world. When you do this—when you respectfully, earnestly, sincerely devote your attention inward to this central channel and breathe up and down through that—you are actually making an enormous contribution to your community and to humanity at large.

To have your greatest impact on the world, you don't need any followers. You don't need to have some grand, externally oriented purpose or mission. You simply need to be more of who you already are—the Soulful Self. The rest will flow from there.

When you turn your complete attention to the inside, it doesn't take time for transformation to occur, because the self that you are awakening to operates beyond space and time. Projects that you were told would take five years to manifest, for example, become lucrative, flowing abundantly, in one year. Inspirations and resources come out of the blue, furthering your progress on your true path. Complicated situations resolve with ease, and in the best interest of all parties. Everyone wins.

As you live more and more in the vibration of love, peace, abundance, and harmony within yourself, you actually begin to perceive those same qualities in your environment. It is as if you are tuned into a TV station where you see, hear, and feel that everything that is happening is serving something "good." Once you give yourself permission to "love no matter what," the outer world has no choice but to reflect back the image of unconditional love. This may take a little time, but it will prevail. It can't *not* prevail! When you live in a space of gratitude, celebration, and joy that includes everyone—where all are welcome and you see yourself in them—the *creator* version finally gets to have the life it came here to live.

Think of the Soulful Self as the *connected* self. As I say in my courses, "There is nothing that we are not." When we live in that space, we automatically see from the vibrational frequency of connection. In fact, it is this connection that we have been seeking since the moment of the Protective Personality's inception. We've spent our life attempting to find that connection through our relationships, our activities, and even our expectations, but eventually we learn that it is literally impossible for that to be the answer, because the outer world is merely a reflection of how we are embodying the "connectivity frequency" within. The more we tend to the singular task of activating ourselves as the Soulful Self, the more its presence in our life and in the world comes into focus. We find the connection we've been seeking. It's been here all along; it's called HeavenEarth. It's the radio station at which we experience our full potential as Creator and live as the truest expression of ourselves. What could be more meaningful, or purposeful, than that?

———

Now that we are at the end of (this leg of) our journey together, I want to share one last important note to help you take what you've learned here back out into the world, and that is . . .

Be deeply intimate. Allow yourself to be deeply vulnerable within. Listen inside to hear what you need to address within you first, and work on that without judging it or writing a story about it. This intimate connection with your true Soulful Self will allow you to perceive where your most effective work will be done, and support you as you begin to engage and express in the world with a greater level of authenticity.

Build a sacred relationship with the *way things go*. How the universe expresses is one of the most profound things you can embrace, because you *are* the universe.

Finally . . . do the work. Do it as often as you can, joyfully and wholeheartedly. This is literally the most important work you will ever do in your time here on Earth.

When you find that you want to share this work with others, give them this book, and then have rich and meaningful conversations with them. When we support one another in our growth, we develop loving trust and create an external experience of what this world was meant to be—an unfoldment in service to our magnificence.

Never underestimate the power of just one person saying yes to their own true Self. Now is the time to choose your life experience. Your own awakening activates the field around you, and your vibrational resonance has *global* impact. It has always been your destiny to realize your power as a divine, energetic being of love. HeavenEarth awaits only your permission to manifest in the here and now. Will you say yes?

This work isn't my gift to you; it's *your* gift to the world, because when you engage with it and embody it, you will step into your full power as a Creator, and the whole world will benefit as a result.

With Great Love, from the heart of my Soulful Self,
Dr. Sue

REFERENCES

Addington, Jack Ensign. *The Hidden Mystery of the Bible.* Camarillo, CA: DeVorss, 1969.

Alder, Vera Stanley. *The Finding of the "Third Eye."* Rev. ed. 1968. Reprint, New York: Samuel Weiser, 1970.

Anderson, James E., MD. *Grant's Atlas of Anatomy.* 7th ed. 1978. Reprint, Baltimore: Williams & Wilkins, 1980.

Ardekani, Ali Mirabzade. "Genetically Modified Foods and Health Concerns." *Iranian Journal of Biotechnology* 12, no. 2 (Spring 2014). doi:10.5812/ijb.19512.

Babbitt, Edwin D. *The Principles of Light and Color.* New York: Babbitt & Co., 1878.

Becker, Robert O., and Gary Selden. *The Body Electric: Electromagnetism and the Foundation of Life.* 1985. Reprint, New York: William Morrow, 1987.

Bhagavati, Ma Jaya Sati. *The 11 Karmic Spaces: Choosing Freedom from the Patterns that Bind You.* Sebastian, FL: Kashi, 2012.

Bohm, David. *Wholeness and the Implicate Order.* London: Routledge and Kegan Paul, 1980.

Brennan, Barbara Ann. *Light Emerging: The Journey of Personal Healing.* New York: Bantam Books, 1993.

Brookie, Kate L., Georgia I. Best, and Tamlin S. Conner. "Intake of Raw Fruits and Vegetables Is Associated with Better Mental Health than Intake of Processed Fruits and Vegetables." *Frontiers in Psychology* 9 (2018). doi:10.3389/fpsyg.2018.00487.

Bryant, Edwin F., trans. *The Yoga Sutras of Patanjali: A New Edition, Translation, and Commentary; with Insights from the Traditional Commentators.* New York: North Point Press, 2009.

Burr, Harold Saxton. *Blueprint for Immortality: The Electric Patterns of Life.* London: Neville Spearman, 1972.

Childre, Doc, and Deborah Rozman, PhD. *Transforming Depression: The HeartMath® Solution to Feeling Overwhelmed, Sad, and Stressed.* Oakland, CA: New Harbinger Publications, 2007.

Chopra, Deepak, MD, and Menas C. Kafatos, PhD. *You Are the Universe: Discovering Your Cosmic Self and Why It Matters.* New York: Harmony, 2017.

Condron, Daniel R., DM, DD, MS. *Permanent Healing.* 3rd ed. Windyville, MO: SOM Publishing, 1995.

de Vendômois, Joël Spiroux, François Roullier, Dominique Cellier, and Gilles-Eric Séralini. "A Comparison of the Effects of Three GM Corn Varieties on Mammalian Health." *International Journal of Biological Sciences* 5, no. 7 (2009): 706–26. doi:10.7150/ijbs.5.706.

Diamond, Harvey, and Marilyn Diamond. *Fit for Life.* New York: Warner Books, 1985.

Easwaran, Eknath, trans. *The Upanishads.* 2nd ed. Tomales, CA: Nilgiri Press, 2007.

Ganong, William F., MD. *Review of Medical Physiology.* 10th ed. Los Altos, CA: Lange Medical Publications, 1981.

Gerber, Richard, MD. *Vibrational Medicine: New Choices for Healing Ourselves.* Santa Fe, NM: Bear, 1988.

Gray, Harry, FRS. *Gray's Anatomy of the Human Body.* Edited by Charles Mayo Goss, AB, MD. 29th American ed. Philadelphia: Lea & Febiger, 1973.

Greenblatt, Matthew, ed. *The Essential Teachings of Ramana Maharshi: A Visual Journey.* 2nd ed. Carlsbad, CA: Inner Directions Foundation, 2003.

Guyton, Arthur C. *Textbook of Medical Physiology.* 6th ed. Philadelphia: Saunders, 1981.

Hawkins, David R., MD, PhD. *The Eye of the I: From Which Nothing Is Hidden.* West Sedona, AZ: Veritas, 2001.

———. *Transcending the Levels of Consciousness: The Stairway to Enlightenment.* West Sedona, AZ: Veritas, 2006.

Hay, Louise L. *You Can Heal Your Life.* 1984. Reprint, Carson, CA: Hay House, 1994.

Holmes, Ernest. *The Science of Mind: A Philosophy, a Faith, a Way of Life.* Rev. ed. 1938. 1st Trade Paperback ed., New York: Tarcher, 1998.

Hunt, Valerie V. *Infinite Mind: Science of the Human Vibrations.* Malibu, CA: Malibu Publishing, 1995.

Iyengar, B. K. S. *Light on Yoga: Yoga Dipika.* Rev. ed. New York: Schocken Books, 1979.

John, Da Free. *The Yoga of Consideration and the Way that I Teach.* Clearlake, CA: Dawn Horse Press, 1982.

Kandel, Eric R., and James H. Schwartz, eds. *Principles of Neural Science.* 1981. Reprint, New York: Elsevier, 1983.

Kelder, Peter. *The Eye of Revelation: The Ancient Tibetan Rites of Rejuvenation.* Edited by J. W. Watt. Booklocker.com, 2008.

Khalsa, Dharma Singh, MD, and Cameron Stauth. *Meditation as Medicine: Activate the Power of Your Natural Healing Force.* New York: Fireside, 2002.

Leeson, Thomas S., MD, PhD, and C. Roland Leeson, MD, PhD. *A Brief Atlas of Histology.* Philadelphia: Saunders, 1979.

Lipton, Bruce H., PhD. *The Biology of Belief: Unleashing the Power of Consciousness, Matter and Miracles.* Santa Rosa, CA: Mountain of Love, 2005.

Maghari, Behrokh M., and Ali M. Ardekani. "Genetically Modified Foods and Social Concerns." *Avicenna Journal of Medical Biotechnology* 3, no. 3 (July 2011): 109–17.

Maximow, Alexander A., and William Bloom. *A Textbook of Histology.* 6th ed. 1952. Reprint, Philadelphia: W. B. Saunders, 1953.

McTaggart, Lynne. *The Field: The Quest for the Secret Force of the Universe.* New York: HarperCollins, 2002.

Moore, Keith L., PhD, FIAC. *Clinically Oriented Anatomy.* 2nd ed. Baltimore: Williams & Wilkins, 1985.

Morter, M. T., Jr., DC. *An Apple a Day?: Is It Enough Today?* Rogers, AR: B.E.S.T. Research, 1996.

——. *Correlative Urinalysis: The Body Knows Best.* Edited by John M. Clark, DC. Rogers, AR: B.E.S.T. Research, 1987.

——. *Dynamic Health: Using Your Own Beliefs, Thoughts and Memory to Create a Healthy Body.* Rev. ed. Rogers, AR: B.E.S.T. Research, 1997.

——. *The Healing Field: Restoring the Positive Energy of Health.* Rogers, AR: B.E.S.T. Research, 1991.

——. *The Soul Purpose: Unlocking the Secret to Health, Happiness, and Success.* Rogers, AR: Dynamic Life, 2001.

——. *Your Health, Your Choice: Your Complete Personal Guide to Wellness, Nutrition and Disease Prevention.* Hollywood, FL: Frederick Fell, 1990.

Myss, Caroline, PhD. *Anatomy of the Spirit: The Seven Stages of Power and Healing.* New York: Harmony, 1996.

Netter, Frank H. *The CIBA Collection of Medical Illustrations.* vol. 4, *Endocrine System and Selected Metabolic Diseases.* 1965. Reprint, Summit, NJ: CIBA Pharmaceutical, 1981.

New, Susan A. "Intake of Fruit and Vegetables: Implications for Bone Health." *Proceedings of the Nutrition Society* 62, no. 1 (November 2003): 889–99. doi:10.1079/pns2003352.

Oschman, James L. *Energy Medicine: The Scientific Basis.* 2nd ed. Philadelphia: Elsevier, 2016.

Oschman, James L., Gaétan Chevalier, and Richard Brown. "The Effects of Grounding (Earthing) on Inflammation, the Immune Response, Wound Healing, and Prevention and Treatment of Chronic Inflammatory and Autoimmune Diseases." *Journal of Inflammation Research*, 8 (2015): 83–96. doi:10.2147/JIR.S69656.

Percival, Harold W. *Thinking and Destiny: With a Brief Account of the Descent of Man into This Human World and How He Will Return to the Eternal Order of Progression.* 1946. Reprint, Dallas: Word Foundation, 1987.

Pert, Candace B., PhD. *Molecules of Emotion: Why You Feel the Way You Feel.* New York: Scribner, 2003.

Pusztai, A., PhD. "Genetically Modified Foods: Are They a Risk to Human/Animal Health?" *American Institute of Biological Sciences* (2001). www.actionbioscience.org.

"The Puzzling Role of Biophotons in the Brain." *Technology Review* (blog). December 17, 2010. www.technologyreview.com.

Rahnama, Majid, et al. "Emission of Mitochondrial Biophotons and Their Effect on Electrical Activity of Membrane via Microtubules." *Journal of Integrative Neuroscience* 10, no. 1 (March 2011): 65–88. doi:10.1142/s0219635211002622.

Rinpoche, Sogyal. *The Tibetan Book of Living and Dying.* Rev. ed. Edited by Patrick Gaffney and Andrew Harvey. New York: HarperCollins, 1994.

Rolf, Ida P. *Rolfing: Reestablishing the Natural Alignment and Structural Integration of the Human Body for Vitality and Well-being.* Rochester, VT: Healing Arts Press, 1989.

Rose, Colin, and Malcolm J. Nicholl. *Accelerated Learning for the 21st Century: The Six-Step Plan to Unlock Your Master-Mind.* New York: Dell, 1997.

Schiffer, Fredric, MD. *Of Two Minds: A New Approach for Better Understanding and Improving Your Emotional Life.* London: Pocket, 2000.

Schimmel, H. W. *Functional Medicine.* Heidelberg: Karl F. Haug Verlag, 1997.

Sheldrake, Rupert. *A New Science of Life: The Hypothesis of Formative Causation.* Los Angeles: Tarcher, 1981.

Sills, Franklyn. *Craniosacral Biodynamics.* Rev. ed. Vol. 1. Berkeley, CA: North Atlantic Books, 2001.

Snell, Richard S., MD, PhD. *Clinical Neuroanatomy for Medical Students.* Boston: Little, Brown, 1980.

Solomon, Eldra Pearl, and P. William Davis. *Understanding Human Anatomy and Physiology.* New York: McGraw-Hill, 1978.

Storrs, Carina. "Stand Up, Sit Less, Experts Say; Here's How to Do It." CNN. August 7, 2015. Accessed January 2018. http://www.cnn.com/2015/08/06/health/how-to-move-more/index.html.

Taylor, Jill Bolte, PhD. *My Stroke of Insight: A Brain Scientist's Personal Journey.* New York: Viking, 2008.

Van Auken, John. *Edgar Cayce's Approach to Rejuvenation of the Body.* Virginia Beach, VA: A.R.E. Press, 1996.

Van Wijk, R. *Light in Shaping Life: Biophotons in Biology and Medicine.* Geldermalsen, Netherlands: Meluna, 2014.

Wapnick, Kenneth, PhD. *Forgiveness and Jesus: The Meeting Place of a Course in Miracles and Christianity.* 6th ed. 1998. Reprint, Temecula, CA: Foundation for A Course in Miracles, 2004.

Yukteswar Giri, Swami Sri. *The Holy Science.* 8th ed., 1990. Reprint, Los Angeles: Self-Realization Fellowship, 2013.

RESOURCES

For information regarding live coursework with Dr. Sue,
please go to drsuemorter.com.

The following resources can be found on our website at drsuemorter.com
/energycodesbook. Please visit the Resources page periodically, as we continually add to and update our offerings to support you better. Please note that no prior experience is needed to do any of these exercises and techniques.

108 Ways to Embody Your Magnificence (book), **Dr. Sue Morter, 2017.**
Tips to manage the stresses and misunderstandings of life, providing a paradigm shift into the abundant reality that "everything serves." Dr. Sue shows us how to shift our perspective into complete empowerment with simple and short recommendations, one message at a time, in this fun, deeply revealing, "open-to-any-page" guide to manifesting the deeper truth of who we are.

108 Ways to Embody Your Magnificence (audio), **Dr. Sue Morter, 2015.**
Audio version of *108 Ways to Embody Your Magnificence*, to help you step consciously into the full expression of the real You. Listen while you drive or walk in the park. Learn while you live, and live while you learn.

BodyAwake™ III—Breathwork from The Energy Codes® Chakras One, Two, and Three (video), **Dr. Sue Morter, 2013, 2nd ed., 2018.**
We are made of energy—sound vibration and light. We are here to learn to masterfully manage that energy, beyond our thoughts and limiting beliefs. Conscious breathwork ushers in the creative, safe space we need to gracefully change our beliefs. Learn to move energy in chakras one, two, and three for clearing subconscious blockages, piercing veils that prevent

integration of all aspects of your consciousness, enhancing vitality, and shifting from survivorship toward creatorship.

BodyAwake™ IV—Yoga Activation (video), Dr. Sue Morter, 2013, 2nd ed., 2018.

For thousands of years, yoga has proven that there are particular body positions that allow for improved physical, mental, and emotional healing in the body. Coupled with conscious breath patterns, this alignment enhances our orientation and disposition in life, helping us see a bigger picture and transmute stress into opportunity. *BodyAwake IV* teaches introductory positions to enhance energy flow and begin utilizing yoga as energy medicine, as described in the Energy Codes practices in this book. Join Dr. Sue for a guided instructional series of gentle, conscious physical exercises and breath patterns that nurture body and spirit.

BodyAwake™ V—Healing Patterns (video), Dr. Sue Morter, 2014, 2nd ed., 2018.

Injuries and stresses can shift and slow the flow of energy as it travels through the body. Bogged energy systems stagnate cellular recovery and rejuvenation. Healing happens when energy regains its natural flow. Here, Dr. Sue teaches you to move energy into and throughout the body, with specific techniques to repattern the subtle energy fields for healing. Study practices for resolving particular pain patterns (whether from injury or unknown onset) and learn to translate these techniques and apply them to other healing needs specific to you.

BodyAwake™ VI—Yoga Practices (video), Dr. Sue Morter, 2015, 2nd ed., 2018.

In *BodyAwake VI*, Dr. Sue shares yoga instruction infused with the Energy Codes breathwork, guiding you to consciously move *prana*—healing energy—through the tissues. Become more flexible, accelerate healing, and find your deeper core presence. These practices are designed to allow you to practice meditation while in motion. Includes a chair practice, a beginner-intermediate practice, and two intermediate practices.

BodyAwake™ VII—Advanced Breathwork from The Energy Codes®, Chakras Four, Five, Six, and Seven (video), **Dr. Sue Morter, 2015, 2nd ed., 2018.**
Activate these chakras and integrate them with additional demonstrations of the Fern Frond Breath pattern for greater healing and creativity. Consciously breathing into specific areas of the body attunes the related tissues that house these higher levels of consciousness, awakening and enlivening them. In this video program, Dr. Sue teaches you breath patterns to activate your ability to self-heal, enlighten, integrate, manifest, and love fully.

BodyAwake™ VIII—Stacking Up the Column—Central Channel Enhancement (video), **Dr. Sue Morter, 2015, 2nd ed., 2018.**
Peace of mind and a sense of well-being come naturally when we learn to release the bind the ego has on our lives. Dr. Sue leads you through a process to direct the mind inward to assist in cultivating that freedom. You will learn to release your overly high-performance, guarded, or protective patterns by developing this deep sense of centeredness and connectivity to your true passion. Dr. Sue guides you into the central core of your being—your essential Soulful Self—allowing greater flow, ease, and abundance to happen in your life automatically. Experience absolute presence by enhancing awareness at the core of your being. Build awareness at the core of your being for strength and vitality, and strengthen your ability to stay aligned under stress.

BodyAwake™ IX—Conscious Calisthenics: Exercise for Everyone (video), **Dr. Sue Morter, 2016.**
Conscious exercise represents a quantum leap above and beyond traditional calisthenic exercise. It raises your vibration and life force, and promotes vitality in the body. Intentional movement of energy through the body, coupled with focused breath, helps us generate new neurocircuitry that carries us to higher levels of consciousness. Use weight lifting, lunges, exercise bands, etc., with BodyAwake breathwork for greater benefit from efforts you are already making toward improving your health. Anchor your consciousness as you develop greater body strength. Use regularly for mind-body-breath integration and strengthening.

BodyAwake™ Yoga for Healing—Three Yoga Practices to Embrace Vitality and Embody Flow (audio), Dr. Sue Morter, 2018.

Dr. Sue guides you through a slow, gentle yoga practice with focused breathwork for moving innate healing intelligence and essential restorative energy throughout the body, specifically for the purpose of physical healing. The Energy Codes Twelve-Chakra System is highlighted, particularly chakras eight, nine, and ten, for the conscious embodiment of high-frequency, subtle energy on the yoga mat. *BodyAwake Yoga for Healing* integrates and rejuvenates mind, body, and soul at the central channel of the body. For a beginner and intermediate practice, this MP3 audio CD contains three yoga practices recorded live at a healing retreat in Evergreen, Colorado. Consult your physician before starting this or any exercise program.

The Bus Stop Conversation—Soul Contracts and Life Purpose (audio with workbook), Dr. Sue Morter, 2014.

We enter this life with powerful soul contracts, agreements made on our way in about what we seek to experience here in the body and on this planet. Discover how everything—from your most painful experiences to the sublime—has occurred not *to*, but rather *for* you. In *The Bus Stop Conversation*, Dr. Sue guides you into a deeply personal exploration through which you will powerfully and profoundly shift your perspective about everything in your life.

Fear into Fire—Tools from The Energy Codes® for Passionate Life Purpose (audio), Dr. Sue Morter, 2015.

Beneath every fear is a suppressed, passionate fire that must return to our daily lives. Prosperity and passion are one and the same. Change your fears forever with a total paradigm shift and learn to: make decisions from that passionate space within you, master the invisible for powerful results, free yourself from the mind chatter of self-questioning, and create a reality shift by turning fear into the powerful tool of transformation that it is meant to be.

Front Side, Back Side—Awaken the Creator Within (audio with workbook),
Dr. Sue Morter, 2013.
If there were a scale for personal empowerment, the Front Side would be the ideal perspective: free and strong. The Back Side would be the victimized perspective: incapable and unworthy. The purpose of your life journey is to traverse to the Front Side of the Model in every aspect of your experience. Dr. Sue guides you on how to use life experience to awaken to your true power. Contains conversational teaching with excerpts from live presentations, meditations, and reflective exercises.

Lineage Yoga—Light Is Your Lineage, Love Is Your Legacy, Three Yoga Practices (audio), **Dr. Sue Morter, 2013.**
Dr. Sue guides you with clear instruction about passionate breathwork while you move through foundational yoga asanas (positions) to cleanse your body, open your core, and find your center in life. Experience a deeper form of embodiment with Dr. Sue's inspiring insights on yoga, based on ancient technologies and civilizations and their teachings. For a beginner and intermediate practice, this audio program contains three classes recorded live at Dr. Sue's Lineage Retreat in Sedona, Arizona.

Passionate Purpose—The Power of Doing YOUR Thing (audio), **Dr. Sue Morter, 2015.**
Passion is not about specific experiences, but about our ability to access and live from the truth of who we are. Purpose is not about what we intend to achieve, but about what we are meant to *be*—it is about revealing our magnificence. You don't need a miracle, and you don't need a guru. You already *are* both. In this two-hour audio program from Dr. Sue, find out how to discover, reveal, and engage your power and passionate purpose for the rest of your life.

Sacred Stream Yoga—Conscious Movement of Prana for Healing, Three Yoga Practices (audio), **Dr. Sue Morter, 2016.**
The complete and abundant flow of energy through the body is essential for healing and vitality. Body movement into ancient and sacred positions, coupled with conscious breath, ignites that flow and returns the body to

its natural self-healing state. Running vertically from your head to the tip of your spine, the Sacred Stream is the flow of energy through the deep central channel of the body. It is here that the eternal, essential Self-Healer resides. This practice is designed to awaken and integrate the profound, innate healing presence at the core of your being. You will anchor your energy field and align to the strength of nature, build conscious presence at your power centers, and learn asanas for accessing your deep wisdom. You will build neurocircuitry for manifesting and self-expression, and experience your essential Soulful Self within the physical realm.

pH Kit
Complete kit to test saliva pH, including litmus paper, acid tablets to challenge pH, and test results interpretation booklet with recommendations for improving pH status.

ACKNOWLEDGMENTS

The Energy Codes has had a blessed path to this point of expression. I first would like to thank Bonnie Solow of Solow Literary for her wonderful stewardship of this manuscript to Simon and Schuster for review. Her belief in this work and in me has indeed been life-changing. Above all, I am blessed by her friendship.

Every book requires a publishing team, and *The Energy Codes* has been so very fortunate to have a tremendously talented one, beginning with my brilliant editor, Sarah Pelz, whose clarity and kind expertise also teamed us with an expert in the field and in the topics of the Codes, coeditor Leslie Meredith. Leslie's astute and polished familiarity with the science alongside her brilliant command of the editorial process shaped this project into a beautiful alchemy of heart, mind, and soul. I am honored by the gifted contributions of these two amazing women.

I am profoundly grateful for the intimate circle of angels who have held sacred space for me since the first moments of my exalted awakening: Marci Shimoff, for her passionate guidance and encouragement to write a book, as well as her expertise in developing its content, and her love and light, from day one. She is my angel and maker of miracles once again. Suzanne Lawlor, for her unwavering presence in my life as a truth holder and an embodied devotee of Divine Love. And to AlexSandra Leslie, for her elevated perspective on all things possible.

The gift of an amazing writer is immeasurable and I was blessed to have the perfect fit for a message requiring the synthesis of tradition and inspiration, Eastern and Western perspectives, innovation and authentic care: Brookes Nohlgren, whose genius at taking my spoken word and formulating a narrative flow for *The Energy Codes* created this book. Her rare form of devotion to grasp and share this content in service toward a better world has touched my heart forever—a thousand blessings on her crown. Bryna Haynes, a most superb content editor, for her wisdom, devotion, readiness, and editing additions and expertise—another blessing indeed.

With my extensive travels, "it takes a village" to live my life. The amazing team around me at Morter Institute affectionately call themselves "The Village People." I am blessed every day to call them my friends and beloved team: Kris Conlin, who has been my right arm of detail and organization as well as devoted editing ally. I am eternally grateful for her integrity and fortitude. This book would not have happened without her brilliance. Andrea Stumpf, whose writing assistance and modeling for the images in the book have made every aspect of this project better. I am forever grateful for her bright spirit and love of goodness. Monica Turner, for her wonderful talent and devotion to creating the artwork within these pages and for her constant friendship. Glynis Pierce, for her air-traffic control of Morter Institute and care for me. Breeze Woodlock, for being there for me all hours and for so many years.

My initial spiritual journey and "ray-of-light" awakening was a most precious time in my life, a time of soulful unfolding. Those soul friends who held me then are imprinted in my heart forever: Melanie Mills, Mary Ann Shurig, Dr. Rebecca Anderson, Arielle Azeez (Pinky), Bill Psillas, Dr. Michael Hermann, Keith Chaon and then Windy Woodland, and our late Julia Moses.

Many of my most beloved teachers are no longer on the planet, and live on through my devotion and teachings every day. My gratitude is nearly unspeakable: Ma Jaya Sati Bhagavati, a most beautiful teacher and guru of unconditional love in my life, who gave me the spiritual name Saraswati Ma Jaya, representing the bridging of science and the arts, long before I knew that was my destiny. I bow. Shirdi Baba, Neem Karoli Baba, Ramana Maharshi, Virginia Essene, and Angeles Arrien, I would not be here without your guidance, physical and ethereal.

Reverend Michael Beckwith, for meeting me in the higher realms and affirming what I know to be true and for encouraging me to emerge and reveal. Lynne McTaggart and Dr. Joe Dispenza, for their wonderful encouragement to take on this considerable project and bring this message to the world audience.

Dr. Vicki Knapke, and my best friend of thirty-plus years, Dr. Scott Cooper, for their love for B.E.S.T. and Morter Institute and for their constant availability for friendship, care, and treatment between my travels.

The yoga studios that held the space for my yoga research and development over the years are imprinted in the fabric of this work and remembered every time I teach my BodyAwake Yoga classes and courses. Thank you: The Yoga Center, Heather Thomas and Karen Fox; Cityoga School of Yoga and Health, Dave Sims; Marsha Pappas and Nikki Myers; and Blooming Life Yoga Studio and School, Lily Kessler.

My heartfelt thanks to Dr. Raj Maturi and Cassie Stockamp for their gracious demonstrations of yoga filmed as resources for this book. And to Ryan Penington for his perfectly creative and professional videography. Deep gratitude to Jeralyn Glass of Crystal Cadence, Music of the Heart, for musical accompaniment to the book's meditations.

The many patients, clients, and students whose stories have helped illustrate this message, and the countless patients and students who have contributed by asking the many questions that led to the answers now called the Energy Codes.

Family is always at the root of our awakening, embodiment, and liberation. Both our origins and our choices reveal our Soulful purpose here. How does one better thank a mother and father than by living into one's own highest self? There are no words beyond: "Mom and Dad, I am blessed to have had you as my own." My gratitude for my brothers, Dr. Ted and Dr. Tom, and their wives, my dear sisters-in-law Janna and Anna, for holding fast to the dream of our father's work and stewarding it as they have all these years, and for loving me. I love them dearly.

And of course, my beloved Dr. Elisa Zinberg, for being there with me every step of the way—each travel, decision, and discovery; for loving Sophie and Gracie so abundantly; and for endlessly caregiving to the countless amount of all things important. Lucy, my forever love and deepest gratitude.

About the Author

An international speaker, master of bioenergetic medicine, and quantum field visionary, Dr. Sue Morter teaches the retraining of the nervous system and subtle energy system of the body through a process called Embodiment. Through her Energy Codes and BodyAwake Yoga seminars and retreats, and her BodyAwake video series, she illuminates the relationships among quantum thoughts, energy medicine, and healing through the repatterning of the nerve impulses through the body by use of the mind and deep breathwork. She retrains the brain, shifts old memory patterns, and then teaches us how to move beyond the brain for sustainable healing. Her ultimate goal and life purpose is to awaken divinity within humanity. To that end, she holds yoga, meditation, and self-healing retreats in Mexico, Bali, Peru, Egypt, India, Ireland, and Easter Island, as well as across the United States.

Dr. Sue is seen in several documentary films, including *The Opus*, *The Cure Is . . .* , *Discover the Gift*, and *Femme*. She has served on professional licensing boards and in human service organizations for thirty years. As a prominent leader in her profession, she has received numerous outstanding achievement awards in the fields of natural health care and transformational leadership.

She is founder and visionary of the Morter Institute for BioEnergetics, an organization committed to teaching individuals self-healing techniques and a new approach to life based on quantum science and energy medicine, the elevation of consciousness, and life mastery. The Morter Institute is an international destination for healing and for wellness education, providing ongoing coursework and treatment for hundreds of thousands of people since the 1980s. Dr. Sue is a master teacher of the

BioEnergetic Synchronization Technique (B.E.S.T.), a powerful energy medicine healing modality developed by her father that is taught to health-care professionals globally.

She draws from her experience as a doctor serving tens of thousands of patients for more than thirty years, inspiration from a life-changing awakening during ancient meditation practices, and her personal passion for cracking the code of life itself. She ignites scientific, personal development, spiritual, and health-care audiences by bridging the worlds of science, spirit, and human possibility. Her greatest joy has been sharing her discoveries with hundreds of thousands of audience members, both live and online, over the past three decades.

As a long-established speaker and facilitator in the self-help health-care arena, Dr. Sue is currently onstage—teaching, leading workshops, or presenting keynotes and other presentations—more than 250 days a year. She has dozens of CDs, DVDs, and online support materials available.

As an active member of the Transformational Leadership Council, she collaborates with many other powerful teachers, healers, and leaders to create a better world.

Between speaking engagements, Dr. Sue enjoys her peaceful home in the countryside near Indianapolis, Indiana, with her partner and two miniature schnauzers. She also lives part-time in Long Island, New York.

For more information on the Morter Institute, BioEnergetic treatment programs, Dr. Sue's Energy Codes coursework, BodyAwake Yoga, Body-Awake Yoga Teacher Training, and JourneyAwake conscious excursions to sacred sites around the world, visit www.DrSueMorter.com.